Indivisible selves and moral practice

Indivisible selves and moral practice

VINIT HAKSAR

EDINBURGH UNIVERSITY PRESS

BARNES & NOBLE BOOKS
SAVAGE, MARYLAND

© Vinit Haksar, 1991

Edinburgh University Press
22 George Square, Edinburgh

Set in Linotronic Ehrhardt by
Koinonia Ltd, Bury and
printed in Great Britain by
Page Bros Ltd, Norwich

British Library Cataloguing
  in publication data
Haksar, Vinit
    Indivisible selves and moral practice
    1. Self – Philosophical perspectives
    I. Title
    126
ISBN 0 7486 0249 6 cased

First published in the United States in 1991 by
Barnes & Noble Books
8705 Bollman Place
Savage, MD 20763

Library of Congress Cataloging-in-Publication
Data is available from the publisher

0-389-20956-2

Contents

Acknowledgements

I am most grateful to the following who read earlier versions of this book and made valuable suggestions: Stanley Eveling, Kit Fine, David McNaughton, Derek Parfit and Timothy Sprigge. I have profited from those whose views I have discussed in this book, especially by the writings of Nagel and Parfit, and I have benefited from discussions with Neil MacCormick and Jeremy Waldron.

An earlier version of Appendix A originally appeared in *Inquiry*, 1981. Earlier versions of some of the chapters were given to the philosophy societies of the following universities: Dundee, Edinburgh, Glasgow, McGill University, Queens University, York University (Canada). Earlier versions of chapters 9 and 10 were given at the politics department seminar at Glasgow University, at the Centre for Crimonology and the Social and Philosophical Study of Law, University of Edinburgh, at a conference in Edinburgh on Parfit's *Reasons and Persons*, organised by Dory Scaltsas in 1987, and at the Departmento de Filosofia del Derecho Moral y Politica, University of Valencia. An earlier version of chapter 5 was given at a seminar in the psychology department organised by John Beloff, where I had the benefit of Colwyn Trevarthen's comments.

I would like to thank Linda Alexander and Joan Steven for typing some of the chapters of an earlier version of the book, and Cheryl Foster for compiling the index.

Introduction

This book examines some of the different theories of the self and some of their moral, social, legal and practical implications. I have stressed the importance of the first person perspective for the study of problems such as personal identity. Some of these problems cannot be properly apprehended without the first person or subjective viewpoint. From an objective or external standpoint there would be no more problem about personal identity than about the identity of other objects.

One of the limitations of the objective approach to the study of persons is that it leaves out the subjective point of view. Nagel believes that there is discord and clash between the objective and subjective approaches and that we are doomed to be stuck with two irreconcilable viewpoints. My own view, which I develop in Appendix A, is that there is no need to embrace such irrationalism. We should try to achieve harmony between the two approaches. The subjective approach provides us with imaginative insights into our own nature. Some of the most important of these insights, such as that we are indivisible selves whose survival does not admit of degrees, cannot be established by the objective approach. But it would be wrong to infer that such views are based on error. I argue that such views are defeasible conjectures, and that it is reasonable to believe in them unless there is evidence to the contrary.

The relation between the subjective and objective approaches has similarities to what happens in science, where scientists form conjectures and then try to test them with possible counter-examples. Somewhat as in science one tries to get a fit between scientific theories and observation statements, so also one should aim for a fit between the deliverances of the subjective approach, as well as of our moral and practical views, and objective facts.

The Buddhists, Hume and Parfit do not believe that there is a persistent self or indeed any self in a deep sense. On this no-self or reductionist view there is a self in the sense that there is a certain psychology and one can talk of earlier and later selves in the life of a human being, the early self referring to the early character the later self to the later character. But there is no self in any deep sense; our continued existence over time just consists in various physical and psychological connections, continuities of our bodies and of our psychologies. On the non-reductionist view these connections are merely evidence of a further fact viz: the persistence of an indivisible self; and our continued existence consists in the persistence of this self. The non-reductionist view involves a realist view regarding personal identity. In chapter 1, I discuss some of the crucial differences between the reductionist and non-reductionist views.

In this book I try, especially in the last three chapters, to work out the moral and practical implications of the no-self view. Such a study shows how widespread the traditional (i.e. non-reductionist) view of the self is. I maintain that a good deal of our subjective, practical and moral life presupposes the non-reductionist view. I also maintain that such considerations provide a defeasible presumption in favour of the non-reductionist view of the self. I examine whether this presumption has been defeated by the reductionists. I try to show that none of the arguments of the reductionists against the non-reductionist view are in fact successful. But I admit that if splitting of consciousness were to occur, then the case for the non-reductionist view would be undermined.

In chapter 1 I contend that the self is indivisible. In chapter 2 I maintain that our practical life assumes unity of consciousness and that it is the non-reductionist self that gives a deep unity to our experience; the reductionist cannot provide any deep unity. In chapters 8-10 I examine some of the moral and practical consequences that would follow from the lack of any deep unity in a person's life. For instance, I stress in chapters 9 and 10 that suffering is much more of an evil when the same enduring and indivisible entity suffers on and on. The view that the self is indivisible has profound consequences in our moral and practical life. Other things being equal, if a group such as a family suffers a lot over a hundred years, this is not as bad as if the same indivisible self were to suffer the same amount for a hundred years. This is because the suffering of the family is borne by several different individuals. If, however, persons are like groups as they are on the Humean view (Hume explicitly compared the soul to a commonwealth) then their suffering too would be borne by their parts, and so will become less of an evil than would be the case on the indivisible self view. I defend this view in chapter 10.

In chapter 1 and elsewhere in the book (especially chapters 8, 9 and 10) I argue that the reductionist view goes against common-sense and that the non-reductionist view is presupposed by a good deal of our experience. Since this is so, there is a defeasible presumption in favour of the non-reductionist view. The onus is on the reductionist to defeat this presumption. The view that it is reasonable to continue to adhere to our traditional practices until they are shown to be false is defended in chapters 3-6.

What reasons do people have for rejecting the non-reductionist view? In chapter 7 I examine some of these reasons and find them unpersuasive. In that chapter I also examine the role of imaginary examples in discussions of personal identity and conclude that the non-reductionist view cannot be refuted by imaginary counter-examples.

One of the most important reasons some people have for abandoning the non-reductionist view is to do with splitting of consciousness. On the non-reductionist view the self is indivisible and there is unity of consciousness, so splitting of consciousness seems to create a problem. On the reductionist view splitting of consciousness presents no more of a metaphysical problem than does the splitting of nations and other groups.

In chapter 1 I maintain that the self is essentially indivisible; it is metaphysically impossible for the self to divide. In chapter 5 I contend that it is physically impossible for a person's brain to split into two halves, such that they each support independent conscious lives, each with memories and dispositions of the old person. If it turns out that it is physically possible to split the human brain in this manner, then my conjecture that the self is indivisible and that it is metaphysically impossible for the self to divide will be undermined.

In chapters 5 and 6 I examine and reject the view that split-brain cases and multiple personality cases show that splitting of consciousness has occurred. But I agree that if splitting of consciousness is shown to occur, this would be subversive of the traditional (i.e. non-reductionist) theory of the self. That is why it is important to discuss whether such splitting has occured. I argue that the split brain and multiple personality cases so far can be explained without postulating splitting of consciousness. The intellectual case for the view that there is splitting of consciousness has not been established. I admit that the intellectual case for the view that such splitting does not take place has also not been established. The multiple personality and split brain cases, as well as other alleged cases of divided mind, are consistent with the view that there is splitting of consciousness and with the view that splitting of consciousness does not occur. I would use the principle of reasonable faith to show that we should opt for the view that splitting of consciousnees does not occur. Since splitting of consciousness conflicts with the traditional conception of the self, we should put the onus of proof on the person who claims that such splitting does take place.

In chapter 2 I distinguish different senses of minds as well as different senses of unity of mind. This discussion is crucial for the case I make in chapters 5 and 6 against the view that splitting of consciousness does occur. For clearly it would be foolish to deny that in some sense the mind is often divided and lacking in unity.

Some philosophers reject the non-reductionist view on empiricist grounds. There is Hume's celebrated argument about never observing the self: 'For my part when I enter most intimately into what I call myself, I always stumble on some particular perception or other, of heat or cold, light or shade, love or hatred, pain or pleasure, I never catch myself at any time without a perception, and never can observe anything but the perception.'[1] Hume's empiricism assumes that the items of experience are the basic units of the world. It is not clear that such a view has any more empirical evidence in its favour than does the old fashioned theory of the self. Do we really observe discrete items of experience existing on their own? I contend in chapter 1 that experiences are modifications or states of the agent. The view that agents or persons rather than experiences are primary makes more sense of our moral and practical life as well as of our subjective experience.

An attraction of the reductionist view is that it appears to avoid the problem of scepticism. Personal identity on this view does not involve any further fact beyond the observable facts such as physical and psychological continuity in a non-branching form, so the problem regarding whether x is the same individual as y becomes in principle soluble. The non-reductionist view involves a belief in a further fact and so it can lead to genuine sceptical doubts of the kind that Kant raised, such as how do we know that there is one person per human being rather than a succesion of persons, each passing on its memories, dispositions, beliefs, etc to the next?

There are many ways of classifying philosophers. One of them is to divide them into the following two groups: those who want to avoid scepticism at all costs and those who think that we can learn to live with it. My own sympathy is with the latter; in chapter 3 I examine some of the objections raised by those in the former group against those in the latter. For instance, in chapter 3, I discuss a principle of significance that Strawson favours and which I reject; this principle, if it is valid, would imply that my views on personal identity, since they lead to scepticism, should be abandoned.

Empiricist minded philosophers want us to base our practical and moral life on facts that can be established by empirical observation. I have argued in *Equality, Liberty and Perfectionism* as well as in this book that such an approach will lead to the abandonment of much of our civilized norms and constraints. Fear of scepticism makes some people prefer the reductionist approach to the non-reductionist approach. But, as I argue in chapters 3 and 4, fear of scepticism should not be allowed to carry absolute weight. In other areas too, such as induction, we have to rely on something like the reflective equilibrium model rather than on an empiricist approach. Indeed as Rawls acknowledges, his use of the model was influenced by Nelson Goodman's use of it in dealing with problems relating to induction and scientific method. Rawls used it to get a fit between our general moral principles and our considered moral judgements in specific cases; when there is a clash between the former and the latter we modify or revise one or the other until the clash disappears.

In chapter 4 I commend the reflective equilibrium method, but in a broader way than Rawls does. For I believe that the fit should also include metaphysical and practical views. Roughly one should aim for consistency, coherence, and comprehensiveness. Coherence involves more than just consistency, it involves that the views that are consistent should mutually support one another. Comprehensiveness is also important. Other things being equal, if one gets a good fit in just a small area this is not as impressive as when the fit is over a larger area. Ideally the fit should be between all areas of knowledge, but in practice we can only strive towards comprehensiveness just as one can only strive towards consistency and coherence.

In this book I commend the non-reductionist view as against the reductionist view by the use of the reflective equilibrium model in conjunction with what I call the principle of reasonable faith. According to the latter, when objective, empirical, scientific and intellectual considerations leave an issue open (as they probably do in the dispute between the reductionists and non-reductionists), in deciding what is reasonable to believe in, we should appeal to practical and moral considerations as well as to our subjective experience. Some such principle is found in William James and is implicit in some of

Kant's writings. The principle of reasonable faith, which I commend in chapter 3, leads to the problem regarding which of the many moralities and practices we should appeal to. To answer this problem I appeal in chapter 4 to the reflective equilibrium model in the wide sense.

I argue in this book that the non-reductionist view rules out not only cases of fission, but also cases of fusion and the creation of replicas of human beings. It might be objected that any view which rules out such cases is doomed to be proved wrong. History tells us how dangerous it is for philosophers and other arm chair thinkers to tell us that certain things can never happen. One famous philosopher said that it is certain that man could never get to the moon. Is it not equally rash to assert that fission, fusion and the creation of replicas are all physically impossible?

What are we to make of this objection? It is wrong to assert dogmatically that certain things cannot happen. But it does not follow that it is wrong to assert in a scientific spirit that some things are physically and metaphysically impossible. For instance, it is perfectly reasonable to conjecture that it is physically impossible for men to fly or that it is physically impossible for men to run a mile in under 10 seconds. From the fact that many of the things that we have believed to be impossible have turned out to be physically possible, it does not follow that nothing is physically impossible.

One must not confuse metaphysical impossibility with epistemic impossibility. It is epistemically possible that one's conjecture about what is metaphysically impossible turns out to be false. I am not committed to the view that it is certain that the non-reductionist view is right. Indeed I believe that the non-reductionist view is falsifiable. If fission, fusion, the creation of replicas etc. start taking place I would abandon the non-reductionist view. It is sometimes thought (for instance by Popper) that belief in essences and metaphysical necessities hinders the progress of science because it makes us think that we have discovered the final truth. But actually one can believe in essences and metaphysical necessities in a scientific spirit; one could and should believe in them as a conjecture that could turn out to be wrong.

So if we believe fission etc. to be physically and metaphysically impossible, we should do so in a scientific spirit. We must be prepared for the possibility that one day we may be proved wrong and have to abandon the non-reductionist view. One of the reasons for discussing the ethical and practical implications of the different views of the self is that if one day the traditional view is undermined, we would be more prepared to deal with our predicament e.g. with the problem about how our ideas of desert, responsibility, egoism etc. will have to be modified or abandoned in such a world. Another reason is that there are already many people who believe in (or at least try to believe in!) the reductionist view. Parfit is the distinguished modern example in the West, but he is by no means the only one. In the East, long before Hume, the Buddhists commended the no-self view. They also tried to work out the moral and practical implications of this view. As a result, there are many people all over the world, who try to live their lives in accordance with what they think are the implications of the no-self view. Another advantage of studying the moral implications of the reductionist theory, according to which a person is really like a group, is that it has relevance to the morality of groups. So one does not need to apologize for spending time in trying to solve the problem of what really are the implications of the reductionist view.

Parfit distinguishes what he calls the extreme view from the moderate view regarding whether our ideas about desert, compensation, fair distribution of resources, rationality of egoistical concern etc, are compatible with the reductionist view of the self. According to the moderate view they are compatible, according to the extreme view they are not.

Of course one could adopt an extreme view with regard to a good deal of our morality and a moderate view regarding other parts of morality. In this book, as in my *Equality, Liberty and Perfectionism*, I argue for the extreme view with regard to substantial parts of our morality but I do admit that there are parts of our morality where the moderate view holds. For instance, our conceptions of pride and shame can be reconciled with the reductionist view. Just as a member of a family can be proud or ashamed of what another does, so too can a later self be proud or ashamed of what an earlier self has done, for it is related to it in close ways. I argue in the last two chapters of this book that the reductionist view would undermine some of the individualist constraints that at present qualify the operation of collectivist and utilitarian moralities.

Parfit argues that both the extreme view and the moderate view are defensible, not just in the sense that the moderate view is true of some of our morality and the extreme view is true of other parts of our morality; even within a particular area of morality the two views are defensible in the sense that though they cannot both be true within the same field, a good case can be made for each of the views. In the last three chapters of this book I make a case for an extreme view with regard to areas such as the rationality of egoistical concern, fair distribution of resources, compensation, moral desert, etc. But I do not deny that even in these areas in some attenuated sense some of these conceptions (such as desert) can survive the change over to the reductionist view.

I have in chapters 8 and 9 tended to discuss the moderate version of Parfit's views because it is these views that are undermined by some of my arguments. In some of his writings he, like the Buddhists, favours the extreme version and here I am in considerable agreement with Parfit. But even here there is an important difference. Those who believe in the extreme view can be divided into two groups; those who think that the non–reductionist view is false and those who do not. If, like Parfit and the Buddhists, you think that the non–reductionist view is false and if you subscribe to the extreme view then you would want the existing morality replaced by a substantially different one. But if, like me, you think that the non–reductionist view has not been shown to be false then the extreme view does not commit you to a radical overhaul of our moral and practical system.

NOTES

1.   D. Hume, *A Treatise of Human Nature*, Book 1 Part 4 Sec.6.

I. *Persons and Personal Identity*

Section 1: Reductionist versus Non-Reductionist Theories

There are several views about the nature of persons and personal identity. There is the reductionist view or the no-self view of the Buddhists, Hume and Parfit according to which there is no self or substance persisting through the different phases of an individual human being's life. This is also called the bundle theory of the self or the empiricist theory of the self. The difference between the no-self theory and the bundle theory of the self is merely verbal. It might be objected that the no-self theory denies the existence of the self while the bundle theory gives a reductivist analysis of the self, so how can the two be the same? The answer is that the no-self view only denies the self in the non-reductionist sense; it does not deny that there is a bundle that consists of the successive experiences, dispositions etc. that one has. Whether one calls this bundle the self is a verbal matter.

Sometimes the reductionist view of the self is called the complex view of the self but in fact the two are not always the same. There are two versions of the complex view. According to the non-reductionist version there is no one permanent self, but there is a succession of temporary selves (which are overlapping in some of the versions) in the life of a human being; the person is a complex entity made up of these selves. According to the reductionist version there is no self in the deep (i.e. non-redutionist) sense at all, not even a temporary one.

Then there is the simple version of the non-reductionist view according to which there is as a matter of fact just one simple self that persists throughout the life of a human being. There are of course other views about the self. For instance, one may, as in the *Bhagwat-Gita* and in the *Advaita Vedanta*, believe in a cosmic self that pervades the whole human race, or even the whole of the cosmos, or, as Herder and others did, in a collective self that pervades a group such as a nation state.[1] These could also be versions of the non-reductionist or metaphysical view of the self. The non-reductionist view is metaphysical as opposed to empirical in the sense that it involves belief in the self as a further fact that is not empirically observable. But the version of non-reductionism that I defend in this book is falsifiable in the sense that if certain facts such as fission of persons occurred, then the case for believing in the non-reductionist view would be undermined.

Some of our moral and practical views, including our subjective hopes and fears, presuppose the simple version of the non-reductionist view of the person according to which there is one indivisible self per person, whose survival is a matter of all or nothing. I shall defend this version of the non-reductionist view; unless otherwise stated all references in this book to the non-reductionist view should be taken to refer to this version.

The non-reductionist view can be contrasted with the reductionist view according to which survival of a person admits of degrees and is rather like the survival of nations and machines. What is involved in the survival of a nation are just certain continuities, such as the continuities of peoples, cultures and political systems. On the reductionist view of nations, the nation's survival consists of the survival of these connections; as they weaken, less and less of the nation survives. Once we know how much these connections have weakened, that is all there is to know, there is no further fact about the survival of nations. The person's survival too on the reductionist view of persons consists of the survival of certain continuities and connectedness, physical and psychological; these continuities are not evidence of any further fact about personal identity or personal survival. On the non-reductionist view our bodily and psychological continuities are evidence of a further fact, viz. the persistence of the self. On the simple version the further fact is the persistence of the simple self; on the complex version of the non-reductionist view the further fact involves the gradual changing of a complex entity.[2]

On the complex version of the non-reductionist view the person is identical to an entity that is complex. Consider, for instance, the view that the normal human being is identical to a compound of two or more selves or persons.[3] On such views we are complex not just in the sense of being composed of something complex but also in the sense of being identical to something that is complex. And so our survival can admit of degrees. It is often said that the difference between the reductionist view and the non-reductionist view is that survival on the former does not admit of degrees. We can now see that this is only true if we are talking about the simple version of the non-reductionist view. The difference between survival on the non-reductionist view, whether on the simple version or the complex version, and survival on the reductionist view is that the former survival is much deeper, for it involves the survival of the self that has the various bodily or psychological characteristics, whereas on the reductionist view it only involves the survival of these characteristics.

On the non-reductionist view survival is in a sense derivative from identity, survival involves persistence of the same self. Since identity is a matter of all or nothing so too must survival be all or nothing. So how can survival admit of degrees on the non-reductionist view? On the complex version of the non-reductionist view the complex entity is identical to the sum of more than one simple entity. The survival of each of these simple entities is indeed derivative from their identity and so it does not admit of degrees, but the survival of the complex entity can admit of degrees in the sense that if one of the simple entities which forms part of the complex entity disappears then less of the complex entity is left. From the first person perspective, we do not think of our survival as admitting of degrees, nor do we think that we can divide into two like an amoeba; we cannot imagine our stream of consciousness splitting into two such that we anticipate great torture in one of these streams and look forward to great joy in the other.[4] So the first person perspective seems to go against both the reductionist and the non-reductionist versions of the complex view. In this book, unless otherwise stated, references to the non-reductionist view should be taken to refer to the simple version.

The feature of the simple view that needs stressing is that the simple self is indivisible in the sense that it cannot divide into selves. There is more than one sense of indivisible self and correspondingly there is more than one sense of simple self. A self can be simple and indivisible in the sense that it can not divide into selves (unless otherwise stated, it is in this sense that I shall, in this book, use the terms indivisible self and simple self). But this is consistent with the view that it is complex and divisible in the sense that it could break up into parts that are not selves. Suppose (what I do not think is the case!) the self is a conscious functioning brain. A functioning brain is clearly a complex and divisible entity in the sense that it is made up of parts. It does not follow that the (conscious) functioning brain is also divisible in the sense that it is divisible into two or more separate (conscious) functioning brains. The split brain experiments do not in my opinion show that the *conscious* functioning brain can split into two separate conscious functioning brains. For there is only one brain stem and it is not established that there has been or can be splitting of consciousness.

The view that the self is indivisible has important consequences in our moral and practical life, particularly regarding suffering (see chapter 10).

There are at least three senses of the term same person. There is
the reductionist sense in which the same person could be said to persist
if the same character or personality persists; there is the non-
reductionist sense in which the same self or substance persists; and
there is the combined sense in which both the personality persists and
the self persists. Similarly we can distinguish three different senses of
personal survival.

Sometimes when a person's character or personality has changed
a lot we say that he is not the same person that he was; here we are
using 'same person' in the sense of same personality. But it could be
that in another sense he is the same person, i.e. the same self. Indeed
in saying that *he* is not the person that *he* was, the two uses of 'he' refer
to the same individual. The same self could manifest different
personalities at different times. Cases of multiple personalities do not
necessarily involve cases of multiple persons (in the non-reductionist
sense).

The case for the view that some of our important moral and
practical views presuppose the reductionist view looks stronger than it
is if one neglects the combined sense of the term same person. Often
we do direct our attitudes such as resentment, love etc, to the agent's
personality which does gradually change in degrees. But it would be
wrong to assume, as reductionists sometimes do, that such attitudes
only make sense on the reductionist view. For they are compatible
with the combined sense. In chapter 4 section 3 I give a few
illustrations of this point from different spheres of practical and moral
life.

There are different versions of the reductionist view some of
which I shall discuss in this book. For instance, there is the version
that treats experiences as atomic units separate from each other and
there is the version which stresses that some of the experiences form
a continuous flow. I discuss the significance of this distinction in
chapters 9 and 10.

Let us now examine some of the differences between the
reductionist and non-reductionist views. We saw that the latter
involves a belief in a further fact. Parfit thinks that on the only
plausible version of the non-reductionist view persons are separately
existent beings, separate not only from their brains and bodies but
even from their experiences. But this is not so. The non-reductionist
can also regard the person and his experiences as inseparable. The

most plausible version of the non-reductionist view asserts that experiences do not exist in themselves but only as states or modifications of the self or agent. So the difference between some of the reductionist views and the non-reductionist view is that on the former view the items of experience are the primary units, are objectively real in the sense that they exist in themselves, while persons are logical constructs out of these experiences; whereas on the non-reductionist view experiences do not exist in themselves and so are not objectively real but have a subjective reality, for they only exist as states of the agent. This feature of the non-reductionist view can explain why my experiences could never in any possible world have been yours.

Another related difference between the two views is that on the non-reductionist view the agent or self can help to explain the way in which the various experiences are unified; there is unity of consciousness when all the experiences belong to the consciousness of the same subject. On the reductionist view, since the subject of experience does not exist in any deep sense but only as a manner of speaking, it cannot be used to explain unity of consciousness.[5]

The agent on the non-reductionist view is primary not only with regard to its experiences; it also plays an important role in explaining actions and distinguishing them from mere bodily movements. Actions, unlike mere bodily movements are guided by the person or agent.[6] On the reductionist view the agent can have no such role for the agent does not exist in any deep sense. Reid who believed in the non-reductionist theory of personal identity said, 'I am not thought, I am not action. I am not feeling; I am something that thinks and acts and suffers'.[7] On the reductionist view too one can admit that I am something that thinks, acts etc, but this would be true because of the way we talk; we could give a complete description of reality without talking of persons; the Buddha said 'O Brethren actions do exist and also their consequences but the person that acts does not. There exists no individual, it is only a convenient name given to a set of elements'.[9] So how can an appeal to the person explain the difference between actions and bodily movement?

Of course, there are several versions of reductionist views, some more extreme than others. The extreme ones deny the primacy of the person and of personal identity. But there is a moderate version, advocated by Shoemaker, which grants that persons are primary but denies that personal identity is primitive. He is a reductionist with regard to personal identity but not with regard to persons.[10] How then do we distinguish such a reductionist view from the non-reductionist view of personal identity? Sometimes, it is thought that on the former view unlike on the latter, identity admits of degrees. It is thought that the reductionist view is true of objects such as chairs where if a part of it is replaced by another then the subsequent chair is partly the same as the old one and partly not; similarly it is argued that on the reductionist view the person can be partly the same as he was earlier. This is not an adequate way of characterizing the difference, for identity is in its logic a matter of all or nothing. A better way of characterizing the difference is that on the reductionist view it is survival that is the basic concept and can be used to explain identity, whereas on the non-reductionist view it is the other way round. On the reductionist view since personal survival consists of certain things such as psychological connectedness and continuity, it is these things that it consists of that ultimately matter; personal identity is of derivative importance, it consists of non-branching personal survival.

Let us now discuss whether non-reductionist survival is deeper than reductionist survival. I believe the answer is 'yes'. On the non-reductionist view personal identity involves a deep further fact.[11] And this fact, if true, would justify important attitudes with regard to egoistical concern, desert, equality etc. I examine some of these implications in the later chapters. Survival on the non-reductionist view is a deeper sort of survival than survival on the reductionist view, where survival just consists of the survival of one's psychology. It is not just that on the non-reductionist view (on the simple version) one survives fully as long as one lives, whereas on the reductionist view one survives less and less in the future. It is also that even in the short run one survives in a very shallow sense. For on the reductionist view survival consists merely of certain relations that hold between certain experiences and a person phase now and certain experiences and a person phase in the future.

Shoemaker believes that survival is not any deeper on the non-reductionist view. He holds that on both views the unity relation between various experiences and person stages of the same person is the co-personality relation; what makes my present person stage and my future person stage stages of the same person is that they are linked by the co-personality relation. On the non-reductionist view this relation is primitive and unanalyzable, on the reductionist view it can further be analyzed into non-branching psychological continuity and connectedness. Why should the relationship being primitive and unanalysable make it especially important for moral and practical life? This objection does have force if one compares the reductionist view to non-reductionism of the kind recommended by Madell where the self is not a substance but a property, and where all that my experiences have in common is that they have the unanalysable property of being mine. Why should the fact that the relevant property is unanalysable make my survival any deeper? But there is another way of characterising the difference between the non-reductionist and reductionist views. On the former view my present person stage and my future person phase are phases of the same substantial self (where the self is not a property) whereas on the reductionist views these phases are merely linked by certain relations such as psychological continuity and connectedness. Of course even on the reductionist view, my present person stage and my future person stage are stages of the same person, but this is a relatively trivial truth; for if there had been branching (e.g. splitting of persons into two or more) the links between the earlier and later phases would have been just as close but they would not have been stages of the same person.

On the non-reductionist view, it is a non-trivial truth that personal identity consists of the persistence of the same subject. From the first person perspective the self is the subject of all my experiences and provides a unity to these experiences. All my experiences are co-personal. On the non-reductionist view the relation of co-personality does not have to be primitive as Shoemaker thinks it does; co-personality can be explained. All my experiences are co-personal because they are experiences of the same self or subject. It is the self and the persistence of the self that are primitive on the non-reductionist view.

Shoemaker who adopts a functionalist approach argues that personal identity plays a vital role on his reductionist view too. 'It seems essential to functional definitions that it makes use of the notion of personal identity in defining particular mental states; for what the functional definition of a state tells us is that something counts as a realisation of that state if it is such that when combined with such and such other states of *the same person* it produces certain effects in that *same person*.'[12] This seems difficult to reconcile with the reductionist view of personal identity where personal identity has a derivative role because it is understood in terms of relations between mental states.

On the reductionist view when there is fission or fusion there is survival without personal identity. The link between the person stages is just as close whether or not there is branching. So how can personal identity be what really matters in explaining what unites the various experiences over time?

On the non-reductionist view personal identity involves the persistence of the self or substance. Shoemaker thinks that such a view is based on a confusion that arises from a failure to distinguish substances in the Aristotelian sense, the sense in which continuants like trees that can survive changes in their composition count as substances, and substances in the sense of portion of stuff, material or immaterial. He argues that it is either false or vacuous to say that the identity of things like trees consists in their being the same substance. If 'substance' means portion of stuff then the claim is false; if it means 'persisting subject of properties' then it is vacuous, for it then boils down to: being the same tree consists in being the same tree.

A tree at a particular time is not identical with the portion of matter it is composed of, and it can survive the gradual replacement of matter that it is composed of. A person too can survive changes in its composition, whether material or immaterial. So even if a person were composed of different souls on different days, he could survive the change of souls. If this is so, people are confused in thinking that it is possible that there is a succession of persons in the same human body, each passing its psychology on to the next. Just as a tree can persist inspite of gradual changes in its matter, and a waterfall can persist inspite of even sudden changes in its water, so also a person could persist in spite of a succession of immaterial souls or substances. Shoemaker[13] agrees with Parfit that if someone's mental states are transferred to a different brain the person goes with the mental states and aquires a new brain. He claims that by parity of reasoning Parfit should admit, as Shoemaker does, that if someone's mental states are transferred from one immaterial soul to another, the person goes with the mental states. If so Kant's example of a succession of substances, in the sense of subjects of experience, within the same human being is incoherent.

What are we to make of this argument? The non-reductionist would deny the above characterisation of his views. For instance, on the Cartesian version of the non-reductionist view, my relation to my soul is not like the relation of objects like trees to the matter they are composed of; I am not composed of a soul, rather I am the soul; I am identical to the soul whereas the chair is not identical to the wood it is composed of. The view that persons are indivisible selves or souls is not meant to be a trivial truth that follows from the meaning of words like 'selves' and 'persons', but a controversial metaphysical claim about the world. If I am the self, the subject of my present experiences, I can wonder in a non-trivial way if this very self will be there in the future as the subject of the experiences that are related to my present experiences by psychological connectedness and continuity.

To return to the problem of non-reductionist survival being deeper than reductionist survival, one answer is to show what a shallow form of survival reductionist survival is. I do this in chapter 8, where I stress that reductionist survival merely involves the survival of one's psychology, whereas non-reductionist survival insists that the person who has the psychology should persist. If I want to write a good book and if my want is an egoistic one then it is essential to the satisfaction of my want not just that the book be written but that it be written by me.

In the next section of this chapter and in chapter 8, I contend that on the reductionist view, at any rate in its psychological version, it is my egoistic concern (which varies with the extent to which I identify with my future selves) which helps to determine my survival rather than my survival which provides me with a reason for egoistical concern. This reflects the fact that my survival on the reductionist view is a shallow form of survival compared to non-reductionist survival where my survival can, without any circularity, provide me with a reason for egoistical concern. Of course the fact that non-reductionist survival is deeper from the point of view of our egoistic concerns does not imply that it is better than reductionist survival from other points of view. For instance, if we want people to live in a group without a sense of their separate individual identity, such a view would be easier to justify if we assume the reductionist view of people.

But given that people do identify with their future selves, whether or not the reductionist view is correct, is not their survival just as deep on the reductionist view as it is on the non-reductionist view? One answer to this is that some people, especially some children, do not identify much with their future selves; some others are dissociated from their past selves: 'It was not I who did it, it was someone else'. Even amongst sane adults some people, such as the Buddhists, try to decondition themselves from their egoistic concerns. On the non-reductionist view, unlike on the reductionist view, one could argue that all such people survive, whether or not they identify with their past and future selves. Non-reductionist survival provides them with a reason for such identification. Of course if the dissociation is severe enough they may need psychiatric or other help, before they can see and follow reason.

Another answer to the above question is that even when people do identify with their future selves their survival is not deep enough on the reductionist view; this point will be further developed in chapters 8 and 10. In chapter 10 I argue that what is specially evil about great suffering is that the same individual keeps suffering on and on; the reductionist view cannot account for what is specially terrible about such suffering, even when people identify with their future selves.

Section 2: Realism versus Ascriptivism
We have seen that on the non-reductionist view persons or agents are real in a much deeper sense than they are on the reductionist view. On the former view they help to explain actions, and to explain how there is unity of consciousness both at any one time and across time. On the reductionist view the language of persons is at best a pragmatically useful way of dealing with the world, which could in principle be described completely without the use of such language.

Since the language of persons is in principle redundant on the reductionist view, it follows that the language of personal identity is also in principle redundant on that view. The contrast with the non-reductionist view is clear, for on the non-reductionist view judgements of personal identity correspond to the way things are and the way things are cannot be completely described without the language of personal identity. On the reductionist view what really matters can be explained in terms of concepts other than persons and personal identity. Thus it is suggested that personal identity can be understood in terms of non-branching survival and survival can be understood in terms of psychological connectedness and continuity.

Our present system involves the realist view according to which judgements of personal identity, even in the most difficult of the actual problem cases have a right answer that is independent of our decisions or choices. On this view, in the multiple personality cases as well as in the split personality cases there is a truth about whether or not there is more than one self per human being, however difficult it is for us to get at the truth.

The realist view of persons and personal identity can be contrasted with the the conventionalist view according to which personal identity judgements are, at any rate in the problem cases, a matter of convention or decision. Thus Wittgenstein thought that our ordinary concept of the person is meant for ordinary situations; where extraordinary situations arise we have a choice: 'Now were Dr. Jekyll and Mr. Hyde two persons or were they the same person who merely changed? We can say whichever we like.'[14] Putnam[15] considers without fully endorsing a conventionalist solution to the split brain cases where there is alleged to be a second consciousness. On the conventional view whether there is a second consciousness is a matter of decision.

In fact we are realists with regard to consciousness as well as personal identity. Nagel points out rightly that if things emerged from a spaceship such that we could not know whether they were machines or conscious beings, there would be a truth of the matter inspite of our not being able to know the truth; whether they were conscious would depend upon whether there was something it was like to be them, and not on the possibility of extending mental ascriptions to them on evidence analogous to the human case. This point applies *mutatis mutandis* to the problem of whether there is a second consciousness in split brain cases.

That the current view of personal identity is a realist one according to which personal survival is a matter of all or nothing and does not admit of borderlines can be seen from the following considerations. If a car is involved in a major accident such that about 50% of its parts have been destroyed and it loses some of its main functions, does it survive the accident? This presents a borderline case and the answer depends on our decision. But if a person has a major accident and loses a substantial part of his mental and physical characteristics, either he has survived (though with an impoverished mind and body) or he has not, there is no borderline. If a person is told that he will suffer a lot after the major accident his egoistic worries do not get less on the grounds that there will be less of him left after the operation. A pain in the future will be either mine or not mine; one does not think of it as something that will be partly mine. One does not argue that from a prudential standpoint one should care less now about oneself in the more distant future (say after forty years) than in the near future (say after one year) on the grounds that there will be less of oneself left in the more distant future. Of course one might attach less weight to things that might happen in the remote future on other grounds; for instance, because the more remote future is more uncertain or because one adopts an ostrich-like policy with regard to it, or even because one does not sympathise much now with the sort of character one might acquire later. One can care less about oneself in the remote future because there will be less of one's psychology left then, but one can argue, by appealing to the combined sense of the term 'same person' (which I explained in section 1 of this chapter) that such considerations are compatible with the non-reductionist view. One can care both for one's psychology, whose survival admits of degrees, and for the survival of the self that has the psychology; the survival of the self does not admit of degrees. I shall further discuss the combined sense of the term 'same person' in chapter 4 section 3.

Chisholm gives the following example: Suppose you need to have an operation, and you have a choice between a very expensive operation where you are subjected to total anaesthesia, and a very cheap operation where there is great pain involved. But the doctor in the second case will give you two drugs. First a drug just before the operation that makes you forget everything with regard to the past and then another drug that restores your former memories but makes you forget totally what happens during the operation.

Some philosophers such as Locke would say that the person who was conscious during the operation was different from the person before and after the operation. Others would say the opposite. But clearly there is something absurd about deciding between these views by appealing to a convention. Suppose the person is very afraid of the pain that he will suffer if he chooses the cheaper operation. He is not going to be reassured if we tell him not to worry since we (his friends, doctors, clergymen etc.) will by convention suitably alter the criteria of personal identity, so that the person who undergoes the operation is not him but another person.

This example does seem to show that our present system is a realist one, but some reductionists would deny this. They would claim that non-realists too could reject a crude conventionalist approach where our say-so determines the correct personal identity judgements. Some of them lay down what I shall call a super-criterion for personal identity, by which I mean a criterion for evaluating criteria of personal identity. For instance Shoemaker[17] says that our criteria of personal identity should be such that our judgements of personal identity should match the special concern that we feel for our future selves. A very similar super-criterion has been suggested by Mackie[18] who says that our personal identity judgements should match the hard facts of biologically determined concern. He commends his proposal on the grounds that it makes such judgements coincide with what is the normal object of one's special concern. He uses his super-criterion for ruling out alternative views; for instance the Lockean view that John Smith becomes a different person when he suffers amnesia is criticized by appeal to the fact John Smith before the amnesia will feel egoistic concern for what happens to him as an amnesiac.

Perhaps one could supplement the above super-criterion with others. For instance it has been suggested that one of the things that tends to make us survivors of our past selves is that we identify with our past selves, e.g. by feeling guilty or ashamed or proud of what we did.[19] Such a super-criterion too could be used to evaluate the rulings that we may give about personal identity and personal survival. To be accurate one should say that on the reductionist view these are super-criteria of personal survival rather than of personal identity. For on that view it is personal survival that is ultimately important.

So on the reductionist view too we are not free to adopt any convention that we like about personal survival. We must keep our judgements in line with the relevant attitudes and emotions. Ultimately one has a choice regarding one's judgement about personal survival only to the extent that one can alter the relevant attitudes and emotions. So this view too is not a crude conventional view where our say so determines the extent to which we survive and where any ruling about personal survival is as good as any other, rather it is our attitudes and emotions (such as guilt, fear etc.) that determine it.

Now whether or not the non-realist view is the correct one, it is not the ordinary common-sense view. The common-sense view is the realist view where judgements of personal identity and personal survival correspond to the way things are and are presupposed by our attitudes and emotions; I feel terrible remorse because it was I who did the terrible deed, my feeling remorse does not tend to make the deed mine. Again, on the common-sense view my egoistic fear about the torture that I shall undergo next year presupposes that it will be I who will be tortured next year; the existence of my fear does not tend to make the future suffering that I am afraid of mine.

Even though the ascriptivist theory of personal identity and personal survival is not the current one, is it the correct view? Should we accept it as a recommendation? It might be replied that the ascriptivist view is an absurd one. For our egoistic concerns and our conceptions of moral guilt and moral responsibility presuppose the realist view of personal identity and personal survival. So how can these attitudes and feelings that presuppose personal identity and personal survival be used to determine it?

Against this the ascriptivist might make a reply similar to the reply that was made by the defenders of the reductionist view in connection with memory and personal identity. The believers in the reductionist view used memory as one of the criteria of personal identity. They had to face the objection that memory presupposes personal identity and so cannot be used as a criterion of personal identity. Reductionists replied to this charge by distinguishing memory from quasi-memory. Quasi-memories are like memories except that they do not assume that the experience one recalls happened to oneself. Like genuine memories they give us knowledge from the past from the inside. Such rememberings of the past from the inside are not something that we establish on inductive grounds.[20] Similarly one might try to explain quasi-egoistic concern as concern which is like egoistic concern except that it does not assume that the concern is for the very same person as oneself. Like egoistic concern, quasi-egoistic concern involves concern for an individual or individuals to whom one is related from the inside as it were. This could include one's offshoots.[21] Such a defence might at best rescue the reductionist from the charge of circularity but there are other problems. In chapter 8 I shall examine some of the attempted reconciliations between the reductionist view of persons and the rationality of egoistic concern.

With regard to some other feelings such as guilt etc, I shall examine in chapter 9 how far some of them can be reconciled with the reductionist view.

Let us now examine some of the different versions of ascriptivism. There are at least two currently popular versions of ascriptivism as applied to personal identity: the individual version and the social version;[22] similarly there are at least two versions of ascriptivism as applied to personal survival.

According to the individual version it is the individual's own attitudes and beliefs that are one of the important determinants of whether he is the same person as a past self or as a future self. We have briefly discussed this view earlier. According to the social version, it is society's attitude that is an important determinant of whether x and y are the same individual. One may of course subscribe to both these versions for it is quite consistent to believe that both the individual and social attitudes are important determinants of personal identity. Illustrations of the social version as well as of the individual version are found in Shoemaker's writings. He asks us to imagine a society where increased radiation has made it impossible for a human body to remain healthy for long. For each person there is a stock of duplicate bodies stored in a radiation proof vault. 'Periodically a person goes into the hospital for a 'body change'. This consists of his total brain state being transferred to the brain of one of his duplicate bodies. At the end of the procedure the original body is incinerated... All of the social practices of the society presuppose that the procedure is person preserving. The brain state recipient is regarded as owning the property of the brain state donor, as being married to the donor's spouse, and of holding whatever offices, responsibilities, rights, obligations, etc. the brain-state donor held. If it is found that the brain-state donor had committed a crime, everyone regards it as just that the brain-state donor should be punished for it'.[23]

Shoemaker says that the imaginary society is right in regarding the brain state transfer as person preserving. He thinks that they mean the same thing by 'person' and 'personal identity' as we do and that personal identity has with them the same connections with moral responsibility, ownership, property etc. as it does with us. But this is not so. In our society, systems of moral responsibility, justice, property etc. presuppose the conception of a person rather than determine it. In our society it is not because the later Brown is considered by society, or by himself, to be morally guilty for the deeds of the earlier Brown that makes him, or even tends to make him, the survivor of the earlier Brown. Rather such judgements assume that he is the same person. Similar remarks apply to society's decision to let the later Brown keep the property that belonged to the earlier Brown.

Individual ascriptivism is also different from our ordinary common-sense ideas, as we saw earlier. So both the popular versions of ascriptivism are alien to our common-sense ideas of personal identity. In chapter 9 we shall see that the social ascriptivist view is also inconsistent with our idea that the person is an end in itself. The ascriptivist view goes naturally with the reductionist view of the person rather than with the non-reductionist view which as we have seen goes with a realist view. Compare the case of nations. If one takes a non-reductionist view of nations and believes that what makes Scotland one nation is the possession of a soul or substance, then it is not the feelings and attitudes of the Scottish people that makes

Scotland one nation; but if one takes a reductionist view and denies that Scotland is a soul or substance, then it is more plausible to argue that the fact that the Scottish people regard Scotland as a nation tends to make them one nation. Again on the reductionist view Europe is not a nation, not because there is no European soul or substance, but because Europeans do not regard Europe as a nation. Similar considerations apply to persons on the reductionist view.

Does the reductionist view necessarily go with some versions of ascriptivism? Later in the book[24] I shall argue that the two do go together, that one cannot reasonably be a reductionist, at any rate in the psychological version, unless one is also willing to embrace ascriptivism with regard to personal survival. So if ascriptivism is counter-intuitive, so too is reductionism!

There are two kinds of ascriptivists. Those such as the Buddhists, Parfit[25] and Mackie who suggest their views as a recommendation, based on a true insight into the way things are, but who would admit that their views are counter-intuitive and that our present system is a realist one, which is based on an error. And those such as Shoemaker and Kathleen Wilkes who argue that even our present system is at least partly an ascriptivist one.

Kathleen Wilkes,[26] like Shoemaker, seems to regard society's attitude as one of the determinants of our present system of personal identity. She thinks that there is powerful evidence arising from a study of multiple personality cases, against the view that there is always one person per human being. But she thinks that society's attitudes pull us in favour of the one person per human being view. Our voting system, our medical practice, our legal, political and social institutions all constrain us to adopt the one person per human body view. So she claims that in some of the multiple personality cases the conception of the person breaks down, for there are powerful considerations both for and against the one person view.

It is wrong to regard the present system as even partly an ascriptivist one. Of course social pressures may influence our judgements of personal identity, but this is not the way the system is meant to work, at any rate when there is a strong intellectual case for making a judgement of personal identity. One should not have to balance intellectual considerations on the one hand against social ones on the other. In the U.S. legal system it used to be debated whether blacks were persons. There were social pressures to say they were not, but surely such pressures were irrelevant to their being persons, though they may have been relevant to whether they were in fact likely to be given the status of persons by society or by the legal system.[27]

If there is a good intellectual case for making judgements of personal identity then such judgements do not become any less true because there are social or practical considerations on the other side. Nor can we say that the present system breaks down in some difficult real life cases and remains intact for the ordinary cases. If it breaks down in some real life cases, then it breaks down altogether. For on the present view survival is a matter of all or nothing and so it does not allow for any indeterminacy. One might suggest that there are some freakish cases of abnormal personality, where the reductionist view applies, while in the ordinary cases the non-reductionist view applies. This suggestion would leave the non-reductionist view intact; for it would not imply that the non-reductionist view breaks down in some actual cases. Although one cannot rule out this suggestion on *a priori* grounds, one can be suspicious of it on empirical grounds, which I discuss in chapter 6. In that chapter I discuss other suggestions which may be more plausible, viz, that in such abnormal cases there is more than one non-reductionist self per person or, the view that I defend, that there is only one indivisible self with switching of consciousness from one personality to another.

It is worth distinguishing the social ascriptivist theory of personal identity which I have criticised from the doctrine of reasonable faith which I defend. The former view is much stronger. On the latter view if the balance of intellectual considerations are on one side, then practical or subjective considerations on the other side must give way; it is only when intellectual or empirical considerations leave an issue open that practical considerations should guide us as to which option we should choose. Secondly, there is the difference that the doctrine of reasonable faith, at any rate in the version that I want to defend, is compatible with the realist view of personal identity. According to it there is a fact of the matter about personal identity that is quite independent of our practical views; it tells us what it is reasonable to believe, whereas on the ascriptivist view the relevant attitudes help to determine the truth about personal identity or personal survival.

Section 3: The First Person Perspective

Some philosophers who attach great importance to ruling out scepticism, have stressed the outward empirical criteria that we use for identifying and reidentifying of persons; we identify individual selves or individual consciousnesses by identifying the observable human being; we have ordinary criteria for identifying and reidentifying of ordinary human beings, just as we have empirical criteria for identity of ordinary objects. Counting of selves on this view is derivative from counting of human beings. On this view though I identify myself from a first person perspective without reference to any outward criteria, this is only because such first person judgements have links with ordinary empirical criteria of identity of human beings. Let us call this the ordinary approach. Among those who adopt some such approach are Strawson[28] and Mark Johnston.[29]

Adherents of the ordinary approach point out that those, such as the Cartesians, who do not adopt this approach have to face the insoluble problem regarding how many selves there are in the lives of a human being, both at any one time and across time. I shall deal with this problem in chapter 3. They also sometimes suggest that their opponents cannot reconcile their views with the common-sense view that we know for certain that John Smith today is the very same person or self as John Smith yesterday. I shall reply to this criticism later.

The ordinary approach has its own problems with regard to the individuation of persons. Why must there be one person or self per human being? I myself defend the view that there is *in fact* one self per human being, as a reasonable conjecture which we should accept unless and until we get evidence to the contrary. But on the ordinary approach the notion of identity of selves is derivative from the notion of identity of the flesh and blood people and so it would be absurd to wonder if there could be more than one self per human being, at any rate in the ordinary case. There are thinkers, such as Puccetti who claim that cases of split brains and multiple personality show that there is more than one self per person not only in these cases but in the ordinary cases as well. I examine some of these arguments in chapters 5 and 6 and conclude that the evidence so far does not justify such a radical view. We should adhere to the conservative view of one person per human being as long as we honestly can. But the radical view is I think an epistemically possible one, and one must not dogmatically rule it out as an absurd hypothesis.

It might be suggested that we should modify the ordinary view in a functionalist or behaviourist direction. Why not adopt something like Shoemaker's approach according to which the mind of a human being, though often it is compartmentalised, is treated as a unit, not because of the dogma 'one human body, one person' but because in the multiple personality and split brain cases that actually occur, the compartmentalisation is incomplete and because we think that it is possible at least partially to restore the integeration of the mind.

I contend in chapter 2 that some such fuctionalist approach may be helpful in dealing with the problem regarding why certain items of behaviour are lumped together in one mind; but it does not help with the problem of unity of mind in the strong sense which is the problem regarding what unites the various items of conscious experiences in one unit. As Brentano[30] and others have stressed such unity can only be understood from the inside.

From the first person perspective[31] one believes in the non-reductionist view, for one thinks of survival as all or nothing. Some philosophers would go further and argue that the first person perspective presupposes Cartesian dualism with the mind and body as two separate substances. My own view is that this has not been established; a dual aspect theory where mental and physical properties are both properties of the person has not been shown to be incompatible with the first person point of view. I shall develop this point during the course of this chapter and also try to examine some though by no means all of the problems that the first person perspective raises.

In introspection one is not present to oneself as an object, neither material nor immaterial. One does not come to know that one is in pain by observing an object in pain and then identify that object as oneself. Indeed in order to identify an object as oneself one would already have to have self-awareness. Suppose an object is in pain. How would I know that that object is me? Is it that it has certain properties that I know that I uniquely have? But in that case I would already need to be aware of myself. It makes no sense to say of an inner conscious state that I am aware of it but I do not know whose state it is. Conscious states only exist as modifications of the agent, who directly ascribes them to himself. It is because experiences only occur as modifications of the agent that the agent cannot wonder whose experience it is; things would be different if experiences were objectively given particulars.

From the first person perspective I see myself as the subject of my experiences. It is often suggested that these experiences are not mine in virtue of being related in a certain way to an object in the external world, such as the brain or the human body. If they were then it would be possible for me to be mistaken in attributing them to myself. In fact though I can be mistaken about the nature of my conscious experiences I cannot be mistaken in thinking that they are mine.

Shoemaker[32] thinks that such considerations do not point towards Cartesiam dualism or towards the view that personal identity is unanalysable. He suggests that it is possible that we are so constructed, as a result of evolution or by God, that when a human being is in a certain conscious state, he comes to believe directly that he is in that state. The reductionist view and the view that the person is a complex object in the world are compatible with the view that he has direct unmediated belief from the inside about himself. Such beliefs count as knowledge because of the reliable way in which they are produced. We are so constructed that such beliefs are reliable.

But this suggests that nature might throw up freaks who are not so constructed! Is it even conceivable that there could be a persistent individual who is self conscious, who is directly aware of a conscious experience but who is not certain if it is he who is experiencing it? I shall presently offer a way in which the dual-aspect theory might be able to account for first person ascriptions of conscious states.

Anscombe gives the example of a person who is locally anaesthetized all over and who is in a state of total sensory deprivation. He can still use 'I' in the normal way and say things like 'I must not let such things happen again'.[33] Anscombe thinks that 'I' does not here refer in absence, so if 'I' is a referring expression it refers here to a Cartesian ego or to a stretch of one. But could not a double aspect theorist reconcile this example with his views without denying that 'I' is a referring expression? The double aspect theorist could say that in this example, even though an essential aspect of the person viz. the physical aspect, is absent, another essential aspect, viz. the mental aspect, is present and so one uses 'I' with an important aspect of oneself present.

Suppose I am having some experiences. If I identify the individual that I am from the outside, for instance by looking at a mirror, then I can go wrong in attributing these inner experiences to their proper owner. But if I refer to myself via the inner aspect, as the individual whose inner aspect I am aware of, and where these experiences are taking place, can I go wrong in attributing these experiences to the individual who has them? Not if I refrain from specifying the nature of the individual that I am. But if I say that I am brain X then I can go wrong if it turns out that I am not that particular brain but another one or if it turns out that I am not a brain at all.

A dual-aspect theorist could grant that I do not infer that these experiences are mine because they belong to this human body or this brain; rather, because they are mine, I know that these experiences belong to the individual (e. g. the human body or brain) whose inner aspect I am directly aware of. So a dual aspect theorist could say that though all the inner experiences I am aware of are mine, I could wrongly attribute these experiences to a certain brain or human body, because I wrongly think of that human brain or body as identical with me. So it is not established that first person ascriptions of experiences necessarily point towards Cartesian dualism.

It might be thought that the simple version of the non-reductionist view involves a belief in dualism, in mind and body as two separate substances. For since survival of a person's body or psychology admits of degrees, if we postulate the simple view, then we have to fall back on some sort of Cartesian immaterial soul which is simple and indivisible. But in fact there are other alternatives. It might be that a person is something primitive which has a dual aspect, a mental aspect and a physical aspect. And though a person's mental life admits of degrees and so does his physical nature, his own survival does not admit of degrees. Even though the physical aspect and the mental aspect are both aspects of the person, it does not follow that the person has no property which its physical and mental aspects do not have. So the person may be simple in the sense that it is indivisible (i.e. it cannot divide into persons) and its survival does not admit of degrees, even though it has aspects of which the survival does admit of degrees.

But one might believe in a dual aspect theory according to which the person that has the dual aspect itself belongs to a primitive category and is not identical to a particular body or brain; the brain is the outer aspect of the person. Even though it is essential to a person that he have a physical aspect, the body or brain that he has could change without the person's survival being affected; for what is essential is not that the person should continue to have the same physical components but that it should continue to have some physical components. Similarly, the view that a person must have a mental life does not imply that a person cannot survive radical changes in its mental life. The view that a mental aspect and a physical aspect are essential for a person to be a person, does not imply that a person's identity or survival is dependent on the identity or survival of the mental and physical make up that it presently has. It may be that a person could survive entire changes in his body and brain; what is essential on this view is that he must always be embodied in some relevant body or brain. Similarly, a person may survive changes in his mental life, even though it is essential to his personhood that he should continue to have some mental life.

A dual aspect theory, at least in one important version of it, is non-reductionist; for according to it the person is primitive and cannot be analysed in terms of his mental and physical components. So it would be dogmatic to assume that the rejection of the reductionist view of the person commits us to a belief in the Cartesian soul.

It may be that all dual aspect theories are incompatible with the non-reductionist view. But this is something that has to be shown to be the case. In the present state of our knowledge, it is epistemically possible that the two are compatible. So when in this book I argue that a good deal of our subjective experience and our moral and practical system presupposes the non-reductionist view, I shall leave it open whether the indivisible self is a Cartesian immaterial soul.

Section 4: The Self As Brain

The view that the self is the functioning brain is the modern successor to the view that the self is the live human body. It is now realised that people can survive the removal of large parts of the human body; in many cases they are actually better off with transplants. The brain or at least some part of it, is the only essential physical part of us; it is the seat of our memories, dispositions etc. True, in order to flourish or even survive in any worthwhile sense we also need other physical parts, but these other parts are in principle replaceable. The vital parts of the brain on the other hand are irreplaceable, or so it is believed. If replicas of the brain could in principle be created then the view that I am my brain would lose whatever plausibility that it now has. For I have argued in chapter 7 that if replicas could be created then we should abandon the non-reductionist view. And I have argued in chapter 8 that if we accept the reductionist view then the view that I am my brain should be rejected.

On one view of the brain, the brain is a construct made up of successive brain stages. This view is clearly incompatible with the view that the non-reductionist persistent self is the brain. For if the brain is made up of successive brain stages, then it cannot be used to provide unity to the various experiences of the person. If my brain is the subject of my experiences, such a subject will not remain the same as one brain stage gives way to another. Then there are philosophers, such as Nagel, who combine the view that the non-reductionist self is the brain with the view that the brain is a complex unit. This view too would seem to be incompatible with our subjective view according to which our survival does not admit of degrees.

The brain clearly is complex in the sense that it is composed of several parts functioning together in certain relations to each other. But is it even certain that the simple version of the non-reductionist view is incompatible with the view that the self is a functioning brain? Nagel believes that his view that the self is the brain involves a partial revision of our existing views of the self; for the brain is a complex organism whose survival is a matter of degree, while on the existing view the self is indivisible and simple. And some people are persuaded by the Leibnizian argument that nothing material, neither the brain nor any physical object like the human body, could be identical with the simple self, for material things are extended and so are divisible. While Leibniz would have denied that the self is the brain because he was convinced that the self is a simple substance, Nagel thinks that we should abandon the view that the self is simple. But they would both agree that the simple self view is incompatible with the view that the self is a brain.

What are we to make of such arguments? It is true that a physical object such as a brain does in a sense have parts. But it does not follow that it must be divisible in the relevant sense. A conscious functioning brain may still be indivisible in the sense that though it has parts, the parts are not capable of independent existence as conscious functioning brains. Compare nations, which not only have parts but the parts themselves are capable of separate existence as nations. Nagel and Parfit are too impressed with split brain experiments; I have argued that such experiments do not show that a self can split into selves.

Does the survival of the functioning brain admit of borderlines? This is an important question, for if it does then its survival is not always a matter of all or nothing, and so it would clash with our existing views of personal identity. This would not of course show the view that we are functioning brains to be false; but it would, in accordance with the principle of reasonable faith, provide us with a reason for assuming that we are not functioning brains, unless and until there is sufficient evidence to show that we should revise our common-sense views.

There are two ways in which a functioning brain may be said to admit of borderlines. Firstly, it may be thought that we can chop and change different brains; we can mix bits of Brown's brain with bits of Smith's brain until we get the fusion of the psychology of Smith and Brown. If such things were possible, they would go against the view that the survival of persons is all or nothing. Are they possible? It is true that some human brain tissues can be transplanted from one brain to another. Thus some brain tissues have been transferred from human embryoes to patients suffering from Parkinson's disease. But such transplants are of small unused portions of the brain and they do not involve a fusion of the psychology of the different individuals. So they do not create borderline problems with regard to the persistence of persons. Nor has it been shown that split brain experiments and multiple personality cases create such problems.

But it might be said that there is another way in which the survival of a functioning brain is not a matter of all or nothing, but admits of degrees and borderlines. Even if the brain as a conscious functioning system is indivisible in the relevant sense, as bits of it wear out there is less of the brain left. Against this it might be said that the brain as a functioning system is not identical to the matter it is composed of and so it could survive changes in its matter, somewhat as a tree survives the shedding of its leaves. But does not the functioning brain survive less and less as the corresponding mental abilities deteriorate? And when the degeneration has gone far enough, is it not up to us to say whether or not the degenarate brain is the same as the old brain?

It might be replied that inspite of the deterioration of the relevant mental faculties, the brain could be said to survive in an all or nothing manner as long as it provides the basis of the same consciousness. But what makes it the same consciousness? Does the brain provide unity to the various items of consciousness or does the 'same consciousness' wear the trousers and provide unity to the brain? If the latter, personal identity is ultimately explained, if at all, in terms of 'same consciousness' rather than in terms of brain identity.

When a human being becomes very senile, has a low level of consciousness and has lost all potential for self consciousness, is he the same individual as the earlier normal human being? Some philosophers think that 'person' is a substance sortal,[34] so that when a person ceases to be a person, he ceases to exist; though the human being lives on in a state of primitive consciousness, the old individual has not lived through the decline. On the other hand if 'sentient being' is the substance sortal, then the person who existed before lives through the loss of personhood, somewhat as a boy lives through the loss of his boyhood. How do we choose between these views? On the present realist view there is a truth of the matter about whether the two are the same individual independent of our conventions and decisions; though of course we can be ignorant of the truth.

But can the view that the self is the brain not be reconciled with this realist view? One might argue for the reconciliation on the grounds that the survival of the brain too does not admit of borderlines; what we think is a borderline is really a case of our ignorance; we just do not know whether the self as a functioning brain survives the loss of the potential for self-consciousness, but there is a truth of the matter.

We distinguish the survival of the non-reductionist self from its flourishing. The self flourishes more at some times than at others but we believe its survival is a matter of all or nothing. Similarly, why not distinguish the survival of the conscious functioning brain which could be a matter of all or nothing from whether it is performing well or badly?

Even if the brain is in an important sense indivisible, it is difficult to think of oneself from the first person perspective as a brain, if the brain is treated as a physical system. For there does not seem anything it is like to be a brain. How can a physical system experience anything? And how can it provide unity to the various conscious experiences, a unity that is grasped only from the inside? There is also the problem that the person transcends any physical system such as a brain or human body.[35] It seems strange to say that people's bodies or brains suffer pain, play games, write philosophy or feel ashamed of themselves. It is the person who has the brain or body that can be said to do or undergo these things. This does seem to be the common-sense view. In chapter 4 I contend that common-sense views should be adhered to until good reasons have been advanced to show that they should be abandoned.

Some people are impressed by what they regard as evidence for the view that the self or the person is the brain. If this evidence is good then we may indeed have to revise our common-sense views (as well as our subjective views) with regard to persons not being brains. But what is the relevant evidence? Some people argue that it is empirically established that the persistence of psychological unity in a person is explained by the persistence of the relevant neuro-physiological evidence. And it is true that the brain is the carrier of the psychological traits, memories and so forth that are stored in the brain. Though the brain stores the potential for our experiences, it does not follow that when the potential is realised in actual experiences, the brain is also the subject of these experiences. The empirical evidence is compatible with the conjecture that the brain is the instrument of the self[36] or perhaps an outer aspect of the self rather than identical with it. The brain may when it attains a certain complexity give rise to a subject of experiences, to a whole world of experiences. But to say this is not to say that the brain is the subject of these experiences.

What more is required to show that the brain is the subject of our experiences? I think it needs to be shown that it can provide unity to one's experiences. In the next section I shall point out some of the difficulties facing the view that the brain can provide such unity.

Section 5 : Subjective Worlds and Brains

Consider the following conjecture: Each separate person is in a sense a separate subjective world or universe.[37] A subjective world or universe is a world or universe that has subjectivity. As long as my subjective world persists I persist; when this world comes to an end, I come to an end and lose consciousness forever. My world has a subjective reality, it is the domain where all my experiences take place. What unites my experiences is that they all take place in my world, in the same subjective domain. My subjective world is different from the objective world though it may inter-act with it. My world is not to be identified with the particular psychology that I have. The person transcends not only his body and brain (for the reasons we mentioned in the previous section), but also the particular psychology that he now has. Had he been brought up very differently from birth he would have had a substantially different psychology, he might for instance have been a psychopath, but he would have been the same self; the consciousness that is now alive would still have been there, he would have have had a substantially different psychology and different sorts of experiences would have inhabited the same subjective world that his present experiences now inhabit.

The fear of extinction, from the first person point of view is not just the fear that my brain or my living body or even my psychology will be wiped out. It also involves, as Nagel eloquently tells us, the fear that 'this consciousness will black out for good and subjective time will simply stop... My death as an event in the world is easy to think about;

the end of my world is not... There will be a last day, a last hour, a last minute of consciousness, and that will be it, "Off the edge"'.[38] Off the edge and into nothingness!

From an objective standpoint my death is an event in the objective universe which will carry on without me, but from a subjective standpoint it involves the expectation that there will be nothing, my subjective world will come to an end. The prospect of nothingness after my extinction involves the prospect that my subjective world would have come to an end.

Nagel poses the paradox that each of us is at the centre of the universe and at the same time an insignificant part of it. His solution is that as an ordinary human being I am an insignificant part of the universe, but as an objective self I am the centre of the objective world.[39] But it seems to me that when I have a conception of the objective world, it is true that the conception is mine, but this does not make me the centre of the world that I conceive. Nor is there any need to postulate an objective self. It is the same self that sometimes sees itself as an insignificant part of the universe, and at other times is the subject of the conception of the objective world. I think the solution to the above paradox is that though I am of course an insignificant part of the universe I am the centre of my subjective universe; indeed I am my subjective universe.

There is an interesting problem regarding whether only self-conscious creatures are each a subjective universe or whether conscious but non self-conscious creatures are too. On one view the experiences of the latter do not have any true unity. Some people believe that external objects such as living bodies or functioning brains do not provide any deep unity to the experiences linked with them. No doubt these experiences all have a unity in the sense that they are all intimately linked with the same external object, they are all attributes of the same body or brain; but the external object does not provide them with any true unity from the inside. In the case of self-conscious creatures there is a self that provides true unity from the inside in a way in which no external object such as the brain can.[40] In the case of non self-conscious creatures their experiences inspite of being all linked with the same external object are just a succession of experiences.

One may argue that the reductionist theory applies to creatures who are not self-conscious, while the non-reductionist theory applies to self-conscious creatures. There are problems with this solution. Can experiences exist on their own? Moreover human beings have a common evolutionary past with non-evolutionary creatures, and if the latter have unowned experiences it will be strange if we do not have any such experiences at all. Is it that a human being, in its early stages, before it acquires self-consciousness, has unowned experiences, gradually as it becomes a self-conscious creature, the proportion of owned to unowned experiences increases? And do we give less weight to suffering when it is unowned then when it is owned, on the grounds that in the case of the latter there is a persistent individual that keeps suffering on and on?[41] On this view the various experiences that V.H. underwent without self-consciousness are not really my experiences. On this view if V.H. is going to suffer a lot when V.H. has a mental breakdown I can take comfort from the fact that if the breakdown is severe enough I might lose self-consciousness and so I will not be there to undergo the suffering. If we take such a view we should not attach so much weight to the suffering of extreme cases of mental breakdown as we should in the cases of mental breakdown where the sense of self is still there. Also this view would make it morally easier for us to inflict pain on animals and on human infants that lack self-consciousness; for on this view creatures without self-consciousness do not suffer on and on.

A more natural view would be that each of us is a separate subjective world. What unites the various experiences of a creature is that they all belong to the same subjective world or subjective consciousness. This is true both of self-conscious creatures and of creatures who are conscious but not self-conscious. Some subjective worlds, such as those of some animals, never acquire self-consciousness as others do. Each separate person is a separate subjective world, though the converse is not necessarily true. There being a separate world is not a sufficient condition of there being a separate person; it is also essential that the separate individual should have the potentiality for self-consciousness. This solution would avoid the difficuties that arise on the alternative view discussed in the previous paragraph. On this solution the individual lives through the acquisition of self-consciousness as well as temporary lapses of self-consciousness. The same individual persists as long as the same subjective world persists.

We can now come back to the problem of how to individuate persons. The view that persons are brains does not by itself tell us how to individuate persons. Do each of the hemispheres of the brain count as a separate brain or parts of the same brain? In chapter 5 I contend that they are parts of the same brain in the sense that they are brains of the same person; there is only one centre of consciousness, i.e. one subjective world, associated with both the hemispheres of the brain. On this view the number of persons per human being would ultimately depend not on how many brains or bodies there are but how many centres of consciousnesses or subjective worlds there are. Some people say that in the split brain experiments there are two persons because there are two centres of consciousness; others, like myself, say that such experiments do not show that there is more than one centre of consciousness and so they do not show that there are two persons.

It might be suggested that the brain cannot be the subject of my experiences in any deep sense unless it provides unity to these experiences. But how can it provide such unity if its own unity is explained by appealing to the idea of the same consciousness or same subjective world? If we use the 'same subjective world' to provide unity to the brain then we could also use it to provide unity to the various experiences. What unites all my experiences is that they all belong to the same subjective world. So what role is the brain performing in explaining the unity of consciousness?

Some philosophers would argue that what makes my brain the brain of one person is not that it is related to just one subjective world but that the behaviour that it gives rise to forms one functional system or rational system. In the next chapter I discuss the functionalist approach and contend that it accounts for unity of the mind in the weak sense but not in the strong sense.

In chapter 2 I argue that the fact that 'same consciousness' has an important role does not show that 'same person' does not also have an important role. Defenders of the view that the person is a brain might argue in a similar vein that even though 'same consciousness' has an important role in understanding unity of consciousness, this is consistent with the view that 'same brain' (i. e. 'same person') also has an important role. But can the brain play this role? Is the brain the subject of my experiences and of my actions? The view that the brain feels depressed, does philosophy, etc. sounds counter-intuitive.

Exactly how (or even roughly how?) each subjective world is related to items in the objective world I do not know. We are very much guessing in the dark when we claim to provide answers to such questions. But I believe that when in doubt it is reasonable to adhere to the common-sense conjecture that the self is simple in the sense of being indivisible and its survival being a matter of all or nothing. Each subjective world is simple in this sense. Or at least it is reasonable to believe in this conjecture until it is shown wrong.

I have maintained that on our present view the person transcends both his body and his psychology. This reflects the truth that our present views are non-reductionist. I have some sympathy for the view that the person is primitive, with an inner aspect and an outer aspect, but it is still quite open whether this is the best of the non-reductionist theories or whether for instance some kind of Cartesian dualism is more acceptable.

One might be tempted to argue that the view that we are each a separate subjective world points in a Cartesian direction. But it seems to me that the view that we are each a separate subjective world appears compatible both with the Carteseian view and with the dual-aspect view. The view that the self is a subjective world implies that the self is a world (or universe) that has subjectivity. It does not rule out the view that the self also has some physical characteristics that are essential to it. So the view that we are each a separate world is not, at least not on the face of it, incompatible with the dual aspect theory.

Nagel[42] has suggested that we combine a dual aspect theory with the view that the self is the brain. The brain has an outer aspect and an inner aspect. The brain on this view is not just a physical system, it has a mental aspect which is not reducible to the physical. I think if we go in for a dual aspect theory it is closer to common-sense to regard the person as primitive; his body, including his brain, being the outer aspect. I agree with Nagel that though the dual aspect theory is attractive in unifying the mental and the physical, it has 'the faintly sickening air of something put together in the metaphysical labora-tory'. As far as I can see to combine this view with the view that the self is a brain lends a pseudo-scientific air to a theory that is not, at least not yet, ready for empirical testing.

On one interpretation of Nagel's dual aspect theory the person is the brain; let us call it brain proper to distinguish it from the physical brain. The brain proper is not identical to the neurophysiological structure or the physical brain; rather it is the entity that has the neurophysiological structure (or the physical brain) as its outer aspect. But in that case how does this view imply, as Nagel thinks it does, that the person does not survive the destruction of the relevant neurophysiological structure? If the brain proper has an inner aspect and an outer aspect why can it not survive the replacement of its present outer aspect? If a person has an inner aspect and an outer aspect then it seems dogmatic to say that the person could not survive with a numerically different outer aspect.

On another interpretation of Nagel's dual aspect theory, the person is the brain, the physical system, but the brain is not just a physical system, it also has a mental aspect. However the brain is not something mysterious and unobservable, which can survive the destruction of the relevant physical system. It cannot survive the destruction of the relevant physical brain because it is this very physical brain. My reservations about the view that the self is the brain, which I mentioned earlier in this chapter, apply to this version too.

I have argued that the view that the person is primitive and has a dual aspect is one of the defensible versions of the non-reductionist view. It has some resemblances to the views of Strawson who also regards the person as primitive with a mental aspect and a physical aspect. But there is an important difference. I think that the person transcends his present physical body and brain as well as his present psychology; and this goes naturally with the view that personal identity cannot be analysed in terms of empirically observable bodily and psychological continuities. Such continuities can at best serve as evidence of the persistence of the person, but they are not logically adequate criteria for the persistence of persons. The persistence of the person involves the persistence of the subjective world, but the persistence of the subjective world is not empirically observable. Since personal survival on the non-reductionist view is a matter of all or nothing, it is hardly surprising that we do not have conclusive objective evidence for such survival. If we look at a person only from the outside as an object, then like other objects, one would expect it to survive in degrees.

I said that the persistence of the person involves the persistence of the subjective world. The converse is also true. The persistence of the subjective world of a person or self involves the persistence of the person or the self. There is mutual dependance here, for on this view the self is a subjective world, i.e. it is a world that has subjectivity or consciousness. Whether such a world has also essentially a physical aspect is left open epistemically. If it does then some sort of double aspect theory would be correct. If not, some kind of Cartesian soul view might be the correct one. In this book I do not adjudicate between these two competing views; rather I defend the non-reductionist view as against the reductionist view. I also argue that the version of the non-reductionist view that our moral and practical system presupposes is the version according to which the self has a unity of consciousness (see the next chapter), is indivisible and its survival is a matter of all or nothing. So I have tried to unearth some of the general features of the non-reductionist view that our moral and practical system presupposes. In this chapter I have also argued that the view that the self is a brain, though it does share some of these features, does not share *all* of these features. Important parts of our moral and practical system do not harmonise with the view that I am my brain. In chapter 7 section 2 I shall argue that the view that I am my brain cannot be refuted by purely imaginary counter-examples. In chapter 8 section 1 I shall argue that the view that I am my brain becomes less plausible if we adopt the reductionist view.

NOTES

1. There is also a reductionist version of the cosmic self view, advocated by Timothy Sprigge in 'Personal and Impersonal Identity' *Mind*, 1988. This version is reductionist because the ultimate ontological units are the momentary items of conscious experiences. The cosmic self here seems to be not a substance (which it has on the non-reductionist version) but a concrete universal that is manifested in the various items of experience. In some of his other writings, however Sprigge seems nearer to the Advaita view, for he commends the view that there is a cosmic consciousness. See his *Vindication of Absolute Idealism.*, Edinburgh University Press, Edinburgh, 1983.

2. Thomas Nagel seems to believe in some variant of the complex version of the non-reductionist view. See his *A View From Nowhere*, Oxford University Press, Oxford, pp. 44-45. Parfit (*Reasons and Persons*, Clarendon Press, Oxford, 1984) does not consider the complex version of the non-reductionist view, he thinks that the only plausible version of the non-reductionist view is the simple version. I shall later consider the suggestion that some of the moderate version of his views , e.g. with regard to distributive justice, egoistical concern etc. might make sense if we adopt the complex version of the non-reductionist view rather than his own reductionist views where there is no self, except as a *façon de parler*, and where each item of experience is a separate atomic unit.

3. See R. Puccetti, 'Brain Bisection and Personal identity' , *British Journal of Philosophy of Science*, 1973, pp. 339-55 and David Lewis, 'Survival and Identity' in A. Rorty (ed.)*The Identities of Persons*, University of California Press, Berkeley, 1976.

4. See ch. 6 p. 128.

5. The view that the reductionist cannot adequately account for the unity of consciousness is discussed in chapter 2.

6. See H. Frankfurt, 'The Problem of Action' *American Philosophical Quarterly*. 1978. R. Taylor. *Action and Purpose*, Prentice Hall, New Jersey, 1966, and R. Chisholm, 'Freedom and Action ' in K. Lehrer (ed.)*Freewill and Determinism*, Random House, New York, 1966.

7. T. Reid, *Essays on the Intellectual Powers of Man*, Macmillan, London 1941 ch.4.

8. See D. Parfit, *Reasons and Persons*, p. 213.

9. Quoted approvingly in *Reasons and Persons*, p. 302.

10. S. Shoemaker and R. Swinburne, *Personal Identity*, Blackwell, Oxford, 1984, p. 101. I find he is trying to reconcile the irreconcilable. For if persons are primary then the persistence of persons would involve the persistence of persons and not just of their psychology.

11. This is Parfit's view in *Reasons and Persons*.

12. *Personal Identity*, p. 99. In chapter 7 Shoemaker tries, I think unsuccessfully to answer charges of circularity.

13. S. Shoemaker, 'Critical Review of D. Parfit, *Reasons and Persons*,' *Mind*, 1986, pp. 443-53.

14. L. Wittgenstein, *The Blue and Brown Books*, Blackwell, Oxford, 1958, p. 62.

15. *Reason, Truth and History* , Cambridge University Press, Cambridge, 1981, pp. 91-92.

16. See R. Chisholm, 'The Loose and Popular Sense of Identity' in N. Care and R. H. Grimm (eds) *Perception and Personal Identity*, Ohio University Press, Cleveland, 1969.

17. S. Shoemaker, 'Comments', in N. Care and R. H. Grim (eds) *Perception and Personal Identity*.

18. *Problems from Locke*, Clarendon Press, Oxford, 1976, p. 197.

19. 'Suppose that he continues to feel responsible for what he did. And suppose that he and others know what the psychological connections are. He can still say, 'It was only my past self'. But all this can do to produce in others the false belief that he does not feel remorse... The remark cannot make it true that he does not feel remorse. So it cannot change what counts for him as the history of the present self.' 'Importance of Self-Identity', *Journal of Philosophy*, 1971, p. 688.

20. See S. Shoemaker, *Identity, Cause and Mind*, Cambridge University Press, Cambridge, 1984, chapter 2.

21. One's offshoots are a result of one's fission and are not to be confused with one's offspring.

22. There was also the divine ascriptivist version, according to which it is the divine will which makes us all into one individual. It can even make us one with the rest of humanity, past, present and future, so

that we could all be guilty of the sins of our ancestors. It is on such grounds that Jonathan Edwards regards us as guilty of the crimes committed by Adam. See *Works of Jonathan Edwards*, ed., C. A. Holbrook, Yale University Press, 1970, volume 3, *Original Sin*, part 4 chapter 3.

23. *Personal Identity*, pp. 109-110. Both in *Personal Identity* and in his Comments in *Perception and Personal Identity*, he subsribes both to the individual version and to the social version. And in 'Comments' he allows individual ascriptivism to trump social ascriptivism, when the two conflict.
24. See chapter 8 pp. 158ff.
25. In footnote 1 on p. 21 we saw that Parfit was in his earlier writing committed to some kind of ascriptivism. In *Reasons and Persons* too he seems to be commited to some form of ascriptivism with regard to personal survival though not perhaps with regard to personal identity. On p. 299 of his book he rightly stresses the importance of normative cconsiderations in determining psychological connectedness. I discuss this point further in chapter 8.
26. 'Multiple Personality and Personal Identity' *British Journal of Philosophy of Science*, 1981, and *Real People*, Clarendon Press, 1984, chapter 4.
27. This discussion applies *mutatis mutandis* to the views of certain anthropologists who write about the conception of the person they observe in different cultures. For instance, it has been argued that personhood is conferred by the Tallensi society upon the individual; see J. S. La Fontaine, 'Person and Individual in Anthropology', in *The Category of the Person*, (ed. by M. Carrithers et. al.), Cambridge University Press, Cambridge, 1985, and M. Fortes 'On the Concept of the Person among the Tallensi' in *Le Notione de Personne en Afrique Noire*, ed. G. Dieterlen, Paris 1973). We are told that full personhood amongst the Tallensi is not conferred on women and children but it is conferred upon crocodiles that live in the tribal area. (Are female crocodiles recognised as persons?) Unless we are to descend into crude relativism we would criticise such a conception of the person. Some societies create a superior class of persons; in Britain they create peers who sit in the House of Lords; something like social ascriptivism applies here; you are a Lord if you have been made a Lord by the appropriate social authorities. One sometimes gets the impression from some of the anthropological literature that the Tallensi may also be busy 'creating' a superior class of people and that they call such people persons. But none of this shows that they do not also have something that corresponds to our ordinary conception regarding what people are. See ch. 4 sec. 3 where I discuss Levy-Bruhl's views regarding two conceptions of the person existing side by

side.

28. P. Strawson,'Self, Mind and Body' in *Freedom and Resentment and Other Essays* , Methuen, London, 1974. See also his *Bounds of Sense*, Random House, New York, 1966.
29. M. Johnston, 'Human Beings', *Journal of Philosophy*, 1987, pp. 59-83.
30. F. Brentano, *Psychology from an Empirical Standpoint*, Routledge and Kegan Paul, London, 1973, p. 160.
31. For the view that the first person perspective is inelimanable, see the seminal work of Hector Castaneda, '" He" A Study in the Logic of Self-Consciousness', *Ratio*, 1966.
32. *Personal Identity*, p. 147-148.
33. See E. Anscombe, 'The First Person' in S. Guttenplan ed., *Mind and Language*, Clarendon Press, Oxford, 1975. Anscombe rejects the view that 'I' is a referring expression partly because she does not like the sceptical implications of such a view, such as that we can never know how many egos there are per human being. I deal with such objections in chapter 3.
34. See D. Wiggins, *Identity and Spatio-Temporal Continuity*, Blackwell, Oxford, 1967.
35. See D. Wiggins, *Sameness and Substance*, Blackwell, Oxford, 1980, pp. 163-4.
36. The view that the brain is an instrument of the self is developed by K. Popper in *The Self and Its Brain*, Springer-Verlag, London, 1977, and by R. Chisholm, 'Human Freedom and the Self' in G. Watson (ed.) *Free-will*, Oxford University Press, 1982.
37. For a similar idea see K. Popper, *The Self and Its Brain*, p. 3; Popper says: 'Each time a man dies a whole universe is destroyed.' See also T. Nagel, *The View from Nowhere*, p. 33 and ch. 11 sec. 3.
38. *The View from Nowhere*, p. 225.
39. *The View from Nowhere*, ch. 4. sec. 3.
40. Some such view is suggested by Colin McGinn, *The Character of Mind*, Oxford University Press, Oxford, 1982, p. 104.
41. See chapters 9 and 10 where I stress the importance of the same individual suffering on and on.
42. *The View From Nowhere*, pp. 40-45.

II. *Consciousness and Its Importance*

Section 1: Minds, Weak and Strong

In the previous chapter I stressed that one of the most important features about our present conception of the person is that it implies the simplicity of the self in the sense that the self is indivisible and its survival is a matter of all or nothing. I now want to stress that an equally important feature is that it involves a belief in the unity of consciousness. We assume that a person has access to his conscious experiences at any given time. On our present system, the view that each of us is an indivisible self is held in conjunction with the unity of consciousness view, and it is thought to explain it, what unites a person's various experiences is that they all belong to the same indivisible self or subject: 'When a person is aware of seeing and hearing, he is also aware that he is doing both at the same time. Now, if we find the perception of seeing in one thing and the perception of hearing in another, in which of these things do we find the perception of their simultaneity? Obviously, in neither of them. It is clear rather, that the inner cognition of one and the inner cognition of the other must belong to the same real unity'.[1]

That our practical life presupposes unity of consciousness can be seen from the following example. Suppose I go to the dentist and he gives me a local anaesthetic and he then bangs my teeth and I say and am convinced that there is no pain. When I say I feel no pain I am referring to the consciousness that I have access to. If there is great suffering going on in another stream of consciousness dissociated from the stream of consciousness that I have access to, it does not concern me in an egoistic way. When I am happily and consciously talking to you, the idea that I could be suffering enormously in another stream of consciousness seems bizarre, from the egoistical first person point of view.

It is this view about the unity of consciousness which shows why belief in the cosmic self or collective self is alien to our ordinary ways of thinking. My *egoistical* fears and concern are with what happens to the one state of consciousness that I have access to and not with the suffering that is part of your stream of consciousness, not even with the suffering that is part of a stream of consciousness dissociated from the consciousness that I have access to. My concern for your pain is altruistic concern which shows that I regard you as different from myself.

While we cannot prove that there is a permanent self, or even a series of temporary selves, we can postulate it as a presupposition of our practical life and subjective experience. It is presupposed by our egoistical hopes and fears and it provides unity to our experiences both at a time (synchronic unity) and and over time (diachronic unity). All my experiences are experiences of the same self, they all belong to the same subjective world. A temporary self could suffice for the purposes of providing synchronic unity, but to provide unity of consciousness over time, we need to postulate a persistent self.

If splitting of consciousness took place, then we should abandon the view that there is a permanent indivisible self and adopt something like the reductionist view of the person. If we abandon the self then we will not be able to account for the unity of consciousness by an appeal to the self. Our belief that there is unity of consciousness in some deep sense will be shown to be an illusion, along with the view that we are non-reductionist selves.[2]

Of course, if one is convinced that there is a proof of the existence of non-reductionist selves, then one will resort to devices to show how one can retain belief in selves in spite of division of consciousness. For instance one might believe in a self with a divided consciousness. .

Since I believe in the non-reductionist self, not because there is a proof of such a view but because it is presupposed by our subjective and practical experience, I do not find much use for the idea of a separate self with a divided consciousness. For such a self does not help to account for the unity of consciousness,[3] nor for our egoistical fears and hopes, which are confined to one stream of consciousness.[4] If there is splitting of consciousness, one could adopt the reductionist view or the cosmic self view according to which there is one self pervading the whole human race if not the whole cosmos; why stick dogmatically to the one self per human being view? Perhaps in the case of the same human being there is the hope that the various divided or multiple consciousnesses will be integrated into one; it is sometimes claimed that in therapy one sometimes succeeds in achieving such integration. Believers in the cosmic self view would say each of our separate consciousnesses has the potential to merge with the cosmic consciousness; and they would appeal to the highest forms of mysticism, where such a merger appears to take place.

In chapter 8 I argue that neither the cosmic self view nor the reductionist view can make sense of our primary egoistical hopes and fears, including our hopes for *personal* salvation, except as a brute fact.I also suggest in that chapter that the facts of mystical experience are compatible with the view that each human being has a separate self.

On the reductionist view there is no diachronic unity in any deep sense. Reductionists tend to explain the unity between the earlier and later experiences by appealing to certain relations between them but these relations would be just as close whether or not there was branching. Yet if there was branching, then unity would be lost. So what is ultimately important on the reductionist view is not unity, but the relations that hold between the earlier and later experiences.

Neither can reductionists explain synchronic unity in any deep sense.[5] Reductionists[6] sometimes argue that they can explain synchronic unity as follows: When I think about philosophy and hear some music at the same time, there is a higher order state of awareness of the simultaneous awareness of my philosophical thoughts and the sound of music. The trouble with this suggestion is that not all the states of consciousness of a person at a given time are always united by a higher order state of awareness. In order to deal with this objection the reductionists might argue that they can be so united. But this raises the problem that once one becomes simultaneously aware of the items of experience, these items may no longer be the same as they would be if one were not simultaneously aware of them. My philosophical thoughts may alter or even disappear once I try to relate them to my consciousness of the music.

In order to deal with this problem, it has been suggested that one should be able to unite these items of experiences in introspection or in memory.[7] After the event I can remember having the philosophical thoughts and hearing the music that took place at the same time as the philosophical thoughts. But I suspect this test provides neither a necessary nor a sufficient test of absence of division of consciousness. It is not at all obvious that one can always remember (even with the help of hypnosis or psycho-analysis or other aids) after the event. Also, to the extent that one can remember, might this not also happen in the case where there has been splitting of consciousness (which the reductionists allow as a possibility) ? That is, suppose there is splitting of consciousness, in one stream of consciousness there are philo-sophical thoughts at time t, in another stream there is the sound of music at time t. And suppose there is fusion of the two streams soon after time t (as the reductionist theory allows), then there may be soon after the fusion a memory of having philosphical thoughts at time t and of hearing music at time t. So the reductionists are still left with the problem of having to account for the unity of consciousness.

Can the non-reductionist account for the unity of consciousness any better than the reductionist can? Non-reductionists would argue that what all my conscious experiences have in common at a particular time or across time is that they are all mine, they are all experiences of the same person. But there is a residual problem for a non-reductionist. Some non-reductionists, such as Madell have argued that even if there is division of consciousness within a human being, all the experiences of the human being belong to the same self; there would be one self with a divided consciousness. Others such as myself would argue that if such division of consciousness occured, then we should abandon the non-reductionist view. But this raises the problem regarding how the disputants here would characterise the division of consciousness. How do we distinguish two streams of consciousness from one? If Madell were to say that each of the streams has its own unity of consciousness (how else would he understand the view that there is more than one stream of consciousness?), then he has to face the problem of what unity of consciousness consists of.

If I am willing to abandon non-reductionism if there is splitting of consciousness, I too must be able to explain what would constitute splitting of consciousness. It seems to me that if there is now a stream of consciousness where there is an agent who has a second order awareness of experiences which he is having, but which I am not now aware of, then that stream of consciousness is not mine. Thus at this moment I feel happy, and am reflecting on this. Now if there is at this time a stream of consciousness connected with some part of my brain, where there is an individual who is reflecting on the fact that he is now suffering a lot, then that individual is not me.

It is an essential characteristic of a person that he can reflect on his various desires, experiences, thoughts, etc. Such higher order reflection at any given time is indivisible. On our present view of the person, my self-consciousness is indivisible in the sense that I cannot go in *simultaneously* for acts of self-consciousness, any of which are cut off from the other. One could widen this point and contend that one cannot have at the very same time higher order acts of conscious awareness any of which are dissociated from the rest. If at this time I am consciously reflecting on my philosophical thoughts then, if I am also at the very same time, consciously reflecting on the music that I am hearing (as opposed to just hearing it) then the two simultaneous conscious reflections of mine cannot be dissociated from each other. The impossibility here is a metaphysical one, not one that can be derived from the meaning of words. The view that there are selves with divided consciousnesses is one that I reject but it is not something that can be shown to be absurd from the analysis of the meanings of words like 'person' and 'consciousness'.

Chisholm[8] has argued that 'same person' rather than 'same consciousness' is the basic notion. He says that in order to understand 'unity of consciousness' one should appeal to the idea that all my experiences are had by the same person. Nothing is gained by adding that they are parts of the same consciousness or that they are co-present in consciousness ; for to say such things means nothing more than that they are all had by the same person.

I would disagree with the above view. 'Same person' as well as 'same consciousness' are both important and related notions. In order to reject the idea of self with a divided consciousness (as well as in order to accept it), one has to appeal to the idea of same consciousness. For as I said earlier, in order to deal with the residual problem regarding the unity of consciousness, one has to appeal to the idea of some of my self conscious and any other higher order conscious reflections not being dissociated from the rest of such reflections at the same time. But to say that they must not be dissociated is another way of saying that they must all be co-present in consciousness! If we *merely* say that what all my experiences at a time have in common is that they are all had by the same person, then we have not ruled out the possibility that there may be division of consciousness. In order to rule out such a division we need to say that they are all parts of the same consciousness in the sense that they are all co-present in the single consciousness of the same person.

'Same person' is also not redundant, it is required, especially in order to understand diachronic unity. For if one just said that what all my experiences over time have in common is that they all belong to the same consciousness then (unless one goes in for a reductivist analysis of 'same consciousness') one is left with the following problem. What is meant by different experiences belonging to the same consciousness, other than that the same person or self is aware of all the experiences?

If one takes the view that ' same person' helps one to understand 'same consciousness' in the case of diachronic unity, one may be asked how one would understand 'same person'? If the answer is that 'same person' is basic or primitive, then one may be asked why one could not just as well say that 'same consciousness' is a primitive notion amd so we do not need 'same person' in order to understand 'same consciousness'.

It seems to me that the idea of person is a basic one. As I said in the last chapter, one's experiences including one's conscious experiences are experiences of a person. It is the person (who has experiences) that acts, not consciousness that acts.

Neither the reductionist view nor the cosmic self view can make sense of some of our subjective and practical experiences. But if there is splitting of consciousness within a human being, then neither will the view that we have separate selves with a divided consciousness be able to make sense of such experience; for as we saw (in the dentist example) such experience presupposes unity of consciousness. If there is splitting of consciousness (especially of self-consciousness) then the corresponding subjective and practical experience will be shown to be based on an illusion. It is not clear why we should prefer the view that each human being has a separate self with the divided consciousness to the view that there is no self or to the view that there is a cosmic self.

It is important to distinguish two senses of mind and correspondingly two senses of 'unity of mind'. Sometimes when we say that an entity has a mind, we use the expression 'mind' in a weak sense merely to indicate that the entity has various mental properties or is subject to psychological laws or tendencies. But sometimes we imply something stronger, we imply that it has an inner life, a stream of conscious experiences, or that there is something it is like to be that entity.[9] We could mark this distinction as the distinction between having a mind in a weak sense and having mind in a strong sense. The mind in the strong sense, unlike mind in the weak sense, has subjectivity: the subjective character of experience is not analysable in terms of an explanatory system or functional states, since these could just as well be instantiated by robots or automata that behave like people without experiencing anything.[10]

We assume, according to our ordinary conception of the person, that each person has a unity of consciousness. We do talk of the unconscious mind, dissociated from the conscious mind, and working simultaneously, but this does not commit us to the view that there is a separate stream of consciousness going on simultaneously which is also a part of us.

There are two views of the unconscious mind. According to one view the unconscious mind does not involve any separate stream of consciousness, it does not involve a mind in a strong sense. According to the second view (which William James believed in) the unconscious mind is only unconscious relative to the main stream of consciousness in the sense that the main stream is not conscious of it, but it (the unconscious mind) has its own stream of consciousness dissociated from the main stream.

We can now distinguish two senses of 'unity of mind'. Some philosophers have argued that Nagel while discussing the cases of split-brain patients exaggerates the extent to which the mind of an ordinary person is unified. Phenomena such as self-deception, weakness of will and doing two tasks simultaneously, such as driving a car while carrying on a conversation, occur even in the case of the normal person (who has not got a split brain); such facts point to the fact that our minds are not so unified. According to Wilkes[11] once we realize this important fact we shall see that the cases of split brain patients, where under test conditions one part of the person acts and behaves in one way, while another part does something quite different, present no new difficulty of principle.

Wilkes has missed the point of Nagel's complaint. For Nagel does not deny the obvious fact that mind in a weak sense can be disunified and disintegrated. What he does insist is that our present conception of a person requires that there should be unity of mind in the sense of unity of consciousness – let us call this unity of mind in the strong sense: 'Roughly, we assume that a single mind has sufficiently immediate access to its conscious states so that for elements of experience or other mental events occurring simultaneously or in close mental proximity, the mind which is their subject can also experience the simpler *relations* between them if it attends to the matter. Thus we assume that when a single person has two visual impressions, he can usually also experience the sameness or differences of their colouration, shape, size, the relation of their position and movement within his visual field and so forth. The same can be said of cross modal connections.'[12]

Functionalists give a different account of a mind's unity. Shoemaker says: 'It is only when the belief that it is raining and the desire to keep dry are co-personal that they tend (in conjunction with other mental states) to lead to such effects as the taking of an umbrella; if the belief is mine and the desire is yours, they will not directly produce any joint effects. And it seems that if a belief and desire do produce (in conjunction with other mental states) just those effects which the functional characterisations of them say they ought to produce if co-personal, then in virtue of this, they are co-personal.'[13]

The functionalist account can explain unity of mind in the weak sense. But it cannot explain unity of mind in the strong sense. It does not capture the subjective element. Some functionalists would stress that they have other arguments to show that they can capture the subjective element. I shall be dogmatic here and say that I do not find these arguments convincing.[14] But even if functionalists are right on this point, this would not destroy the distinction between mind in the weak sense and mind in the strong sense; rather it would show that this distinction can be reconciled with the functionalist account. In chapter 6 I give some reasons why we should not adopt the functionalist approach.

Even if one does allow that there is another stream of consciousness connected with some part of my brain where there is intense pain, the dentist example has shown that as long as it is dissociated from my mainstream of consciousness, I do not identify with it from the egoistic point of view. Of course such a view of the self *may* be false but it is presupposed in our prudential reasoning. Our egoistic hopes and fears are based on just one stream of consciousness. Our present conception allows breaks in the stream of consciousness, such as during sleep, amnesia, alternating personalities. But, as the dentist example shows, it does not allow us to identify egoistically with two simultaneously separate and conscious stream of consciousness. That is why alleged cases of co-consciousness,[15] where there is more than one separate and conscious stream within the same human being, present much more of a problem for our view that there is one person per human being than do cases of alternating personalities.[16]

Although he is often aware of it, Nagel *sometimes* neglects the significance of the distinction between the two senses of mind. He is impressed by recent experiments on split-brain patients and makes out a good case for the view that there is a second mind associated with the minor hemisphere of the brain. But he thinks the trouble does not stop here, for we are on a slippery slope: 'the mental operations of a single hemisphere such as vision, hearing, speech writing, verbal comprehension etc. can to a great extent be separated from one another by suitable cortical deconnections: why then should we not regard *each* hemisphere as inhabited by several co-operating minds with specialized capacities? Where is one to stop?' It seems to me that if we are talking of minds in the weak sense then it may well be the case that there are several such minds within one person, but this does not cause any problem for the one person per human being view. But if we are thinking of minds in the strong sense, then Nagel has not provided us with any reason for thinking that there are within one human being several minds co-operating with each other.

In chapter 5 I shall examine the case for the view that there is a *separate* mind (in the strong sense) associated with the minor hemisphere. I shall argue that the case, though it has some plausibility, is far from proven. Nagel thinks that the case is overwhelming for the view that the separate mind associated with the right hemisphere is not just an automaton (i.e. the mind in the weak sense) but that it is a subject of experience and action. But he nowhere argues for the view that the '*several* co-operating minds' are each subjects of experience and action, that there is something it is like to be such minds. So it is not clear why the existence of several such minds should cause such havoc to our beliefs about persons.

The distinctions between the two senses of mind and of 'unity of mind' are essential for an understanding of problems arising from split brain and multiple personality cases. There are roughly two approaches to such problems: the approach that I adopt which stresses consciousness and subjectivity, and the approach that does not. In my view there can within one person be alternating personalities, such as Jekyll and Hyde, but at any given time there is only one unitary subject of consciousness. If and when there is more than one stream of consciousness within one human being *at the very same time* we can have a case not just of multiple personalities but also of multiple persons.

The other approach stresses that being a separate person involves having unity of mind in the weak sense. On this view persons are rational systems or functional systems, each with a separate unity of the kind described earlier in the quotation from Shoemaker. The unity of mind (in the weak sense) is never complete; parts of the mind work in isolation from others or in conflict with other parts, even in the normal person. Multiple personalities, on this view, are an extreme case of lack of integration that is found in the ordinary person. The treatment of such conditions involves integrating the different personalities into one rational system. Though the degree of integration achieved as a result of the therapy is never complete, the treatment may be considered successful if the degree of integration achieved is roughly the same as is found amongst ordinary persons.

On this alternative view under consideration one tends to distinguish temporary and curable cases of multiple personalities from permanent and incurable ones in the following way. The former are capable of fusion into one rational system, whereas the latter are irreducibly multiple, no amount of therapy will succeed in integrating the different rational systems into one. In the latter case we have more than one person, in the former case there was just one person which had temporarily lapsed into more than one personality.[18] It follows that if therapy does not succeed and there remains more than one personality, we can conjecture but cannot ever know that there is more than one person; for we cannot rule out that in principle fusion of the different rational systems into one is possible, only we do not know how to achieve it.

Critics of the consciousness approach point out that subjective consciousness is something not publicly verifiable and so it is better to have tests of personhood that do not appeal to such unverifiable entities. But such critics do not realize that the alternative approach that treats persons as functional systems also cannot be wholly free from such problems. For on the functionalist view the judgement that there is more than one person per human body is, as we have seen, at best defeasible. Such judgements cannot be shown to be correct, but are liable to be rebutted if and when fusion of the different rational systems into one is shown to be possible. We cannot ever show that in a particular case fusion of different personalities into one is physically impossible.[19] If in very similar cases in the past, fusion has never been achieved, the most that would follow is that fusion is technically impossible.

In the Beauchamp case, which I shall discuss in chapter 6, Sally never got fused with the other personalities. Suppose that in the future, cases similar to the Beauchamp one turn up, and suppose that we manage to integrate the various personalities into one. We may then have grounds for saying that in the Beauchamp case too it was physically possible to fuse Sally with the others, only the technique was not available at that time. So the view that it was physically impossible to fuse Sally with the others is falsifiable. Of course there are many cases where we do not so far know whether or not fusion is possible. For instance we do not know that it is physically possible to have a fusion of Parfit and Greta Garbo. Would it follow from this that on the functionalist view we do not know that they are different persons? Perhaps one might claim that on such an approach the view that they are different persons is a conjecture that is falsifiable. I have argued in this book that the version of the non-reductionist view that I favour is also falsifiable in some sense.

It is worth stressing that I am not rejecting the functionalist approach in all areas. It seems to me illuminating to use this approach to the mind in the weak sense. There is, even in the ordinary person, considerable disunity of mind in the weak sense. In the abnormal cases such as split brains cases and multiple personality cases which I discuss in chapters 5 and 6, the disintegration is much more extreme. Geschwind tells us how the method of treating the person as a unitary structure, while useful in some areas, can be very misleading. He points out how useful it can often be to study the person, not as a unit but as a union of loosely joined wholes. He tells us how when he was studying his brain damaged patient, confusion would often result from a failure to treat the patient as made up of connected parts rather than as an indissoluble whole. 'We were constantly dealing with questions such as "If he can speak normally and and he knows what he's holding in his left hand why can't he tell you?" We had to point out that we could not say that "the patient knew what was in his left hand" and that "the patient could speak normally", since that part of the patient which could speak normally was not the same part of the patient which "knew" (non-verbally) what was in the left hand.'[20]

Though the functionalist and the atomistic approach can help us to understand our minds in the weak sense and a good deal of the resulting behaviour, it does not follow that we should regard a person's consciousness (or mind in the strong sense) as split. In chapters 5 and 6 I argue that the one consciousness per human being view has not been falsified. Since a person's behaviour often reflects both the mind in the strong sense as well as mind in the weak sense, it would not be surprising if both the holistic approach (which treats the mind in the strong sense as an indissoluble whole) as well as the functionalist-cum-atomistic approach (that philosophers like Dennett adopt) help us to understand human behaviour.

The distinction between the two senses of mind is important for understanding the problem of scepticism with regard to other minds. If we talk of minds in a weak sense it is easier to show that other people have minds. Thus it has been argued[21] that there are other minds because by postulating other minds we can explain behaviour which cannot otherwise be explained. For instance jealousy accounts for some human behaviour, and until a better explanation of such behaviour turns up, it is reasonable to assume that jealously does exist. And since such explanations involve mental terms, minds do exist or at least can be presumed to exist until a better explanation turns up. This argument at best shows that there are other minds in the weak sense; even the belief in such weak minds could be shown to be wrong if a better explanation of other people's behaviour turns up.

Be that as it may, how do I know that there are other minds in the strong sense, how do I know that there is something it is like to be other people? I know that there is something it is like to be myself, but how do I know than the devil has not played a big joke on me by creating other human beings who are programmed to say that they have minds in the strong sense, even to write long introspective accounts of what it is like to be them? My friend could tell me in some detail about how it feels to have pain, etc. but his doing so may be a result of his being programmed to say so when he is asked certain questions, and so the fact that he uses such introspective language does not prove that his statements correspond to the way things are in his stream of consciousness. Perhaps he has no stream of consciousness at all. Perhaps I am a freak, the only human being who has an inner life.

If one takes a realist and anti-positivist line, one cannot rule out the possibility that there could be a devil who has played such a joke on me. But although this is logically possible, is it not unreasonable to think that it is in fact the case? Is it not more likely that I am not such a freak? The answer to this last question is yes. But this raises the problem of what the standards of reasonableness are. It seems to me that there is no way of demonstrating that the devil hypothesis is unreasonable. Ultimately such a hypothesis involves an intuitive judgement on our part and one cannot appeal to criteria such as that of simplicity, in order to rule out such a hypothesis.[22] Elsewhere, I have stressed that in moral and political philosophy we need to resort to perfectionist judgements which also involve our making intuitive judgments, since there is no other method of making such judgments.[23]

Another area where the distinction between the two senses of mind is important is the case of group mind. It is sometimes argued that corporations and nations have a mind, just as real as the mind of the individual human being. For we can use mental terms such as the Russian character to explain their behaviour, which cannot be otherwise explained. Moreover, such mental terms are not always reducible to the behaviour of individual human beings.

Even if these claims are correct, the most that follows is that nations have a mind in the weak sense. There is no reason to postulate a group mind in the strong sense. There is not anything it is like to be Russia or Germany; there is something it is like to be individual Russians or individual Germans. It is these individuals who instantiate the Russian character or the German character. Individual Russians have a different consciousness when they are together in their group than when they are not; it does not follow that the group is the subject of consciousness in a sense which is not reducible to the consciousness of individual human beings. Group consciousness may also exist in the sense that the *content* of the consciousness of the members of the group involves an irreducible reference to the group but this is compatible with the view that the subjects of such consciousness are separate individual selves and that the group is not the (irreducible) subject of such consciousness.

The view that the behaviour of groups is not reducible to the behaviour of individual human beings is compatible with the view that the consciousness of the group is reducible in the sense we have just explained. So I do not deny that a holistic approach to the study of group behaviour may be the correct one. What I see no reason to accept is the view that the group is an irreducible subject of experiences. The suffering of the group is ultimately borne by the members of the group. In chapter 10 I shall argue that this is very important from the point of view of how evil the suffering is.

We presume that other human beings have an inner life partly because they tell us about their inner lives, but nations (as opposed to their spokesmen or their members) do not tell us about their inner lives. Also, we saw that it is reasonable to believe that I am not a freak. If other human beings did not have inner lives, I would be a freak, the only human being who had one. But if nations and corporations did not have inner lives, there would be nothing freakish about me. So scepticism with regard to other individuals is not on par with scepticism about groups being the irreducible subjects of experience.

But are such arguments not too strong? Would they not also show that animals and babies too do not have minds in the strong sense, only in the weak sense? For neither animals nor babies tell us what it is like to be animals or babies. Some philosophers such as Descartes would be quite happy to accept the conclusion that animals do not have minds in the strong sense. But most of us do believe that animals have an inner life, that there is something it is like to be an animal. Are there good arguments to support this view?

One can use mental terms such as jealousy, vanity, anger, to explain not only human behavour but also animal behavour. And until such behaviour can be explained in some other way is it not reasonable to postulate a mind? We saw that some such argument has been used in an attempt to deal with scepticism with regard to other human minds. A similar argument is sometimes used to show that animals have minds. But it only shows that there are minds in the weak sense.[24] And it implies that if one day we can give a physicalist explanation of other people's behaviour, then our belief in their having minds would be undermined. It rejects the possibility that minds in the strong sense can exist as an epiphenomena, even if physical explanations have made mental explanations redundant.

Mary Midgley admits that anger, hunger and the like can sometimes be unfelt or unconscious, but points out 'But then equally bricks can sometimes be unseen or unfelt. That does not stop bricks being, in general, tangible and visible objects.'[25] This analogy of Midgley's only shows that the fact that there is a mind in the weak sense does not stop there being a mind in the strong sense. But this does not answer the sceptic with regard to the mind in the strong sense. For the sceptic need not deny that the existence of unfelt anger, hunger and the like is *compatible* with anger, hunger and the like being felt. He can still raise the question, but what reason do we have to believe that these animals do *feel* anger, hunger, and the like.

In the case of scepticism with regard to other human minds the sceptic could ask, I know that I have a mind in the strong sense, but is it not possible that other human beings only have minds in the weak sense? I suggested earlier that it is unreasonable to believe that I am a freak. But this leaves open the logical possibility that I am a freak, the only human being with a mind in the strong sense. Perhaps there is a devil who has played a big joke on me. In the case of scepticism with regard to animal minds, one grants that human beings in general have minds (in the strong sense) but wonders whether animals have minds in the strong sense. Here one can use an argument from analogy; for animals resemble human beings in some important respects. We share a common evolutionary past with animals. The human brain resembles animal brain. With human beings there are different degrees of consciousness, from the very primitive to the very sophisticated; when humans behave in a primitive, animal-like way, or when they are in a drowsy state, they may still retain some consciousness. Animal behaviour resembles human behaviour, especially primitive human behaviour.

One of the main tests of consciousness is the way an individual looks, his voice, his touch etc;[26] let us call this the expressive test of consciousness. Often we cannot tell from the mere content of what is said, whether there is consciousness. There are cases of automatic writing, where there need be no accompanying consciousness, yet the same words spoken in a certain manner may reveal a conscious mind. Again we can sometimes tell from the expression in a person's eyes whether he is conscious or whether he is speaking without any accompanying consciousness. Even when there is no speech or language used, such factors as the expression in the eyes, and voice can reveal consciousness. Now animals do to some extend resemble human beings in their expression.

So we can argue by analogy that animals (or at least the higher ones) too have consciousness. For their brains, behaviour and expressions all have important resemblances to human beings. The traditional argument from analogy has been used to solve the problem of other minds: granted that I know from my own experience that I have a mind, how do I know that others have a mind. According to this argument since my behaviour is correlated with my experiences, so must other people's behaviour be correlated with their experiences. This argument from analogy has been criticised on the grounds that it involves generalizing from one case, namely my own. But I have not used the argument from analogy to solve the problem of why I should believe in other minds in general. My argument for believing that there are some other minds was a different one, namely that it is unreasonable to suppose that I am a freak, the only individual with a mind.[27]

I used the argument from analogy to solve another problem, namely, granted that human beings have minds, what reason do we have to believe that animals have minds. Here the argument from analogy is not a weak one; it does not involve an inference from one human being, but from a whole set of human beings. It might be objected that still one is generalizing from one species, the human species. But it is not the case that we are generalizing from one species to all species; rather we are noticing an analogy between many human beings and many animals. We need not grant that lower forms of life that do not resemble human beings in the relevant respects also have consciousness. They may have consciousness but if we do not have grounds for attributing consciousness to them, then it is not so reasonable to be confident that they have consciousness. Perhaps some of them only have minds in the weak sense.

A similar argument could be used to defend the view that human babies have consciousness, even though they cannot speak a language. There are important analogies between adult human behaviour and expressions and the behaviour and expressions of babies. The view that a child acquires consciousness only when he has learnt to speak a language seem dogmatic and arbitrary. How sophisticated does the mastery of the language have to be before one can be said to acquire consciousness? Do we have to wait till the child can tell us about his subjective experiences? Surely not, if only because such a child may (if only he were articulate enough!) confirm that he now has memories of times when he had consciousness even when he was not linguistically competent to describe his subjective experiences. Should we then say that a child aquires consciousness as soon as he begins to acquire a language? There is gradual transition from pre-verbal thinking to verbal thinking and it is not clear why the first occurrence of consciousness should coincide with the first occurrence of verbal thought. Should we then say that a child who has learnt to tell us about his subjective experiences has had consciousness ever since the times he can now recall having consciousness? But this is to confuse some of the evidence for his having consciousness with the first occurrence of his consciousness. It may be that a child had consciousness at an earlier time even though he has now forgotten about it.

One suggestion is that a foetus acquires consciousness when there is electrical activity in its brain.[28] But this is controversial. Though consciousness is normally (perhaps always) accompanied by electrical activity in the brain, the converse is not true. There can be cases of unconscious behaviour accompanied by electrical activity of the brain. While some philosophers, such as William James, would say that in such cases there is a splinter consciousness, split off from the main stream, this is far from obvious.

Assuming that adult human beings have consciousness, if we are to infer that others such as animals and babies have consciousness, it would be better to argue on the basis of behavioural similarities (including similarities in the expressions) as well as brain similarities, rather than just brain similarities. As we have seen, brain activity can accompany unconscious mental activity. Even in the case of behavioural similarities, one has to be careful. For people under general anaesthetic sometimes shriek, though they do not seem to feel any pain. How then does one decide whether the brain and behavioural similarities are enough to make it reasonable to claim that there is consciousness. Perhaps the crucial test is the expressive test of consciousness, i.e. the one concerned with the expression of the individual, in his eyes, smile, voice, touch etc. The man under general anaesthetic fails this test.

As an infant (or a foetus) grows, its expressions resemble human expression more and more, and so we get more evidence that he too has consciousness. Even if consciousness or an inner life is something that he acquires all of a sudden, our evidence for his existence gradually becomes stronger as the child grows. And if we think it wrong to kill an individual with a human form and consciousness, then the older the child (other things being equal), the greater the chances that we would be involved in killing such a creature. It is sometimes argued that a foetus or a child acquires a greater right to life, the longer he has lived. Normally this view goes with the reductionist view of the person, where an individual gradually becomes a person. But such a view may be defended even on a non-reductionist view. Of course, if we are talking about a natural right to life, then this view becomes bizarre, at any rate if the individual's nature is used to include his potential; for then the embryo (on the non-reductionist view) would have just as much of a natural right to life as an adult.[29] But our duty not to kill an infant or a foetus can become greater as the infant or the foetus grows, because the chances that killing him would involve killing a person become greater as the child grows. We do not know when a foetus or an infant becomes a person but the older he is the more the chance that he is a person in the relevant sense.

The argument from analogy, in the way that I have used it, does not preclude the use of other arguments to show that there is consciousness. Indeed in the case of infants, I have reinforced the argument by appealing to the view that children have an inner life before they learnt to tell us about it. It is not easy to refute a sceptic who doubts if any one has consciousness; it is much easier to refute a sceptic who claims that human beings do not have consciousness until they begin to tell us about it.

In the case of animals too there are other considerations that can reinforce the argument from analogy. Thus it has been pointed out that the possession of consciousness would have given animals an evolutionary advantage, for it helps these animals to understand animal behaviour from the inside; because they have a consciousness, they can imaginatively enter into the consciousness of similar creatures and this can help them to predict the behaviour of these creatures.

In the case of alien creatures, who have different 'brains' and behaviour and expressions from us, the argument from analogy may not be able to show that such creatures have consciousness. But we must not be chauvinistic and conclude that therefore such creatures do not have consciousness. Rather, we can remind ourselves that the fact that the argument from analogy does not show they have conscious-ness is compatible with the view that other considerations may show that they have consciousness.

Thus, suppose such creatures had a language which we eventually decoded and suppose that in their language they described their subjective experiences in great detail. Even here we have to be careful before we infer a mind in the strong sense. It might be possible to programme machines in such a way that when they received certain inputs, they printed certain 'outputs' such as 'I am in intense pain'. The mere existence of such print-out would not show that there was an inner life in such machines. If it did, how easy it would be to construct machines with an inner life! If the details of the print-out can be explained as a result of programming without any appeal to their subjective experiences, then such print-outs would not provide evidence of the existence of an inner life. In the case of alien creatures, even if we have decoded their language which is rich in subjective experience, we have to consider the possibility that they are mere machines; and that though there is evidence of consciousness, it could be that there is consciousness among those who constructed these alien creatures rather than in the alien creatures themselves.

Section 2: Consciousness and the Moral Life

I have stressed that persons must possess consciousness in the sense of an inner life, for I believe it is a necessary condition of there being a person that he should have an inner life, and that it is a necessary condition of there being a separate person that there should be a separate inner life, with a unity of consciousness. Of course it is not a sufficient condition. There are other requirements of personhood such as possession of rationality, will, self-awareness. I shall maintain that possession of an inner life is essential for there to be moral agents and for there to be moral subjects.

It might be objected that the possession of an inner life is not essential for personhood. Minds in what I call the weak sense can suffice. Mental concepts such as understanding are to be understood in terms of dispositions to perform in publicly observable settings rather than in terms of the occurrence of inner mental processes. Some extremists would deny the occurrence of inner mental occurrence, while a more moderate view would be to grant that they occur, but to deny their importance.

Many philosophers belittle the importance of the inner life even in cases of moral qualities: 'Again consider what is involved in judging a person's moral qualities. Perhaps Mr. Bumble experienced a great feeling of generosity while he doled out the gruel to Oliver Twist and his companions. But this is not what we would ordinarily mean if we were to describe him as a generous man'.[30] His generosity is to be understood in terms of his dispositions to perform overt acts in appropriate circumstances.

But from a Kantian standpoint one does not deserve moral credit for one's actions, unless one has overcome one's feelings. For instance, if I strongly feel like spending money on myself, but exercise my will, overcome my temptations, and give the money to someone in distress, then I deserve moral credit. A person who was not subject to temptations, who always did the right thing without any inner struggle, would not get moral credit.

On one interpretation of Kant, what is morally admirable about human beings is that they are rational. But if mere rationality were sufficient, then computers (especially computers in the future) that instantiate rational systems would be as morally admirable as we are. Moreover, if rationality were all that matters to Kant, why should he have bothered to stress the primacy of practical reason over theoretical reason? What is so morally admirable about human beings is not the mere fact that they are rational but that they can exercise their will, rise above their feelings, temptations etc and act in accordance with reason.

William James[31] rightly points out that what gives significance to human life is that we can set ourselves ideals or goals, and then pursue them with zest, overcoming obstacles in the way. If there was no struggle in our human endeavours, there would be nothing heroic about us. When we admire someone for his struggle against his temptations, or his heroic struggle against a disease like cancer, or his heroic attempt at conquering mountains, or solving difficult mathematical problems, we are appealing to an inner life. If a computer solves a mathematical problem, however ingenious its solution, there is nothing heroic about its achievement.[32]

It might be objected that one can understand the duty versus temptation battle without appealing to an inner life; one may give a dispositional analysis of temptation as well as of overcoming it. But I think such an approach does not succeed. We can only make sense of concepts like agency and free-will if we assume the internal point of view. If we look at things purely from an objective point of view, neither the presence of determinism nor its absence can make sense of our agency and freedom.

Subjectivity is required not only to make sense of our ideas of agency and freedom; it is also required to make sense of our idea of moral subjects.[33] In order to be a moral subject, i.e. to be deserving of consideration for its own sake, one needs to be a sentient being, which involves having a subjectivity. It is because there is something it is like to be an individual, to suffer, to love, to be happy, to lead a meaningful life, that it makes sense to give him moral consideration. Some robots may be rational creatures in one sense of that term, for they may instantiate rational systems, but we feel they are neither moral agents nor moral subjects. We don't owe them moral consideration for their own sakes. We feel we can dismantle them and use their parts to construct more useful robots, without violating their rights; and we often adopt a similar attitude towards corporations. It would have been legitimate to do something similar to human beings if human beings had no subjectivity.

Some philosophers give a non-phenomenological analysis of terms like pleasure, plain, suffering etc. But unless there is something it is like to suffer pain, it is not clear why pain is an intrinsic evil. Wittgenstein maintains that our attitudes of sympathy and pity towards someone who exhibits pain behaviour is not explained by our belief about his inner state. At the level of explanation Wittgenstein may be right, for part of what he is saying is that out attitude is quite primitive and not to be explained by any belief about the other person's inner mental state. But at the level of justification we do not take our attitude as primitive. If we see someone under general anaesthetic groaning, whether we ought to come to his aid will depend upon whether he is experiencing pain. Again, if some actions of ours cause behaviour among animals that resembles human pain behaviour, whether we ought to worry about our conduct would depend upon whether the animals are actually experiencing pain. Similar remarks apply with regard to our attitudes towards Martians, human infants or human foetuses.

NOTES

1. F. Brentano, *Psychology from an Empirical Standpoint*, Routlege and Kegan Paul, p. 160.
2. This point is argued by Parfit (*Reasons and Persons*, sec. 88 and pp. 214 and 275). Where Parfit and I disagree is that he, unlike me, thinks that splitting of consciousness has been shown to occur.
3. *Reasons and Persons*, pp. 250-1.
4. See chapter 6, p. 128.
5. See P. Carruthers, *Introducing Persons*, Croom Helm, London, 1986, pp. 54-57.
6. See *Reasons and Persons*, p. 250-1.
7. See H. P. Grice, 'Personal Identity' in *Personal Identity*, ed. J. Perry, University of California Press, Berkeley, 1975, C. F. Marks, *Commissurotomy, Consciousness and Unity of Mind*, Bradford Books, Montgomery, 1980, pp. 12-16.
8. R. Chisholm, *The First Person*, Harvester Press, Brighton, 1981, p. 88.
9. See T. Sprigge, 'Final Causes' *Proceedings of Aristotelian Society*, suppl. vol. 45, 1971, and T. Nagel, *Mortal Questions*, Cambridge University Press, Cambridge, 1986, chapter 12.
10. T. Nagel, *Mortal Questions*, pp. 166-7.
11. K. Wilkes, 'Consciousness and Commissurotomy' *Philosophy* Vol. 53 pp. 185-199.
12. T. Nagel, *Mortal Questions*, p. 160.
13. *Personal Identity*, p. 94.
14. For a discussion of functonalism see N. Block (ed.) *Readings in Philosophy of Psychology*, Volume 1, Harvard University Press, Cambridge, Mass., 1980.
15. 'Co-consciousness' in this sense is quite different from another sense of 'co-consciousness', according to which two items of experience are co-conscious if they belong to the same consciousness.
16. That some such view is the current view of the person is conceded even by many philosophers, such as Mackie and Parfit, who think this view is false and ought to be reformed.
17. It might be suggested that even in the case of alternating personalities, there may be two separate consciousnesses; they may not ever be both present simultaneously, not because they are the same consciousness, but because for some unknown reason a human body can only accommodate one consciousness at a time.
It seems to me that while one cannot rule out such a possibility, the

evidence for the view that there are two persons would be much
stronger if there were two different consciousnesses present at the
same time. In the case of alternating personalities there is always the
very real possibility that the same consciousness is manifested in the
two alternating personalities.

18. Some such view is advocated by S. Shoemaker, *Personal Identity*,
    pp. 96-97.

19. Nor can we show that it is impossible to fuse two different human
    beings or indeed thousands of human beings into one grand indi-
    vidual.

20. Norman Geschwind, 'Anatomy and the Higher Functions of the
    Brain', *Boston Studies in the Philosophy of Science*, Volume 4, 1969,
    p. 130 ff.

21. For instance by H. Putnam, *Philosophical Papers*, Cambridge Univer-
    sity Press, 1975, volume 2

22. H. Putnam, *Philosophical Papers*, vol. 2, p. 358-361.

23. See my *Equality, Liberty and Perfectionism*.

24. See Appendix A.

25. M. Midgley, *Animals And Why They Matter*, Penguin Books,
    Harmondsworth, 1983.

26. It is the neglect of such considerations that make the Turing test so
    inadequate. The Turing test is meant to tell us whether a computer is
    conscious. This involves our carrying on conversations, that are not
    face to face, with a computer and with a human being. The conversa-
    tions are carried out via an intermediary such as an electric type-
    writer, so that we cannot see, hear, touch or smell the human being
    or the computer. If under such conditions we cannot (inspite of
    asking several questions and getting replies) tell which is the compu-
    ter and which is the human being, then the computer is conscious.
    It seems to me that this test can more easily tell if the computer has a
    mind in the weak sense; it cannot reliably tell us whether the compu-
    ter has a mind in the strong sense.

27. The traditional argument from analogy is more vulnerable than the
    freak argument because it makes a stronger claim; it claims that all
    persons have minds whereas the freak argument only claims that I am
    not the only one who has a mind. A more modest version of the
    argument from analogy could be constructed which would be less
    dissimilar to the freak argument in its claims. For instance, I might
    argue by analogy that you have a mind; since my behavour is
    correlated with my experiences, your behaviour is correlated with
    your experiences. This argument would not be as vulnerable as the
    traditional version, for it only extrapolates to your case, not to all
    cases. But even this involves a bolder claim than the freak argument,
    for the latter does not claim that any specific person (other than

myself) such as yourself has a mind, but only that someone other than myself has a mind.

28. See B. Brody, *Abortion and the Sanctity of Life*, Boston, 1975.
29. See my *Equality, Liberty and Perfectionism*, ch. 6.
30. O. Hanfling *Body and Mind*, Open University Press, Milton Keynes, 1980, p. 40.
31. *Talks to Teachers on Psychology and to Students on Some of Life's Ideals*, New York, 1899.
32. See T. Nagel, *Mortal Questions*, ch. 3 and C. A. Campbell, *Selfhood and Godhood*, Allen and Unwin, London, 1957.
33. G. Sheridan in his perceptive paper 'Can there be Moral Subjects in a Physicalist Universe?', *Philosophy and Phenomenological Research*, June 1983, pp. 425-447 argues convincingly for the view that there can be no moral subjects in a physicalist universe, but unlike me he thinks that there can be moral agents in a physicalist universe.

III. *Scepticism and Practical Life*

Section 1: Scepticism and Practice

The version of the non-reductionist view that I favour can lead to sceptical problems, for on this view bodily and psychological continuity and connectedness are at best evidence of personal identity, not logically adequate critieria of personal identity. In this chapter I shall examine how one can cope with some of the sceptical problems that arise for such a view.

Mark Johnston says that an adequate theory of personal identity must enable us to reconstruct our everyday practice of reidentifying people as an unproblematic source of knowledge. My view, where we are reduced to making defeasible conjectures, seems to flout Johnston's constraint and therefore seems to go against the common-sense view, according to which we know that John Smith whom we met yesterday is the same as the John Smith that we met today. This criticism, if true, would undermine my claim that my view is in harmony with common-sense.

It is true that we cannot know that a person persists through time if person refers to something that is indivisible, whose survival is a matter of all or nothing and whose persistence involves the persistence of his subjective world. For all we know John Smith today inhabits a different subjective world from what he inhabited yesterday, yet we know that he is the same person. Does this not show that the subjective world that he inhabits is irrelevant to his essential nature?

No, it does not. We must distinguish what is epistemically possible from what is metaphysically possible. [1] We do not know what a person's nature is, but if we are right in our conjecture about what his nature is then he necessarily has that nature. There is also the point that it may be metaphysically impossible for one's subjective world to dissapear while leaving everything else, such as one's psychology, as it is. If such a traumatic event as the disappearance of one's subjective world made no perceptible difference at all to anything at all, one should of course wonder if it had any importance at all. Rather than embrace the view that I am a subjective world whose presence makes no difference to the various observable characteristics of V. H. , I would abandon my belief in the non-reductionist view.

The view that we do not know but can only conjecture that a

person survives in a non-reductionst sense over time is compatible with the common-sense view that we know that persons survive in some sense over time. We can know that John Smith that we met yesterday survives as John Smith today. What we cannot know but can only conjecture about is how deep this survival is. [2]

Johnston's approach is too dismissive of the sceptic who denies knowledge in some strong sense. Compare other areas such as induction. It would be inappropriate to criticize the sceptic who says that we do not know in some strong sense that the sun will rise tomorrow, by pointing out that this would conflict with our common-sense practice of inferring the future from the past.

There is a positivist principle of significance that many philosophers such as Strawson commend. According to it you cannot talk sense about a thing such as subjective world or soul, or telepathy, unless you know at least in principle how it might be identified, unless you could tell that you have a case of it, unless you could tell one from another and (where appropriate) say when you have the same one again. Let us call this principle of significance 'No entity without identity'. [3] We shall interpret this principle broadly to include the views of those such as Mackie who dissociate themselves from verificationism as a theory of meaning but who insist that one should be able to operate the relevant conceptual scheme in a rational manner. Thus in the case of simple selves, John Mackie grants that such ascriptions are made by our ordinary concept of personal identity and that they are meaningful, but he objects that no reason has been given for making one such ascription rather than another, not merely in problem cases but even in those that we take to be non-controversial:

"If we allow for a moment that there are such unitary subjects of consciousness what ground have I, or has any one else, for identifying one such subject with John Mackie throughout his life?... If we are to admit immaterial substances, why is it not just as likely that there should be a whole series of them associated with each human body, and with each network unity of consciousness? Above all, what ground is there for asserting the necessary unity of each subject of consciousness, not only at one time but also through time, so that its identity is unequivocal, non-arbitrary, and not a matter of degree...?" [4] According to Mackie judgements about simple selves though meaningful are wholly arbitrary.

There is an anti-sceptical argument which many Kantian philosophers, such as Strawson, use according to which the sceptic is inconsistent when he accepts a conceptual scheme and yet repudiates one of the conditions of its existence. Similar in effect to this argument is another Kantian anti-sceptical argument, also employed by Strawson,[5] according to which our practical and moral nature presupposes certain views, and so as practical and moral beings we are committed to believing in these views. Strawson uses this argument in connection with freedom. But one could also use it in other fields, e. g. with selves and with subjective worlds. Let us call such arguments transcendental arguments (without necessarily using this term in the way it was used by Kant) or less grandly we could call them practical arguments.

There is some tension between the principle 'No entity without identity' and the transcendental argument for the existence of a thing. For it is possible that our belief in a thing such as a simple self or freedom is justified by appeal to a transcendental argument, yet the principle, 'No entity without identity' shows that we must not talk about such things since we cannot distinguish one case of it from another. Nor is this possibility a mere logical possibility. As practical and moral beings, we are in fact committed to a belief in freedom and responsibility, as Strawson has eloquently argued. Practices such as resentment and indignation (at any rate in their sophisticated forms) which are so much a part of our civilised life presuppose freedom and responsibility; we cannot as practical beings adopt the objective stance towards each other all the time. There is a similar argument in Nagel[6] who claims that from the subjective point of view human beings are committed to a belief in agency, freedom etc.

But neither Strawson nor Nagel seriously tackles the problem of how to distinguish free actions from unfree ones. Kant too was aware of the difficulty of distinguishing actions for which we are morally responsible from those where we are not 'Our ascription of moral responsibility can only be related to our empirical character. How much of it, however, is a pure effect of freedom, how much of mere nature, nobody can ascertain, from which it follows that nobody can judge with complete justice.' The sceptic may take an even stronger line and claim that the problem is even deeper, for no one can judge with even incomplete justice.

We can now see one important way in which scepticism can arise. The transcendental argument shows we are committed to various practices. But the principle 'No entity without identity' can be used by the sceptic to show that the practice operates in such a way so as to violate this principle.

Strawson thinks that the problem of distinguishing a particular of a kind from another particular of that kind can be solved as follows: 'You can identify the individual because you can identity the form, and in principle track the space-time path of a particular characteristic manifestation of it.'[7] On his view, if we are to talk sense about things like non-reductionist selves or subjective worlds, we must be able to distinguish one such entity from another and to be able to reidentify the same entity. If we cannot make such identity judgements, then this would imply that our conceptual scheme that involves talk of such entities is irrational, based on false or meaningless presuppositions.

But now such results may conflict with the transcendental argument e. g. that talk of non-reductionist selves is presupposed by our practical life and subjective experience. One way out of this dilemma is to stick to the principle of significance (viz the principle 'No entity without identity') and to reform the conceptual scheme where necessary. Thus we could argue that we should give up that part of our conceptual scheme which involves talk of entities where we do not have empirically applicable criteria of application. Parts of our conceptual scheme are irrational in the sense that they are based on false or nonsensical presuppositions.

But while discussing our practical commitment with regard to freedom and responsibility Strawson thinks that such practices do not come up for review as particular cases can come up for review within these general practices. And he points out that if we could have a choice in the matter, which we do not, 'then we would choose rationally only in the light of assessment of gains and losses to human life, its enrichment or impoverishment; and the truth or falsity of the general thesis of determinism would not bear on the rationality of this choice.'[8] Here, in the case of freedom, Strawson is appealing to practical considerations. One may appeal to such practical considerations in the case of selves, too. Thus one may think that we cannot give up belief in the simplicity of the self and even if we could, we could choose rationally only in the light of the assessment of the various gains and losses to human life.

We can now see that it is possible for the principle of significance to clash with such conclusions. For if we cannot distinguish one non-reductionist self from another, then according to the principle of significance it is in an important sense *irrational* to continue to operate with the conceptual schemes which presuppose talk of such entities.

Strawson[9] points out that even if determinism is true, we shall be unable to give up belief in freedom. But he is wrong if he thinks that this shows that freedom is compatible with determinism. For an alternative possibility would be that even if freedom and determinism are incompatible, we may as practical agents have to retain belief in freedom as a practically necessary illusion. Even if a belief in freedom is compatible with determinism, it would not follow that freedom is compatible with determinism.

And this alternative possibility mentioned in the above paragraph shows that Strawson's general anti-sceptical argument is not conclusive. For the sceptic is accused of entering the conceptual scheme and yet repudiating one of its conditions. But the sceptic could reply that he enters the conceptual scheme because it is practically necessary for him to do so, and the beliefs he has as a practical agent could be practically necessary illusions.

Lakatos posed the following problem to Feyerabend:[10] where is the epistemological anarchist who out of sheer contrariness walks out of the window of a 50 storey building instead of using the lift? Feyerabend's reply to this was that the epistemological anarchist could admit that he is a coward, a creature of custom or habit, which is why he is afraid to jump out of the window and cannot control his fear. The sceptic too would make a reply similar to this. And similar replies could be made in other areas, such as free-will, belief in the self. Thus a sceptic may admit that he often acts as if other people have freedom, but he is only acting as a creature of custom or habit.

It may be objected that the trouble with such replies is that as moral and practical beings we do not see ourselves as just acting in a mechanical or habitual manner. We assume that we are acting reasonably even though we may not be able to spell out the standards of reasonableness. And when we are afraid to jump out of the window of a 50 storey building, we actually believe that we shall get hurt.

But scepticism has not been refuted. For the sceptic can point out that it is possible that some of the assumptions we make as practical and moral agents are illusory. The most we can show is that qua practical and moral being the sceptic too regards such assumptions as true; so we can have a sort of *ad hominem* argument against the sceptic.

I said earlier that when the principle of significance conflicts with the conceptual scheme that we adopt as practical agents, one way out would be to reform our conceptual scheme. We now see that this way out will not always be there. It may be there in some cases where we can reform it and where we find it worthwhile to do so (because there is no serious net impoverishment for human beings in giving up the relevant practice). But in other cases where we do not have this option we may find it reasonable to carry on with the conceptual scheme but regard the beliefs as practically necessary illusions. On one interpretation of Hume, this is what Hume did with regard to the self. Thus while discussing metaphysical issues he regarded talk of unity of the self as an illusion, yet while discussing morals he thought that such talk is presupposed by our practical life.[11]

There is also a third possibility that we should explore. When there is a clash between the principle of significance and the relevant conceptual scheme that we are operating, we should try to interpret the principle of significance in a liberal way so that the clash disappears. We have already seen that Mackie allows that judgements about immaterial substances can be meaningful even if one cannot distinguish one such substance from another. But he thinks that such talk is irrational unless we can give good reasons for making the relevant judgments of identity. This requirement is a sensible one but one should interpret it more broadly than Mackie does.

The narrow sense of the principle of significance insists that we must have logically adequate grounds for making such judgements; these grounds exclude the use of non-objective reasons for making such judgements. The liberal or broad sense of the principle also admits that we must be able to make the relevant judgements of identity. But it allows us to use, in addition to any objective evidence available, practical or subjective reasons for making such judgements.

On the broad sense of the principle of significance, even when there is no positive objective evidence in favour of identity judgments, we may make such judgments tentatively by appealing to the purposes of the relevant conceptual scheme. Let me illustrate. If we want to distinguish one simple self from another, we need to appeal to the rationale for postulating the existence of such selves. We postulate the simple self because it is presupposed by our system of moral blame and punishment and by our subjective point of view and prudential fears. Now if we appeal to such considerations we can rule out certain possibilities. For instance, take the doubt regarding whether there is one non-reductionist self per human being throughout his life or one self per person per year. The former rather than the latter is presupposed by our prudential fears, as well as by our system of punishment and moral blame. So given certain practices, certain identity judgements come more naturally than others. We can also appeal here to the principle of parsimony, which would imply that we must not postulate more selves than we have to. None of this of course constitutes a proof that such identity judgments are valid, and that is one reason why scepticism can raise its head even here. But as practical and moral agents we often operate our practices even when we do not have proof.

Similarly, one may apply the principle of significance broadly in order to make judgements about free will and responsibility. We postulate free-will and responsibility because they are presupposed by our moral and practical (and subjective) experience. But this transcendental argument still leaves us with the problem of distinguishing free actions from unfree actions. The sceptic can point out that we never have adequate objective evidence to show that in any particular case we acted out of our own free-will. For often in the past a person's behaviour appeared free but later as we learnt more about the unconscious determinants of his behaviour we found that his action was not really free. How do we know that there is an area of genuine freedom which is not subject to such doubts? The answer probably is that we can't know this. But as a second best what we do is to assume that adult people have free-will until we can show (e. g. in extreme cases of insanity) that they do not. That is one reason why the criteria of freedom tend to be defeasible.

The principle of significance was used by Kant to rule out transcendent (or speculative) metaphysics. Metaphysicians who tried to give us knowledge about the nature of reality in itself violated this principle of significance. But Kant allowed the use of soul and God as useful regulative ideals even though such use violated his principle of significance. My own suggestion is that by interpreting the principle of significance in the broad way suggested earlier, we can use terms like simple self and free-will without violating this principle. However I agree with Kant in rejecting transcendent metaphysics. For the transcendent metaphysician claims that we can have *knowledge* with regard to the nature of ultimate reality. The liberal use of the principle of significance only shows that it can be permissible to use terms even when we do not know whether the term applies; we can do so because we can presume or conjecture that the term applies in a particular case, and such a presumption can be rebutted if the relevant evidence is forthcoming.

So we can see some sort of connection in general between the transcendental argument, the principle of significance, scepticism and the view that the relevant criteria tend to be defeasible. The transcendental argument sometimes makes us postulate some unverifiable entities, such as the simple self, or free will. This raises sceptical problems such as how do we know there is such a self, or there is free-will, how do we distinguish one self from another and so on. We can use *ad hominem* arguments against the sceptic, viz. that he himself enters the relevant conceptual scheme. But of course this by itself does not answer problems such as how to distinguish cases of free-will from cases where free-will is absent, cases where the same self persists from cases where there is a different self. Perhaps we cannot really give satisfactory answers to such questions. So what do we do in those cases where we need to continue to operate the relevant conceptual scheme? If we do not abandon belief in such unverifiable entities, perhaps we have to fall back on the view that the relevant criteria tend to be defeasible e. g. we presume free-will unless it can be shown in particular cases that free-will is lacking.

It is interesting to compare this view with J. L. Austin's view that freedom is a negative term, that the various specific excuses such as accident, mistake, duress, insanity etc. wear the trousers. There are obvious similarities. But the difference is that Austin is not at all sympathetic to the sceptic's case. He thinks the problem of freedom can be solved or dissolved fairly easily by "examining all the ways in which each action may not be 'free' i. e. the cases in which it will not do to say simply 'x did A', we may hope to dispose of the problem of Freedom. Aristotle has often been chided for talking about excuses or pleas and overlooking the 'real problem': in my own case it was when I began to see the injustice of this charge that I first became interested in excuses."[12]

On my view there is a real problem of Freedom, of distinguishing free actions from unfree ones, and the sceptical problem about whether any act is free. We presume free-will, not because we have any objective evidence in favour of free-will but because we engage in practices that presuppose it. The presumption of free-will can be defeated in particular cases. At least in extreme cases such as extreme idiocy or extreme lunacy we do have evidence that free-will is lacking. The view that the criteria of freedom are defeasible is a practical device we use to operate our system, because we cannot ever get positive knowledge of the existence of free-will, so the sceptic who asks do we ever have free-will has not been answered.

Elsewhere I have argued that Austin's view that the various excuses such as accident, mistake, insanity, wear the trousers, gives rise to serious problems. It seems to me that free-will is a term that is needed to understand specific excuses such as insanity. For instance, not all cases of insanity excuse. In order to understand which ones do we need terms like free-will or responsibility;[13] for instance, under the Homicide Act it has to be shown that as a result of the mental abnormality the defendant's mental responsibility was impaired. So such terms do play an important role. It is just that we cannot get positive evidence to show that we have free-will, so we have to fall back on a presumption that we have free-will, until this presumption is defeated in particular cases.

So while Austin was quite content with his disposal of the problem of Freedom, on my present view if we appeal to defeasibility theory this is only because we cannot get any better way of operating our system of responsibility.

Section 2: William James and The Principle of Reasonable Faith

I said earlier that we presume that a person has free-will and is a non-reductionist self, unless this presumption is defeated. But what justifies such presumptions? The mere fact that there is no positive objective evidence in favour of the non-reductionist self or free-will is hardly an argument for presuming their existence. We might as well presume that devils and ghosts exist until this presumption is defeated!

In order to deal with this problem of justification, we can appeal to William James' principle of reasonable faith according to which when objective evidence alone does not tell us whether or not a proposition (such as the existence of free-will) is true, in deciding whether or not to believe in it, it is reasonable for us to take into consideration how far it coheres with our other beliefs, especially moral and practical beliefs.[14]

Of course this principle of reasonable faith will not always succeed in getting agreement between all people, for people have different sets of beliefs. This principle may show that what is reasonable for one set of people to believe is not so for another. This conclusion is not counter-intuitive. It was reasonable a thousand years ago to believe that the earth was flat, it is now no longer reasonable to believe that. Similarly what is reasonable to believe in one society may not be so in another. What is reasonable to believe can vary both with the evidence that is available at the time and with the body of knowledge and practical beliefs that people have.

It might be objected that those who use the principle of reasonable faith are arguing in a circle, that to do so is (to use an example of Wittgenstein's) like buying a second copy of the same newspaper to confirm what is in the first. But this criticism is not quite fair. The use of James' principle has similarities not so much to Wittgenstein's newspaper example but to Wittgenstein's view that 'It is not a single axiom that strikes me as obvious, it is a system in which consequences and premises give one another mutual support.'[15]

It also has similarities to the reflective equilibrium model. And it is interesting to note that similar charges of circularity have (equally unfairly!) been made against those of us who use the reflective equilibrium model.[16]

Of course those who use the principle of reasonable faith (or the reflective equilibrium model) cannot answer the radical sceptic who does not share the relevant beliefs. What one can try to do is to widen the area of mutual support, so that the arguments one uses within the system are persuasive to all those who subscribe to the network of beliefs. One can point to the sceptic the cost of giving up a particular belief (e. g. belief in free-will or in the simplicity of the self) by showing how much else hangs on that belief. And one can challenge him to produce an alternative set of workable beliefs with which civilized men can regulate their lives.

Let us now see how William James himself used this principle of reasonable faith. He rejected the view that there was scientific evidence in favour of the persistence of a simple self (or substance) or for the existence of free-will. Nor did he think that belief in the simplicity of the self or in free-will could be disproved. He used his doctrine of reasonable faith to defend free-will and to reject belief in the simple view.

My application of James' general doctrine of reasonable faith to the problem of personal identity gives different results from James' own views on personal identity. James believes in the reductionist theory of personal identity and in the existence of several simultaneous streams of consciousness within the same person. I think his general doctrine of reasonable faith can be used to criticise these views; in chapter 2 I argue that our practical life assumes unity of consciousness. And in this book, as in my *Equality, Liberty and Perfectionism*, I argue that the reductionist view of persons goes against much of our practical and moral life.

James thinks that the chief reasons for believing in the non-reductionist view have been practical ones. But he goes on to argue that this doctrine is not really presupposed by the practical life of civilized men, though he admits that certain primitive forms of practical life do presuppose it. He believes instead in a stream of consciousness view which does not presuppose any substance.

He thinks that people have appealed to the simple view because it seems to guarantee immortality. A stream of thought 'for ought that we see... may come to a full stop at any moment, but a simple substance is incorruptible and will by its own inertia persist in being so long as the Creator does not by a direct miracle snuff it out'.[17] James objects that the simple substance does not guarantee immortality of the sort we care for: 'The enjoyment of atoms like the simplicity of their substance in *soecula soeculorum* would not to most people seem a consummation devoutly to be wished. The substance must give rise to a stream of consciousness continuous with the present stream in order to arouse our hope, but of this the mere persistence of the substance *per se* offers no guarantee.'[18]

This argument of James' at best shows that the persistence of the simple substance is not sufficient to arouse our hopes; it does not show that it is not necessary to arouse our (prudential) hopes. To meet this last objection, James would claim that such hopes too could be aroused without belief in such a substance if our stream of consciousness persisted in a meaningful way. No doubt this would not ensure immortality but we must not crave for a guarantee of immortality but should be content with the hope that our stream of consciousness continues in a meaningful way. In chapter 8 I discuss how far egoistical concerns are compatible with the reductionist view.

It seems to me that even if the simple view does not by itself arouse our hopes, it can by itself arouse our (prudential) fears about the future. The fear now of boiling in hell in the future does not get any less if we are told that before being made to boil we shall be given an injection which will cause a substantial weakening of psychological connectedness between us then and our past selves. Among Hindus who believe in the Law of Karma and re-incarnation, there is fear that if they commit misdeeds now they will suffer in their next life even though they won't remember anything of their past lives.

Of course nowadays many people do not believe in Hell or in reincarnation, so such arguments won't move them, but similar arguments can be used to show that our ordinary egoistical fears in this life presuppose the simple view. Our ordinary egoistical fears assume that our survival is a matter of all or nothing, such fears do not get less if there is weakening of psychological connectedness.[19]

Another reason, according to James, why many people believe in the soul is to do with our forensic responsibility before God. Locke's view was that continuance of memory was really important, rather than the continuance of a substance or soul. God would not on the day of judgement make us answer for things we remembered nothing of. This view of Locke's was, according to James, considered scandalous for it was supposed that our forgetfulness could deprive God the glory that comes from inflicting retributions. Ayer[20] gives the impression that James agreed with Locke's view that divine retribution does not presuppose the continuance of the simple substance. But in fact this is a misinterpretation of James, for James'[21] view was that divine retribution does presuppose the persistence of the simple substance. He rightly agreed with the view according to which the mere stream of consciousness with its lapses of memory cannot possibly be as responsible as a simple substance which is at the day of judgement all that it ever was. James then goes on to point out that retribution is a primitive idea which civilized societies ought to do without. And so to modern readers who are not obsessed with retribution, the view that retributive ideas presuppose the simple soul, though true will not have any importance.

It is true that most modern readers do not believe in divine retribution. But may similar arguments not be used to show that retributive theories of punishment (of the secular kind) also presuppose the simple view in some form? For only on the simple view can we claim that the person being punished is all that he was at the time of committing the crime. On the reductionist view the 'self' that committed the crime gradually fades away and so the person being punished is not all that he was at the time of committing the crime. So how can it be just to inflict retribution on the later self for the crimes of the earlier self? I shall discuss this point again in connection with the views of Hume and Parfit in chapter 9.

According to James one great use of the simple view has been to guarantee and to account for the the closed individuality of each personal consciousness. The thoughts of one person are all supposed to unite into one self and must be eternally insulated from those of every other soul. James rejects this reason for postulating the simple view. He says that with some individuals at least there can be splitting of consciousness with consequent loss of unity of consciousness. Also he rejects the view that each self is insulated from every other one on the grounds that there can be thought transference, mesmeric influence, etc. between one person and another.

I am not convinced by the evidence produced by James. I argue in chapters 5 and 6 that the case for the view that there is splitting of consciousness is not as strong as it may appear. As for phenomena such as thought transference, it seems to me that the facts that we may observe would be compatible with the view that each person is a separate substance from every other. We never observe that the two persons literally share the same thought or experience.

NOTES

1. See S. Kripke, *Naming and Necessity*, Blackwell, Oxford, 1980, pp. 35-6.
2. See p. 6ff.
3. P. F. Strawson, 'Entity and Identity' in H. D. Lewis (ed) *Contemporary British Philosophy*, fourth series, Allen and Unwin, London, 1976, pp. 193-220.
4. J. L. Mackie, *Problems From Locke*, Oxford, 1976 pp. 195-5.
5. 'Freedom and Resentment' in P. Strawson (ed) *Studies in the Philosophy of Thought and Action*. O. U. P. 1968.
6. *Mortal Questions*, chapter 3.
7 'Entity and Identity' p. 199.
8. *Freedom and Resentment*, p. 84.
9. *Freedom and Resentment*, p. 83-4.
10. Feyerabend, *Against Method*, London 1978, Appendix 4.
11. See T. Penelhum, 'Self Identity and Self-Regard' in A. Rorty (ed) *The Identities of Persons*, University of California Press, 1976.
12. J. L. Austin, *Philosophical Papers* O. U. P. 1961, p. 128.
13. V. Haksar, 'Responsibility', *Proceedings of the Aristotelian Society*, Suppl. Vol. 1966.
14. See William James, 'The Will To Believe', *New World*, June 1896. James also attached importance to how far the proposition coheres with our religious beliefs. Of course those who do not have religious beliefs will not be impressed with how well a proposition coheres with other people's religious views.
15. L. Wittgenstein, *On Certainty*, Blackwell. Oxford, 1977, paragraph 142
16. See Adina Schwartz's review of V. Haksar, *Equality, Liberty and Perfectionism*, *Ethics* 1981.
17. *Principles of Psychology* Vol. 1. Dover Publications, New York, 1980, p. 348

18. ibid. p. 348.
19. See chapters 1 and 8. Also, R. Chisholm 'The Loose and Popular and
     the Strict and Philosophical Senses of Identity' in N. Care and R,
     Grimm (eds.), *Perception and Personal Identity*, G. Madell, *The
     Identity of the Self*, Edinburgh University Press, Edinburgh, 1981 and
     R. Swinburne, 'Personal Identity' *Proceedings of Aristotelian Society*,
     1974
20. A. J. Ayer, *The Origins of Pragmatism*, Macmillan 1968, p. 264.
21. See W. James, *Principles of Psychology*, p. 349

IV. Gambling in the Dark and Reflective Equilibrium

I maintained in the last chapter that it was reasonable to accept certain beliefs if they are presuppositions of our practical life and if they have not been shown to be false. In this chapter I shall explore the view that we need to weigh the costs involved in keeping such beliefs against the costs of abandoning such beliefs. None of this answers the sceptic who wants a theoretical proof of our factual beliefs and who is unimpressed by the need to lead a practical life. But I offer a defence of the reflective equilibrium model as a method of achieving harmony between our practical life and our factual beliefs. And I stress that the non-reductionist view is even more prevalent than may appear at first sight.

Section 1: Some Gambles with Truth
When scientific considerations leave an issue open, besides appealing to our practical and moral life (in the way we saw earlier) there is a prudential test of whether or not it is reasonable for us to believe in the relevant view. One can appeal to the relevant gains and losses to the agent somewhat in the way that Pascal did in his celebrated argument for believing in God. If God does exist but we do not believe in him, we shall lose an enormous amount, even an infinite amount, whereas if he does not exist and we do believe in him we do not stand to lose anything substantial.

Similar arguments can be used in other areas. We do not know whether induction holds. It is reasonable to believe in it, because if induction does not hold we do not become any worse off in terms of predicting the future by believing in it than we would if we did not believe in it (though we would be worse off in the sense that we would believe in a false view); whereas if induction does hold and we do not rely on it, we shall have missed out on the only method that could have helped us to predict the future. This argument assumes that Popper is wrong in his view that we can make reasonable predictions without relying on inductive procedures.

Similarly in the case of the external world, if it does exist we shall lose a lot if we assume that it does not, for we won't be able to come to terms with the external world unless we assume that it exists. If however the external world does not exist and we assume that it does, we shall not lose much, except perhaps in the sense that we (if we existed without the external world!) would be involved in believing an untruth. Avoidance of error, as William James rightly stressed, should not be given absolute importance. Suspension of belief would lead to an avoidance of error, but it would also make practical life impossible, and even growth of knowledge impossible.

Again, free-will cannot be shown to exist. But it might be argued that it is reasonable to believe in it because if we have free-will and we do not believe in it, we would have lost the opportunity to exercise our freedom,[1] whereas if we have not got free-will but believe we have it, then our belief in it was not something that was freely chosen but was out of our control; for instance, because we were fated to believe in it or because our belief in it was a random occurrence over which we had no control. But does not responsibility involve a cost? If we carry the burden of responsibility is this not a loss if our freedom turns out to be illusory; we would have carried this burden in vain? This objection can be easily met. For if we do not have free-will then our assumption of the burdens of responsibility was out of our control, and so we cannot rationally kick ourselves for having assumed it.

It might be objected that sometimes if a person is mentally ill and lacking in free-will, it may be better to encourage the person to have therapy rather than to carry on in the illusion that he has free-will. The latter policy can at least sometimes be damaging for the person who is in real need of therapy. Perhaps we could meet this objection by admitting that when in particular cases free-will can be shown to be lacking, then it is reasonable not to believe in it; this is compatible with the view that until free-will has been shown not to exist, it is reasonable to assume that we have it. This proviso is in harmony with our general assumption that it is only when theoretical and scientific considerations leave an issue open, is it reasonable to appeal to practical considerations of the sort that we considered. Moreover, even in the counter-example under discussion those who have to decide whether to advise the mentally sick person assume that they (the advisers) have free-will. If they take up a fatalistic attitude and as a result do nothing, they could have missed out on the opportunity to do something worthwhile, if in fact they had free-will.

Similarly in the case of physical determinism, as long as scientific evidence leaves its truth open, it would be reasonable not to believe in it, or so it would seem to those of us who think that physical determinism (the view that every physical event has a physical cause) clashes with human freedom[2] and so it clashes with our practical life. Some philosophers[3] have some faith in the truth of physical determinism. If one believes that physics will eventually explain all areas of human knowledge, this faith runs contrary to what many of us think is required by our moral and practical life. Which faith is it reasonable to believe in? It seems to me that for an area of inquiry such as physics, or economics, or psychology or sociology to progress we do not need to assume that it will succeed in explaining everything. How then do we decide how far an area of inquiry can be extended? The answer is to rely on common sense hunches and on trial and error. For instance, there may be economic explanations for the rise and fall of religions, and there may also be psychological and sociological ones. The one that we choose is the one that in fact helps to explain the relevant phenomena. We do not need to assume that everything can be explained by any one science, or even that everything can be explained.

A science can progress and in some cases even flourish without assuming that it can explain all cases of knowledge. Physics can try to progress without assuming physical determinism; economics can try to progress without assuming economic determinism; psychology can try to progress without assuming psychological determinism; and so on.

Quantum mechanics does not assume determinism even in the areas where it applies. And even determinist physics can be qualified so that it does not assume that every physical event is determined; it need only assume that things within its scope are determined. Even if a substantial part of human behaviour cannot be fully explained by any of the sciences, the sciences (including the social sciences) can still progress by explaining other parts of the physical system not affected by human behaviour, as well as in explaining parts of human behaviour such as human behaviour in the aggregate and abnormal human behavior (where freedom is lacking). Also we can discover functional relationships between things without assuming universal causation. The truth of physical determinism is not necessary for the development of physics though it is perhaps necessary to justify a take over bid by physics of all areas of knowledge. Similarly the truth of economic determinism is not necessary for the development of economics though it would help to justify a take over bid by economics of all the social sciences.

So it might be suggested that freedom is essential for civilized life and morality in a way in which physical determinism (which implies the absence of freedom) is not essential for the development of the sciences. It is worth taking a gamble and assuming that freedom exists until it is shown not to exist, or at least until it is shown that it is likely not to.

The view that determinism is incompatible with civilized morality is, of course, controversial. There are philosophers who believe that determinism, including physical determinism, can be reconciled with freedom.[4] So the view that we should take a gamble and assume that determinism is not true is also controversial. It will not appeal to those who think that physical determinism and freedom are compatible.

What is less controversial is that we should assume fatalism to be false. For if fatalism is true, it would not be up to us what we assume, nor would it matter what we assume. But if fatalism is false, and we had assumed it was true, we would have let things drift when we could have been in charge of our destiny.

But even the belief that fatalism is false can involve certain losses. For it is possible that such a belief, in spite of all its bad effects, does bring a certain peace of mind to the people concerned. Of course if fatalism is true, then it is not up to us what we believe. But if fatalism is false, it may be rational for us to believe it is true if this gives us peace of mind. My own view is that such gains would be more than offset by the bad effects of believing in fatalism.

Can the prudential argument (*a la* Pascal) be applied to the self? We do not know whether or not there is a persistent self but it is reasonable, from the prudential point of view, to assume there is one, for if we embrace the no-self view and it turned out that there is a persistent self, we would have abandoned a good deal of our moral and practical life (that part of it which presupposes the persistent self), whereas if we believe in the persistent self and the truth is that there are no persistent selves, there would be no substantial loss for us. Even if there was a loss, we would not be there to suffer it!

Mystics tell us that belief in the ego is a great obstacle to our spiritual liberation, it prevents us from reaching our true destiny, which is union with the cosmos. Parfit, in a similar vein, tells us how the non-reductionist view keeps us ignorant, causing us to be afraid of things like death. The man liberated from such a belief in the self can face life with greater peace and equanimity. But though such considerations show how such liberation can lead to an increase in total bliss and happiness, it would hardly be imprudent to miss out on such happiness if there is no self. If I am not a persistent entity, then it is not reasonable for me to kick myself for missing out on such wonderful experiences. Pascal's wager appeals to our prudential point of view. If there is no self, there can hardly be a prudential gain for us. So it is reasonable to assume (from prudential point of view) that there is a self. This is consistent with the view developed in chapter 8 that in order to be happy one must not live a self-centred life; the view that one must not (if one is to be happy) be obsessed with the self is consistent with the belief that there is a self.

It might be objected that even if there is no persistent self, as a matter of fact John Smith does have a desire that John Smith should be happy. And his liberation does tend to satisfy this desire and he will be worse off if he is not liberated. Yes, but on this view he is worse off only assuming that he has this desire. If a person could decondition himself from this desire, why would he be any worse off?

Of course there are well known problems with Pascal's wager. Some of these are specific to the case of believing in God. But there is one general sort of problem which has analogues in the other areas where I have applied Pascal's wager argument. Even if Pascal's argument shows that it is rational to believe in God, which God is it rational to believe in, Allah or Krishna or the Christian God or the Jewish God? Belief in one of them may even turn out to be fatal if it angers the god who really exists. Believers in false gods may be doomed just as much as atheists are. In the case of induction, even if the wager argument shows that it is rational to believe in induction, there still remains the problem of choosing between different inductive practices, a problem that was highlighted by Nelson Goodman.[5]

Again, in the case of free-will, even if the argument shows that we should believe in free-will, there still remains the daunting task of distinguishing free actions from unfree ones. In the case of the external world too, even if we believe in the external world, there remains the problem of distinguishing our dream world from the external world. Similarly in the case of the self. Even if from a prudential point of view we should believe in the self, there remains the problem of choosing between different conceptions of the self.

How then should we choose between different conceptions of the self? How for instance do we choose between the simple view according to which survival is a matter of all or nothing and the complex version (of the non-reductionist view) according to which survival admits of degrees, there is a self but it gradually fades away.

And if Parfit is right in thinking that it is defensible to argue that the reductionist view is compatible with an egoistical point of view, then how do we choose between his conception of the person and others?

Broadly we may distinguish two sorts of considerations that may be brought to bear in exercising such choices. The first are intellectual and scientific considerations. If certain conceptions of the self are undermined by certain scientific or intellectual considerations, then they must be rejected. I shall argue that if fission were to occur, then the simple view would be undermined. There would be several other competing conceptions of the person to choose from (such as the complex version of the non-reductionist view, and the cosmic self view). There are other intellectual considerations one could bring in to adjudicate between them. But if we still have more than one conception of the person left, we can then appeal to the principle of reasonable faith that I discussed earlier. In fact fission has not occured and the simple view is still among the competing conceptions of the self. It harmonises better with our moral and practical life than the reductionist views do. I argue in this book and in *Equality, Liberty and Perfectionism* that the reductionist views would involve a much more radical overhaul of our moral and practical system than is sometimes realised. This would still leave the problem of why we should not adopt the more extreme practical and moral system that goes with the reductionist approach? How then do we choose between different practical systems, with their different presuppositions, assuming that scientific considerations have not been able to decide between the different conceptions of the self?

Section 2: Some Common-sense Principles and Reflective Equilibrium

Besides appealing to the prudential argument in the way we saw earlier, we can appeal to our subjective convictions and to a defeasible presumption in favour of those of our ordinary practices whose presuppositions appear correct to us. It is reasonable to believe in these practices until they have been shown to be based on presuppositions that no longer appear reasonable to us.

Hume had argued that we should believe that some of our actions are genuinely altruistic, that not all our actions are selfish. He thought it reasonable to believe this for it is the way things appear to us in ordinary life. We could reject our ordinary views if and when some hypothesis is discovered which by penetrating deeper into human nature may prove the former (altruistic) affections to be modifications of the latter (selfish) affections.[6]

Chisholm[7] has suggested that we should be guided by those propositions that we presuppose in ordinary activity. He thinks that we have a right to believe in these propositions in the sense that whether or not they are true, we should regard them as epistemically innocent, until we have found some positive reason for thinking them guilty.

Swinburne[8] commends the principle of credulity according to which one should believe what one is inclined to believe until we have evidence against it. He rightly points out that without some such principle we could not have a body of knowledge.

It seems to me that these philosophers are all appealing to similar principles, which have much to commend them. Roughly the principle is that we should accept common-sense views until they are shown to be wrong. This common-sense principle leads naturally to the reflective equilibrium model. If one allows common-sense presumptions to be defeated by recalcitrant facts, one must also admit that there is a problem when one common-sense belief conflicts with another. For, at any rate, on the realist model, reality does not admit of inconsistencies. So one would need to modify our common-sense beliefs until one gets a good fit with the facts as well as with other common-sense beliefs.

We can now come back to the problem of culture relativity that arises for those who want to adopt the Hume-Chisholm-Swinburne approach, for those who believe in William James's doctrine of reasonable faith, as well as for those who appeal to the reflective equilibrium model. The problem is that different practical systems presuppose different propositions and what seems to be the case to one set of people is sometimes quite different from what seems to be the case to another set of people.

The way to cope with this problem is to accept the propositions that seem reasonable to you. Sometimes different sets of people will accept different propositions, but there is nothing very odd in this. Just as what is reasonable to believe can vary with the available evidence (so that it may have been reasonable for the primitive man to have believed in the flat earth) so also what is reasonable to believe can sometimes vary with different practical and moral life styles and with different subjective intuitions.

Meiland has convincingly argued that if two people, the wife and the wife's detective possess some evidence about the husband's alleged infidelity, the evidence may justify the detective in believing the husband has been unfaithful but it may not justify the wife in so believing. For quite apart from any contrary evidence about the husband's character that the wife may or may not possess, the wife 'has a duty to her husband arising from their commitment to one another over a long period, to require a stronger basis for belief in his treachery than does, say, the private detective.'9 Of course this is not to deny that the wife will be justified in believing the husband has been unfaithful if stronger evidence turns up.

It would be foolish for her to argue that she has a duty to trust her husband, therefore he can never be unfaithful to her. But it is quite reasonable for her to require higher standards of proof than would satisfy the private detective. The inference from inconclusive evidence of the husband's infidelity to the conclusion that the husband is unfaithful involves a gamble that may be reasonable for the detective but may not be reasonable for the wife for whom so much more is at stake.

Suppose free-will is presupposed by much of our civilized practical and moral life. And suppose that it is not presupposed by 'barbaric' life styles, where people are condemned without reference to their freedom. In some of these societies retributive condemnation has extended not only to human beings, but to animals and even to inanimate objects. Again there are certain countries that practise collective responsibility and their presuppositions may be quite different from ours.10 It would be lunacy for us to give up our civilized life styles and adopt some 'barbaric' practice where children are punished for the crimes of the father, where talk of excuses and the individual self is by-passed. Of course it is another matter if we get converted to the 'barbaric' practice and its presuppositions. We must believe in what to us seems reasonable, not what seems reasonable to another set of people. Even if we cannot tell from an objective point of view that our life style is based upon sounder presuppositions than theirs, it is reasonable for us to believe in our life style if its postulates appear more convincing to us.

This is not to deny the importance of trying to see the point of view of other cultures. There should be a constant dialogue between different viewpoints and we should try to discuss the pros and cons of different moral and metaphysical systems. As a result of such a dialogue we may modify our beliefs, and sometimes even get converted to another world view.

The reflective equilibrium model has been unfairly criticised on the grounds that it allows several consistent moral (and metaphysical) systems, each of which is internally consistent and coherent; the model offers no way of adjudicating between such different systems. My own worry with the reflective equilibrium model is the opposite, viz. in practice (at any rate among the civilized options) there is not a single viable moral and metaphysical system which is free of tensions. So the problem of how to choose between several moral and metaphysical systems each of which is internally consistent and coherent hardly arises. And if such a problem did arise, the way out would be for you to opt for the system that squares best with your intuitions; it would be lunacy to use someone else's, unless it is your judgement that the other person's judgements in general are sound.

The real problem is to choose the least implausible system. What we need is a dialogue between different systems, discussing the pros and cons of the different systems. For instance, one can raise difficulties for the Buddhist morality and metaphysics, e. g. if there is no self, why should I bother with my liberation?[11] Or if there is no self, is it just that the later self should suffer for the deeds of the earlier one as the law of Karma, which the Buddhists believe in, asserts?[12] Consider also the debate between rights based theories and utilitarianism. Each tries to defend itself from criticism and also to point out the difficulties involved in the other view. None of these systems are wholly coherent and consistent and free of tensions.

So we should accept the system that appears most reasonable to us. Others will accept the system that appears most reasonable to them. Though different people have different starting points, they can engage in a dialogue. And one must keep an eye open for new discoveries in factual matters. New facts can sometimes undermine traditional practices. One will never reach a point where one can say 'Now we have got a final solution where everything hangs together in a consistent and coherent manner'. At best such a final solution works as a regulative ideal. We aspire to rid our practices and theory and our intuitions of inconsistencies and incoherences.

Both those such as Mackie who think that our practical choices should be based upon facts, and those who believe in the reflective equilibrium model (as well as those who believe in William James's principle of reasonable faith) agree that we should try to get some sort of consistency between theory and practice. But some philosophers take a more radical line. Nagel thinks that there can be inconsistency between the objective and the subjective approach which is inherently insoluble. In appendix A I have argued that there is no need to adopt Nagel's irrationalism. Bernard Williams thinks that the demand for consistency only applies to theoretical systems, not to practical ones. At the practical level inconsistency can be endemic, which is why we have tragic moral dilemmas, so that we do wrong whatever we choose.

But is it not reasonable to achieve a fit between facts and values in the sense that if a certain practice presupposes certain beliefs which are false, then we may need to revise our practice? One of the tasks of a philosopher is to work out the different moral implications of different metaphysical views. For instance, it is important to see how much of our moral system would have to be altered if we abandon the non-reductionist view of the self. Some philosophers argue, as against Parfit, that even if the reductionist view is true, we should still carry on much as before. I reject this view in chapters 8, 9 and 10.

We regard infanticide as wrong. It seems proper to ask, if infanticide is wrong, is not abortion (especially late abortion) also wrong? There may be a difference between the two cases, but it seems reasonable to ask what the relevant difference is. If the newly born infant is a human being, is not the nine-month foetus also a human being? Williams thinks there is no need to answer such questions. It is certain that the infanticide is wrong, and no amount of reasons given will provide as much certainty as the direct intuition that killing a child is wrong.[13] But even if this is so, it is not certain that the killing of a mature foetus is not wrong. The view that it is certain that infanticide is wrong, does not imply that abortion is not wrong. What the reflective equilibrium model does is to examine some of the rationale behind our certain intuitions, and then it can give a ruling on the controversial cases. If infanticide is wrong because it involves killing a child, abortion of a mature foetus is also wrong because it involves killing a child.

Williams admits that public agencies have to be answerable to the public and so they have to give reasons and answer charges of inconsistency. But he thinks that this is not so at the private level. So he concludes that the need to reduce conflict is not an inherent need of the practical life, but only a special need of public agencies, arising from the fact that they are answerable to the public.

But if my arguments are correct, they show that even at the personal level one must be willing to give reasons. One cannot take feelings as just brute facts, especially as many of them can be explained away. Thus one reason why we do not feel as strongly about the killing of the mature foetus as we do about the killing of a newly born child is that we have not seen it. But is this morally relevant? If we refused to even allow the raising of such doubts at the private level, the door is left open for people to continue to hold bigoted views.

Williams says that if our moral life is to have depth and conviction and be worthwhile human beings must 'feel more than they can say, and grasp more than they can explain'. Those of us who believe in the reflective equilibrium model can grant that we can feel more than we can say and that we can grasp more than we can explain or justify. Indeed, something similar could also apply in other areas such as metaphysics. Thus from the first person perspective we feel that the non–reductionist view of the person is the correct one. Scientists often make important conjectures which they cannot justify in the sense of proving them to be true or even probable. The reflective equilibrium model attaches importance to our intuitive judgments. But it also submits them to critical scrutiny, somewhat as a scientist makes a conjecture (which he cannot prove) and then submits it to criticisms and possible refutations.[14] Our intuitions are as important as our starting point, but they are not beyond criticism as they seem to be on Williams's account. On the reflective equilibrium model there is a constant dialogue between different views and as we saw earlier, we try to widen the circle within which we can get agreement.

While some philosophers would reject the reflective equilibrium model because they think that inconsistency is part of the moral life, the reflective equilibrium model has also to face the opposite charge, viz. that it too is irrational. R. M. Hare thinks he has a proof of his ethical views and tends to be contemptuous of those of us who use the reflective equilibrium model. He thinks that it provides no checks against our prejudices.

But it is wrong to think that if we do not have a rational proof of our views, then we have to fall back on arbitrary choice. As Mill pointed out there is a larger meaning of the word 'proof' in which such questions can admit of proof. Considerations can be brought to the attention of the cognitive faculty.[15] Even Hare[16] in other areas rightly admits that it is reasonable for us to hold views that we cannot prove. He thinks religious views can be reasonable even though they cannot be proved. And our common sense views, such as that people are not trying to poison the paranoic cannot be strictly proved. The paranoic is wrong, we are right, even though the paranoic cannot be proved wrong.

Indeed in many other branches of knowledge, such as history, we make judgements that are considered reasonable without there being a proof. Why then must we insist on a higher standard in morals? As for the charge that the reflective equilibrium model only serves to reinforce our prejudices, the version of the model that I commend would ensure that we have a constant dialogue with other viewpoints. We subject our intuitions to criticisms in the way we saw earlier, and even if we are in a sense involved in circular reasoning, we can (as we saw earlier) try to widen the circle within which we get agreement.

Mackie[17] is critical of the Kantian view that gives primacy to the practical over theoretical. He thinks that practical choices should be based on factual beliefs, not the other way round. What is rational to do depends upon what the facts are, but we cannot take what we are inclined to think it is rational to do as evidence about those facts. He asks us what we would say of the general who inferred from the following three premises that the enemy were not advancing in overwhelming numbers:

1. If the enemy are advancing in overwhelming strength, then if we do not withdraw, our army will be wiped out.
2. We must not allow our army to be wiped out.
3. We must not withdraw, because that would mean letting down our allies.

Again Mackie asks us to consider the following syllogism: 'Eat no animal fats; you may eat butter; so butter is not an animal fat. ' Mackie comments that the premises do not establish the truth of the factual conclusion, but he thinks that the person who coherently commends the first two premises, is committed to believing that butter is not an animal fat.

These examples do not constitute a refutation of the reflective equilibrium model. For at most what the model would justify is that certain views go together - that if we subscribe to certain premises, then we should also subscribe to the conclusion. If we subscribe to certain practices, then we must also subscribe to the presupposition of those practices. It does not urge us to blindly accept the presuppositions. If there is some evidence to show that the presuppositions are false, then we must take note of such evidence. We must critically test the presuppositions to the extent that it is possible to do so. If the presuppositions turn out to be false, then we may have to revise our practices, though we may find that the practice is so essential to us that we have to carry on with it, even when it is based on a presupposition which is false. We may in such cases believe in practically necessary illusions. But if the presuppositions have not been shown to be false, we should not assume that they are false. It could be quite reasonable to believe in say non-reductionist selves or free-will until they are shown to be false. We know that it is false that butter is not an animal fat but we have not shown, not even on a balance of probabilities that free-will does not exist, or that non-reductionist selves do not exist.

Sometimes it is quite reasonable to take a gamble and trust our subjective intuitions even though they have not been confirmed by objective facts. If we give a high priority to avoidance of error then the rational strategy would be suspension of judgment. But such a strategy would prevent us not only from getting on in our practical life but even from an epistemic point of view, it could prevent us from acquiring a body of knowledge which is true. Acquiring a body of knowledge involves conjectures which may turn out to be false. If we gave absolute priority to the prevention of error, scientific activity and the pursuit of truth in general would come to a halt.

Mackie commends Sidgwick's view that we should not believe for purposes of practice what we are not inclined to believe as a speculative truth. This point raises deep issues. Mackie and Sidgwick seem to think that we can build a body of knowledge from empirically given data and indubitable rules of inference. If this were so, then indeed it would be reasonable to think that our ethical and other practices should be based on such a body of knowledge.

But we should be suspicious of claims to build such a body of knowledge. Scepticism cannot be answered without an appeal to our practical life[18] and our subjective inclinations. Even Sidgwick admitted that 'if... we find that in our supposed knowledge of the world of nature propositions are commonly taken to be universally true, which rest on no other grounds than that we have a strong disposition to accept them, and that they are indispensable to the systematic coherence of our beliefs - it will be more difficult to reject a similarly supported assumption in ethics without opening the door to universal scepticism'.[19]

Mackie gives us a stark choice: 'Practical choices must be based on factual beliefs, not the other way round'. But there is a third possibility, viz. our values and our beliefs about facts are mutually adjusted in an attempt to get a harmonious fit. Those who believe in reflective eqilibrium would not deny that the fact that butter is an animal fat should be used to undermine one of the premises in Mackie's example.

Section 3: Pervasiveness of the Non-reductionist view

To come back to the self, Pascal's wager does not provide any reason for adopting the prudential point of view, rather it assumes the prudential point of view. But it does reflect how pervasive the belief in the prudential point of view is. The person who goes in for Pascal's wager in different spheres of life, such as, with regards to the existence of God, free will or the self, is appealing to his self-interest and so is involved in rejecting the reductionist view of the self, as well as the cosmic self view. But of course the prudential point of view is not the only point of view. One might argue that from a social point of view or from a cosmic point of view, it is no longer rational to assume that there is a separate self for each human being. The cosmic self view or the no-self view may, if generally adopted, lead to a net reduction of human sorrow. How then do we choose between different conceptions of the self?

I have argued that there is a defeasible presumption in favour of the view that appears to be true to us. If our subjective consciousness points in the direction of the non-reductionist view, and if the non-reductionst view coheres with much of our moral and practical life, it is reasonable to believe in it, until it is shown to be implausible and until a more plausible and viable alternative is produced. Moreover it is an advantage of my version of the non-reductionst view that it is falsifiable.

The prudential point of view is not the only point of view, but it is, at least among ordinary people, one of the important points of view. Only some sages may have transcended it. So it important to see if the no-self view can be reconciled with the prudential (or egoistical) point of view. In chapter 8 I argue that such a reconciliation will not work. I also argue that the view that there is a gradually changing self would cause havoc in our practical and moral life.[20] I briefly argue in chapter 9 that the cosmic self view would undermine our non-utilitarian moral constraints.

None of this of course provides a proof that the non-reductionist view is correct. What one can try to point our are the costs involved in adopting the different views of the person. And even the extent to which something is a cost may depend upon which point of view one adopts. Thus a utilitarian may welcome the fact that non-utilitarian rights based constraints may be undermined if one abandons the non-reductionist view. A Buddhist may welcome the fact that the no-self view is incompatible with the rationality of egoistical concern, for the Buddhist thinks the world would be a better place if we abandoned egoistical concerns.

But it would be wrong to infer that everything is culture-relative in such matters. That certain views of the self have certain implications is often an objective matter of fact. One of the important tasks of the philosopher is to work out the ethical and practical implications of different conceptions of the person. One can also argue against certain views by pointing out that they try to combine elements that do not hang together. Thus I argue on such grounds against Parfit and against some of the Buddhists.

In this book I stress how deep seated and pervasive the prudential point of view and the non-reductionist view are. But it might be objected that one must not exaggerate the importance of the simple view, by concentrating just on one sort of culture. There are other cultures where people have held different views of the person. Thus many Hindus have believed in some sort of cosmic self pervading the whole universe, whereas Buddhists have believed in the reductionist view. The Buddhists not only anticipated Hume's reductionist theory of the self, they also, unlike Hume but like Parfit, drew some important ethical conclusions from it. They argued, that since there is no ego, egoism is irrational. Selfishness presupposes a self. So the no-self doctrine ought to lead to a saint-like detachment.

But it seems to me wrong to infer that in such cultures the non-reductionist view is totally rejected. One must beware of confusing theory with practice. Even if certain views are professed by certain societies, one cannot infer that such views are generally practised in such cultures. In fact the opposite is more likely to be true. In societies where certain virtues are praised, you can be pretty certain that the opposite vices are practised. The truth is that Indians, among whom Buddhism flourished and Hinduism still flourishes, are just as egoistical as any other set of people. Non-attachment is stressed as a virtue because it is recognised that the people are in fact very attached to their egoistical goals. Moreover, the law of Karma (which both Hinduism and Buddhism believe in) does not make sense if one gets rid of the self. For according to the law of Karma the person gets his just deserts in this life or in subsequent ones.

If you do a wicked deed you will in the future suffer for it,[21] if you do a good deed you will reap an appropriate reward in the future. There would be no intrinsic justice in this law if the reductionist view were correct. Why should the fate of the later self be determined by the action of the earlier one? Of course, even if the reductionist view is correct, there will as a matter of fact be an intimate relationship between what the earlier self does and what happens to the later one – if the earlier self spends a lot of time reading certain books the later self is likely to acquire the corresponding knowledge. But if the reductionist view is true there is no intrinsic moral fittingness (of the kind that the law of Karma assumes) between the actions of the earlier self and the fate of the later self. Why is it just that the later self should prosper because of the good deeds of the earlier self?

No doubt, a utilitarian God could so arrange things that the later selves suffer for the deeds of the earlier ones. Even if the later self is different from the earlier one, the earlier one is likely in fact to be concerned with the fate of later one (though is that not because it assumes rightly or wrongly that the later self is the very same self as itself. And so a utilitarian God could deter bad behaviour by having a law where the sins of the earlier self are visited upon the later self. But would there be any intrinsic fittingness in such a law? Of course according to certain primitive views there is a certain fittingness even in the sins of the father being visited upon the sons. But the Hindus claim that their doctrine of Karma is superior to the primitive ethics presupposed by the version of the Christian religion according to which people now suffer for the sins of Adam. This superiority could only be argued if one assumes that on the law of Karma the one who suffers later on is the very self-same individual as the one who committed the wicked deeds.

It is sometimes argued that the Hindus in fact (and not just in theory) do not have a proper conception of the individual self. They see themselves either (at the metaphysical level) as an *atman* which is identical with Brahman, the cosmic self, or (at the empirical level) in terms of their various social roles. For instance, it is said that the Hindu 'cannot be thought as having a bounded ego or an enduring ego in the Western sense... An Indian thinks of himself as a father, a son, a nephew, a pupil and these are the only identities he ever has... It is very common in Indian households to hear a person referred to as "Rekha's mother" or as "Babu's father"... The self is not available as an object to itself in India, and so introspection as a psychological project does not exist. Self-knowledge, in traditional Indian lore, is not knowledge of the empirical self but of the real self which is Brahman... The Indian self lacks reflexive awareness of itself'.[22]

But it is wrong to claim that in fact the average Hindu sees himself in his ordinary life as one with Brahman. The view that he is one with Brahman is one that he may aspire to comprehend; with the exception of the sages and the mystics it is a truth that people are, at best, only dimly aware of. His ordinary life is so full of his egoistical drive, which is why he needs to be reminded by himself and by others of deep truths which stress his identity with the cosmos. According to the doctrine of *Advaita* there is indeed just one Brahman or the cosmic self pervading us all, but as long as the people are in the grip of *Maya* or illusion they will believe that they have separate egos and attach themselves to illusory goals.

The ordinary Indian does have reflexive awareness of himself. Even when others see him as a bundle of social roles, he does not see himself as just a composite of these roles. From the first person perspective he can make judgements such as 'I am Babu's father and I am so and so's son. This body is my body. These thoughts are my thoughts. This suffering is my suffering. The causes of my suffering are my bad deeds in my previous life'.

It is true that some ideologies are primarily individualistic, while others stress the importance of society or the group. It is also true that ideologies often have a profound influence on the way the individual sees himself vis-a-vis society and the cosmos. But there is a limit to which individuals get conditioned. Consider, for instance the position of women.

Agehananda Bharati, a noted Professor of Social Anthropology, tells us 'The key term in Bengali matrimonial transactions is *rasa*, literally "juice" and a woman merges and loses her entire personality into her husband's *substance* at the wedding. This is not of course some sort of disguised romantic kitsch – it is hard ritualistic situation with no nonsense about it. The same concepts are held by all Dravidian groups in the south. It is not only that the *gotra* (lineage with a mythical seer as apical ancestor) of the bride dissolves into her husbands *gotra*, it is not only that she merges the gods of her family of origin with the family gods of the husband; she merges it with his quite literally ... in a truly material sense. For instance, south Indian women... eat their food from the plantain leaf from which the husband has just eaten his meal – totally unthinkable for any other two persons in India'.[23]

There are analogous practices in North India which encourage the woman to merge into the husband's family. Amongst Kashmiri Brahmins (the community I was born into) the traditional practice was that at marriage the wife not only acquired the husband's surname or family name, she lost her first name too, often in a way that reflected her status as an appendage to the husband. My grandfather was Shiva Haksar. At marriage his wife was given the name Shivanti Haksar.

Fortunately, such conditioning is seldom completely successful. Even women who have gone through such brainwashing, retain some spirit and sense of their separate identity. For instance when they are unhappy with their husband or his family, or when they suffer some bereavement, or when they quarrel, they are quite aware of their separate individuality, of their unfulfilled needs, of their suffering. Often a woman would attribute her suffering to her own past Karma – the Law of Karma is a highly individualistic Law.

The fact that force and violence is used against women from time to time (as in cases of Sati or more commonly nowadays in cases of dowry deaths) is another sign that they have not been completely brainwashed but retain at least some sense of separate identity. For every Sati who voluntarily went to her husband's funeral pyre there were many who were forced.

Indeed I suspect that many, if not all, group cultures (i. e. cultures that stress the group as the moral unit) have elements of the individualistic culture co-existing side by side.[24] For instance, in Hindu society the holistic and group culture coexists with the highly individualistic Law of Karma according to which the fate of the individual depends upon his present and past actions in this life as well as in previous ones. Again there are societies where the corporate groups such as villages impose collective responsibility on each other but the group would administer a system of individual responsibility within it. Thus if a member of a village has caused harm to people in another village the latter group will seek vengeance or demand reparations from the former village, but the 'offending' village will use a system of individual responsibility within its frontiers to punish the individual offender.[25]

Levy-Bruhl[26] describes some primitive cultures where the social group, clan or sib is the real unit of which the individual is a mere element. He reports that among the Indians of Guiana, if a human being falls ill not only he but his relatives and others fast. Brothers are considered the same individual rather than separate beings.

He illustrates this theme in many ways, but I shall just mention two of the incidents that he reports. There were a husband and wife who had been married for several years. They had a child. The husband had a brother who took a strong fancy to the woman. Secretly, he often asked her to live with him but in spite of his persistence she kept refusing him. 'Then his brother's love began to change to anger. He cherished vexation in his heart toward the woman and asked her, "Why do you always refuse me? You are the wife not of a stranger, but of my brother. He and I are one, and you ought to accept me." But she persisted: "No, I don't want it." Finally, he tried to enter her and she killed him.'

Levy-Bruhl tells how in 'another story (of the Ogone region) a brother angry with his brother's wife, who was resisting his advances, killed her one night in the forest whilst she was on the way to visit her parents. He was seen and denounced by the woman's son. "Then all the townspeople gathered around him, being horrified at the news of the woman's death. The husband called them all to a council, and the palaver was held at his house. There the grandfather and the lad told the whole story.

The brother-in-law began to enter a denial, but the husband said: "No! You are guilty! And because we are brothers, and we are one, the guilt is also mine, and I will confess for you".

But the wife's family said to the husband: "We have no quarrel with you. We want only the person who killed our sister, and a fine of money for our loss".'

Levy-Bruhl rightly goes on to contend that these two stories show clearly that among these 'natives' a very strong sense of their own individualistic personality co-exists with the non-individualistic view of the person according to which the two brothers are one individual.

One does not have to go as far as Levy-Bruhl's 'natives' to observe such phenomena. In Britain the Christian idea of the unity of husband and wife (which was reflected in the British Legal System - for instance, the wife could not give evidence against her husband, since that would violate the law against admitting self-incriminatory evidence,) co-existed with the individualistic conception of the person.

So the presence of alternative conceptions of the person in a society does not imply that the individualistic egoistical (non-reductionist) conception of the person does not also flourish in the society.

It is the contention of this book that the individualistic view of the self, according to which each of us is a separate and indivisible self, is presupposed by a substantial part of our moral and practical system. I do not want to deny that other views of the self may be presupposed by other parts of our moral and practical system; it would be surprising if our moral and practical system formed a wholly consistent system. But I would claim that the separate self view does not conflict with anything like as much of our moral and practical experience as its critics would have us believe.

It may be argued by some of my critics that even in the modern western culture (where Oriental, African and other exotic conceptions of the self are excluded) there are at least two other views of the self that are more prevalent than I seem to recognise. Firstly, there is the view that human beings are essentially social. Secondly there is the reductionist view.

As for the view that human beings are essentially social, I would argue that the element of what is obviously true in this view can be reconciled with the individualistic view of the self.[27] It is useful to distinguish the following claims. 1. Human beings develop their potential in a social context. Without human society, a human being would be extremely impoverished. Consider, for instance, human beings who have been brought up by wolves. 2. The particular social and psychological characteristics that a human being has, are constitutive of his identity. If he was brought up in a different environment he would be a different individual from the one that he is now.

The separate self view (i.e. the version of the simple self view defended in this book) is consistent with the first claim. As for the second claim, the separate self view is consistent with the view that if I was brought up in a different environment, I would have a different personality from the one that I now have. The social and other environmental conditions do probably help to determine the essence of my personality; it does not follow that they determine the essence of my self. On my view the same self though not the same personality would have existed if I had been brought up differently. The combined sense of the term 'same person' which I introduced in chapter one, is consistent with the view that I am now the same self, but in a sense a different person (because a different personality) from what I would have been if I had been brought up differently. The more radical claim that the identity of my self and not just of my personality is constituted by the social and other environmental conditions that I have grown up in, is indeed inconsistent with my views. But this radical claim is quite counter-intuitive.

For instance, suppose you have injured me in the past, and I now try to sue you and get compensation. On the radical view you could rebut my claim to compensation, by the argument 'If I had not injured you, "you" would now be a different self from what you are now. Indeed, you would not exist but for the injury. For the injury that you received has helped to form the self that you now are. You owe your very essence to me. And as long as it is better for you to exist than not to exist, you should if anything be grateful to me for helping to bring you into existence'.

So we see that what is obviously true about the view that we are essentially social beings has not been shown to be inconsistent with the view that each of us is a separate and indivisible self. Let us now turn to the objection that the reductionist view is more prevalent than I seem to grant. Reductionists sometimes grant that the reductionist view is not the current view; they claim that it is the correct view. At other times some of them seem to argue that it is also the current view in at least some of the areas of our practical life.

It is often suggested that some people do at least in some of their reactive attitudes imply the reductionist theory of the self. Many people such as Hume think that a convict deserves less punishment for his crime if the relevant bits of his psychology have changed. Some lovers drop their beloved when the beloved has changed. Parfit gives some examples from literature, such as the following: 'Nadya has written in her letter: "When you return…" But that was the whole horror, that there would be no return… A new, unfamiliar person would walk in bearing the name of her husband and she would see that the man, her beloved, for whom she had shut herself up to wait for fourteen years, no longer existed'.

'Innokenty felt sorry for her and agreed to come… He felt sorry, not for the wife he lived with and yet did not live with these days, but for the blonde girl with the curls hanging down to the shoulders, the girl he had known in the tenth grade.'[28]

In fact it is wrong to think that such reactive attitudes only make sense on the reductionist view. Such attitudes can make sense if we use 'same person' in what I earlier called the combined sense. In this sense the same person persists if both the same self persists and the same personality persists. When we love a person we can love his/her self and his/her personality (and body). Similarly, when we have resentment against a criminal, this can be directed at a particular self as long as he has certain psychological traits.

We may love Dr. Jekyll while he is normal and hate Hyde (who is the abnormal manifestation of Dr. Jekyll). Such an attitude would be consistent even if the non-reductionist view of persons is correct and Dr. Jekyll and Hyde are the same self.[29] The view that they are the same person or self is compatible with the view that Dr. Jekyll is not responsible for the crimes of Hyde. A person or self could have commited crimes and yet be excused on grounds of mental disorder.

It is true that many of us have a reluctance to punish a reformed criminal, many years after the crime. One might be tempted to argue that this shows that we presuppose the reductionist view. But we would also be reluctant to punish a replica of the criminal for the crime committed by the criminal and this tends to shows that we presuppose the non-reductionist view that the persistence of the same self is necessary for punishment and that the persistence of the personality is not enough. If we appeal to the combined sense of the term 'same person', we can explain both why we are reluctant to punish the reformed criminal, and why we are reluctant to punish the replica of the criminal. Some reductionists can also explain why we are reluctant to punish in the two cases, for they could appeal to the brute fact that we identify a person, including the criminal, with his psycho–physical make up. But the purely psychological reductionist such as Parfit would not be able to explain (in the sense of justify) our reluctance in the second case.

Parfit uses the following view of Proust's in support of his own reductionist views: 'Our dread of the future in which we must forego the sight of faces, the sound of voices that we love, friends from whom we derive today our keenest joys, this dread far from being dissipated, is intensified if in the grief of such a privation we reflect that there will be added what seems to us now in anticipation an even more cruel grief; not to feel it as grief at all – to remain indifferent; for if that should occur, our self would then have changed. It would be in a real sense the death of ourself, a death followed, it is true, by a resurrection, but in a different self, the life, the love which are beyond the reach of those elements of the existing self that are doomed to die'.

In fact the above view of Proust's is inconsistent with Parfit's views. On the latter view the death of one's psychology involves the death of the person, and there is no room for resurrection of the same person with a different psychology.[30] The non-reductionist view is compatible with such talk of resurrection, for on the non-reductionist view the self can persist and be resurrected with a different psychology.

The following example from Leibniz has been used to show that the non-reductionist view is irrelevant to our egoistical concerns. 'Suppose that some individual could suddenly become King of China on condition, however, of forgetting what he had been, as though being born again, would it not amount to the same practically, or as far as the effects could be perceived, as if the individual were annihilated and a King of China were at the same instant created in his place? The individual would have no reason to desire this.'[31]

I think this at most shows that psychological connectedness is a necessary condition of our egoistical hopes. This is compatible with the view, defended in chapter 8, that the persistence of myself (in the non-reductionist sense) is also presupposed by my primary egoistical hopes.[32] Leibniz himself seemed to be aware of this. For his above mentioned remarks were preceded by the following: 'Further, the immortality which is demanded in morals and religion does not consist in this perpetual subsistence *alone,* for without the memory of what one had been it would not be in any way desirable'.[33]

It could be that much of one's egoistical hopes presuppose personal survival in what I call the combined sense, i. e. survival of one's self and the survival of one's psychology. In the case of egoistical fears it is more plausible to claim that such fears can make sense even when there is a break in psychological continuity and connectedness, as in amnesia.

One normally distinguishes between a person's survival and the survival of his psychology; and this distinction is undermined on the reductionist view.

In this chapter and in other parts of the book (e. g. ch. 1 sec. 2 and chs. 8, 9 and 10) I have argued that our common sense view and the prevailing view is the non-reductionist view according to which each of us is a separate indivisible self. I have also maintained that there is a presumption in favour of the non-reductionist view, on the grounds that it is the common-sense and prevalent view. In the next four chapters I shall defend the non-reductionist view against various attempts to show that this presumption has been rebutted.

NOTES

1. Also, much of our civilized life would have to be abandoned if we did not assume freedom. See P. F. Strawson, 'Freedom and Resentment' in *Studies in Thought and Action.*

2. The view that physical determinism clashes with freedom is covincingly argued by G. Warnock 'Action and Events' in D. F. Pears (ed), *Freedom and the Will*, and by E. Anscombe, *Causality and Determination*, Cambridge University Press, Cambridge, 1971.

3. For instance, B. Williams, *Descartes*, Penguin Books, London, 1973, p. 246.

4. See A. Kenny, *Will, Freedom and Power*, Blackwell, Oxford, 1975.

5. N. Goodman, *Fact, Fiction and Forecast*, Bobbs-Merrill, New York, 1965.

6. *Enquiry Concerning Principles of Morals*, ed. L. A. Selby-Bigge, Clarendon Press, Oxford, 1963, Appendix 2.

7. *Person and Object*, pp. 15-16.

8. *Personal Identity*, S. Shoemaker and R. Swinburne

9. 'What Ought We to Believe', by Jack Meiland, *American Philosophical Quarterly*, Jan. 1980 p. 21

10. May be, not must be. Some tribes practise collective responsibility *vis a vis* other tribes, but individual responsibility within their own tribe. (See S. Moore, 'Legal Liability and Evolutionary Interpretation' in *The Allocation of Responsibility*, ed. Max Gluckman, Manchester University Press, Manchester, 1972). Different conceptions of responsibility can co-exist in the same society, even within the same individual, somewhat as we saw that different conceptions of the self can co-exist in the same culture.

11. See ch. 8.

12. See pp. 87-90.

13. *Moral Luck*, Cambridge University Press, Cambridge, 1981, Chapter 4.

14. See K. Popper, *Conjectures and Refutations*, Routledge and Kegan Paul, London, 1963.

15. J. S. Mill, *Utilitarianism*, first published 1961, several editions available, chapter 1.

16. R. M. Hare, in *New Essays in Philosophical Theology*, edited A. Flew and A. MacIntyre, Macmillam, New York, 1955, pp. 96-108.

17. *The Miracle of Theism*, Clarendon Press, Oxford, 1982, chapter 6. pp. 112-3.

18. See David Hume, *Enquiry Concerning The Human Understanding* (ed. L. A. Selby-Bigge, 2nd edition) sec. 12 part 2 pp. 158-160 and L. Wittgenstein, *On Certainty*, Blackwell, Oxford, 1977, para. 204.

19. *Methods of Ethics*, MacMillan, London, 1907, p. 509.

20. See chs 8 and 9 of this book and my *Equality. Liberty and Perfectionism*

21. Even when you have lost all memories of your earlier misdeeds!
22. T. G. Vaidyanathan, 'Authority and Identity in India', *Daedalus*, Fall 1989, pp. 150–151.
23. A. Bharati, 'The Self in Hindu Thought and Action' in *Culture and Self*, eds. A. Marsella et. al., Tavistock Publications, London, 1985.
24. The converse may also be true. Many, if not all, individualistic cultures are likely to have elements of the group culture existing side by side! Even individualists often feel pride or shame at the conduct of the group with which they identify.
25. See Sally Moore, 'Legal Liability and Evolutionary Interpretation' in M. Gluckman (ed.)*The Allocation of Responsibility*, Manchester University Press, Manchester, 1972, ch. 2.
26. Levy-Bruhl, *The Soul of the Primitive.* , Allen and Unwin, London 1965, chapter 2.
27. For a good defence of moral individualism (i. e. the view that the individual is the morally basic unit) against the arguments of the communitarians, see George Sher, 'Three Grades of Social Involvement', *Philosophy and Public Affairs*, 1989.
28. *Reasons and Persons,* p. 305.
29. To deal with connoisseurs of the human body we might have to add the requirement that there should be enough physical similarity.
30. See T. Penelhum, 'The Importance of Self Identity'. Parfit attempts to make some sort of room for the notion of resurrection by appealing to the notion of 'phoenix Parfit'. This move is I think rightly rejected by Nagel in *A View From Nowhere*, p. 45.
31. Quoted with approval by S. Shoemaker in 'Comments' p. 127.
32. In chapter 8 I allow that my secondary hopes can be satisfied without my persistence.
33. Leibniz, *Discourse on Metaphysics*, Manchester University Press, Manchester, 1053, p. 58, italic mine.

V. *Split Brains*

The distinctions that I made earlier in chapter 2 between the two senses of mind as well as between two senses of unity of mind are crucial to my defence of the traditional conception of the person. In this chapter and in the next I argue that cases of split brains and multiple personality do not conclusively show that there are multiple persons per human being. I shall maintain that in some of the cases it is reasonable to believe that there has been a switching of consciousness from one set of dispositions, memories etc. to another; there may be several minds in the weak sense, but there is only one subjective consciousness per human being. One cannot provide objective evidence for this view, but I offer it as a reasonable and defeasible conjecture. Since the one consciousness per human being view harmonizes with our practical and subjective life, the onus is on its opponents to show that it is false.

In this chapter I shall examine the challenge posed to the traditional view of the person by cases of fisson, imaginary and real. In the first section I shall examine how we should deal with some imaginary cases of fission, if they were to occur. In the second section, I shall examine the problems posed by some actual split-brain experiments. My view is that though the traditional conception of the person (i. e. the non-reductionist view) is falsifiable in the sense that we can conceive of cases which, if they were to occur, would undermine the traditional view, the actual cases that have occurred so far have not undermined the traditional view.

Section 1: Some Imaginary Cases of Fission

Let us imagine a case that David Wiggins[1] considers. Suppose we split Brown's brain and house it in different bodies. And suppose the transplanted persons, Brown 1 and Brown 2 each have to an equal degree the apparent memories and character of Brown. Can the indivisible self view cope with such cases or will it have to be abandoned if such cases became possible?

The following are some of the solutions that have been suggested to deal with the problem of splitting:

1. Brown is identical with either Brown 1 or with Brown 2 (but not with both). However, there is no way of telling, even in principle,

which of the two is identical with Brown.

2. Brown is identical with both Brown 1 and Brown 2.

3. Brown is identical with neither Brown 1 nor with Brown 2.

4. There were two Browns all along. Before the split they were both living harmoniously in Brown's body. After the split they go in different directions.

Some of the above solutions may be quite plausible, but I think that none of them can be plausibly asserted by a defender of the indivisible self view. The first solution has been criticized on the grounds that since Brown 1 and Brown 2 have equally good claims to be considered identical with Brown, it makes no sense to allow the claim that one of them is identical with Brown but the other is not. Some of the advocates of the non-reductionist view are not worried by this criticism. They reject the positivist criterion of significance. A non-positivist could say that after the split one of them is the original Brown even though there is no way of telling even in principle which one is. Indeed one could make this reply even more forceful by arguing that the non-reductionist view and the positivist criterion of significance are incompatible. If one believes in the non-reductionist view, one cannot accept the positivist criterion of significance; for there is no empirical evidence in favour of the non-reductionist view.

As I said earlier, the non-reductionist view is presupposed by much of our practical and moral life but we cannot show it to be true. So it may be asked why splitting would present any special problem for the non-reductionist view. If you are a positivist you will not believe in the non-reductionist view anyway, whether or not splitting occurs. If you reject positivism and opt for the non-reductionist view, then you will not be worried by the fact that you have to reject positivism in order to solve the problem of splitting; for that is something you had already done when you embraced the non-reductionist view.

Nor can one rule out the first solution by appealing to the principle according to which importantly different judgements should only be made when there are different grounds for the two judgements. The first solution does not need to assert that it can judge which of the new Browns is the same as the old Brown.

However, the first solution (when combined with the non-reductionist view) is not wholly satisfactory, not because it conflicts with positivism (which it does) but for other reasons. It seems to be very counter-intuitive. It is difficult to deny that in some important sense Brown survives as both Brown 1 and Brown 2. But on the first solution, the defender of the non-reductionist view, has to deny just this. For since (on the non-reductionist view) survival is a matter of all or nothing and implies identity, the first solution when combined with the non-reductionist view would imply that Brown only survives as Brown 1 or Brown 2 but not as both. Suppose that Brown 1 is identical with Brown. In that case the first solution (when combined with the non-reductionist view) would imply that Brown does not survive as Brown 2. So if Brown 1 dies a second after the split, Brown would not survive even though Brown 2 was flourishing. It seems strange to deny that Brown survived as Brown 2. Brown 2 (like Brown 1) is created out of the cerebral material from Brown 1, we can even explain why Brown 2 has the relevant memories, character traits and so forth.

Once we allow that after the split one of the Browns, say Brown 2, is not the old Brown, we can ask how Brown 2 originated as a new person and what its relations are with the old Brown. Suppose we resort to something like the complex view or Kant's elastic balls model to account for Brown 2, e. g. Brown passed on, at the time of the split, various of his properties to Brown 2 in the way one elastic ball passes on its momentum, speed etc. to the successive one that it hits. This can make us wonder whether Brown 1 also originated in the same way. It can encourage us to be sceptical with regard to Brown too. Compare: Descartes had raised the sceptical problem that since our senses sometimes deceive us, how can we rule out that they deceive us in other cases too. Similarly, if the elastic ball model works in some cases, it is natural to suspect that it works in other cases too. Brown 2 seems just as much a person as Brown 1.

Is it that Brown 2 is an indivisible self, only a different indivisible self from Brown 1? Or is it that Brown 2 is not a indivisible self at all? The latter alternative seems to have radical implications. For Brown 2 seems both in his behaviour and in his feelings to be as much a person as you and I and if he is not an indivisible self, then perhaps nor are we! If his egoistic concerns are based on an illusory belief about the persistence of a non-reductionist self perhaps ours are too. The former alternative (viz. that he has a non-reductionist self but one that is different from Brown's) is also disturbing, though perhaps it is not quite so absurd as the latter alternative. If Brown has passed on various of his properties, qualities, etc. to Brown 2 without passing on his self, could the same not be the case with regard to the relation between

Brown and Brown 1? Once we admit that Kant's elastic ball model sometimes works, it is difficult not to think that it could work in other cases too. Once we allow one indivisible self to succeed another, the stage seems set for some sort of version of the complex view which allows for a succession of selves.

The first solution is not logically incoherent. But it does not seem very plausible. It seems a desperate and *ad hoc* device to save the view according to which there is one non-reductionist self per person.

Let us then consider the second solution, according to which Brown is identical with both Brown 1 and Brown 2. The trouble with this solution is that since identity judgments are transitive, this would imply that Brown 1 and Brown 2 are identical with each other. This consequence may be acceptable in cases where splitting is not full blooded, where one of the offshoots does not have a separate mind in the strong sense. But in cases of full blooded splitting envisaged by Wiggins this solution won't work. For Brown 1 and Brown 2 from the time of the split lead separate lives, they have different inner lives, different egoisitic concerns, they communicate inter-personally and so forth. Brown 1 will worry in an egoistic way about what happens to Brown 1 in the future, whereas Brown 2 will worry in an egoistic way about what happens to Brown 2 in the future. Brown 1 will seem responsible for the acts of Brown 1 and not for those of Brown 2. They each seem to be separate autonomous normal agents. How can two separate autonomous moral agents form one person?

It has been suggested that we could drop the requirement that identity judgments be transitive. So Brown could be identical with Brown 1 and with Brown 2, but Brown 1 and Brown 2 need not be identical with each other. But I don't think this view can be combined with the non-reductionist view. For if Brown is identical with Brown 1, then if Brown 1 died, it would follow that Brown also dies (since on the non-reductionist view identity and survival go together.) But then how can Brown also be identical with Brown 2? For Brown 2 could survive the death of Brown 1. There is the suggestion that neither Brown 1 nor Brown 2 are separate substances. They are both phases in the life of the one substance Brown. So that when Brown 1 dies, there is no extinction of a substance since the substance survives in Brown 2. But to talk like this is to give up the common sense idea of the person, according to which each human being is a separate person or substance.

It might be objected that according to the common sense

conception only ordinary human beings are separate persons. This conception does not imply the same about extraordinary cases such as Brown 1. But is Brown 1 not as much a separate person as you and I? Moreover our common sense conception of the person combines the non-reductionist view with the unity of consciousness view. So Brown 1 and Brown 2 would be different persons since they have different streams of consciousness, there is no unity of consciousness between them. In chapter 2 I gave some reasons for not talking of one person with a divided mind in such cases.

Again there have been suggestions that if such full blooded splitting took place perhaps we should treat person as a concrete universal[2] which could be manifested in more than one human being, or we could distinguish a type person from token persons who are manifestations of the type-persons.[3] Brown 1 and Brown 2 would be manifestations of the same concrete universal Brown or of the same type person. If splitting were to occur, such suggestions may have much to commend them, but to adopt them would involve abandonment of the non-reductionist view. For on the non-reductionist view it is the individual human beings such as Brown 1 and Brown 2 who are the only real persons. The problem of what became of the person Brown (who existed before the split), still remains. Which, if any, of the new Browns is the old self? If the suggestion is that both Brown 1 and Brown 2 manifest the same self, then we have abandoned the special version of the non-reductionist view which combines simplicity of the self with unity of consciousness.

Moreover if one of our main reasons for postulating the non-reductionist view is that it is presupposed by our subjective, practical and moral life, the view that Brown 1 and Brown 2 share the same self seems to be weird. For as we said earlier they each have different egoistic concerns, from the time of the split onward they are responsible for different actions, and so forth. Our practical and moral life would assume that Brown 1 and Brown 2 are different persons.

The third solution viz. that neither Brown 1 nor Brown 2 is identical with the old Brown is also one that is not open to the defenders of the non-reductionist view. For since on the non-reductionist view, loss of identity implies extinction, the view that Brown is not identical with anyone after the split would imply that Brown has ceased to exist as a result of the split. But this is counter-intuitive. As Parfit asks, how can a double success be a failure? And Shoemaker rightly points out that splitting is something one lives through. Now if we abandon the non-reductionist view the problem disappears for then we could argue, that though Brown is not identical with anyone after the split, he still survives after the split. For survival on the reductionist view does not require the persistence of self; it merely requires the presence of certain relations, such as psychological connectedness. On the reductionist view splitting of individual human beings presents no more of a philosophical problem than does the splitting of a nation, such as Germany, into two nations. Neither East Germany nor West Germany was identical with the old Germany, but the old Germany did survive in both East and West Germany.

Let us now consider the fourth solution according to which there were two Browns all along.[4] Until the split they were in the same body, after the split they are in different bodies. This view is on the face of it compatible with the non-reductionist view; a normal human being (i. e. one who has not, or not yet, split) is a compound of two simple selves, after the split the two selves go in different directions. What are we to make of this solution? One must not be dogmatic and insist that there must be one person (or self) per body. Elsewhere I have argued that it is plausible to maintain that in the case of some identical twins before segmentation two individuals exist in one body.[5] But how can two grown up autonomous individuals exist in one body without signs of considerable conflicts, much more conflict than is in fact found in the life of an ordinary individual?[6] Sperry has argued that since the two individuals get similar inputs (in terms of stimulus from the environment) it should not be surprising if their outputs (e. g. their decisions) are also similar. But it seems to me that if they are each moral agents with free-will one would expect them often to reach different conclusions about what should be done.

What is perhaps possible is that at least one of the two individuals before the split was not an active autonomous moral agent, but led a slave like existence, even though he had the potential to lead an autonomous life. A master and slave could perhaps have lived in relative peace before the split; the roles of the two could be complementary rather than in conflict. The slave could carry out the orders and the will of the master. But in that case one would expect after the split, at any rate to start with, one of the Browns to be slave-like. The existence of a master and a slave before the split cannot explain how immediately after the split we get two Browns each of whom behaves as a full blooded active moral agent. So the fourth solution won't work in the case of full blooded splitting of the kind envisaged by Wiggins. But something like it might work if the splitting was of a different kind, e. g. if one of the Browns after the split was hesitant and slave-like. Even here whether the fourth solution works will depend upon certain other factors also. For instance, it would be helpful if after the split the slave-like Brown tells us what it was like being a slave before the split.

In fact human beings have two brain hemispheres, and there are philosophers who maintain that there is a separate person connected with the minor hemisphere but that the person connected with the 'minor' hemisphere is dominated by the person connected with the main hemisphere. They even talk of liberation of the person who is connected with the minor hemisphere.[7] But if there is a person being treated like a slave, we would expect some relevant evidence to be forthcoming, e. g. if the 'major' hemisphere was removed, the former slave would gradually get liberated, he would tell us something about what life was like for him in the past (i.e. before the 'main' hemisphere was removed) as a slave-like individual. Yet in the case of patients who have had their major hemisphere removed, they do not tell us of what life was like for them in their pre-liberation days, of what it felt like to be a slave of another person within the same body.

It is true that aphasics cannot speak, and yet we do not deny that they have consciousness. Some philosophers have argued that there could be a second person connected with the minor hemisphere, the mere fact that it cannot speak, does not rule out the fact that it has consciousness. But there is this difference. In the case of aphasics, once they recover, they tell us about their past, about how they had consciousness as aphasics even though they could not speak. In the case of the alleged second person associated with the minor hemisphere, the view that there really is such a second individual would become more plausible, if after the major hemisphere was removed, the patients told us what it was like (in the past) to be a second person connected with the minor hemisphere. Yet in fact such patients do not recall such a time, which makes us suspicious of the view that they really did exist as a separate person, apart from the 'main' person.

There is a deeper difficulty which arises if we are to defend the non-reductionist view by resort to the fourth solution. The non-reductionist view we maintained was not something that has been proved to be true; it is postulated because it is presupposed by much of our practical and moral life and by our subjective experience. But if we are to admit more than one non-reductionist self in one body, there will be havoc in our moral and practical life. For instance, is it just to punish and blame one of the individuals for the crimes of another? Even if we have identified which of the two individuals committed the crime, how do we punish him without making the other one suffer equally? Compare: We do not think it just to execute a pregnant mother because another life is involved. Do we give two votes to people with two hemispheres intact, and one vote to people who have had one of the hemispheres removed? In order to obtain consent to an operation (especially a brain operation) how do we get the consent of both the individuals?

No doubt, if there is positive evidence in favour of the existence of an individual, we should not rule it out merely because it conflicts with our moral and practical life; instead we may have to revise our moral and practical life so that it fits with the way things are. But in the case of non-reductionist selves we do not have such positive objective evidence in favour of their existence. The sole reason for postulating the non-reductionist view was a practical (and subjective) one. And so the practical case for the non-reductionist view would be underminded if we admitted a second non-reductionist self in the same human body, for we could then no longer consistently defend the non-reductionist view by pointing out that it is presupposed by our practical and subjective life.

I do not deny that some evidence might one day turn up (e. g. if patients who had the major brain hemisphere removed recalled their days of enslavement) which favoured the two person per human being hypothesis. My conclusion so far is that though some of the suggested solutions to the problem of splitting may work if splitting took place, none of them could rescue the non-reductionist view very convincingly. If one believed in the non-reductionist view, perhaps the most plausible solution is the first one. But as we saw, even that solution was not very persuasive. It seems to me that if full blooded splitting of the kind envisaged by Wiggins took place, the non-reductionist view would be undermined. It would then become rational to opt for one of the other views e. g. Parfit's reductionist view or the view according to which persons are concrete universals or the view according to which there is a cosmic self pervading us all. Of course as practical and moral beings we may find we are unable to abandon the non-reductionist view, but this only shows that we may have to carry on with it as a practically necessary illusion.

The fact that the non-reductionist view would be undermined by full blooded splitting, does not of course show it to be a false view. Indeed, in a way it is a point in favour of it, for it tends to show that is a scientific view. Though it cannot be proved to be true, we can conceive of conditions which would undermine it. It might be objected that for a theory to be scientific it should be falsifiable; the non-reductionist view however would not be shown to be false, it would only be undermined. It would not be disproved for the first solution, though implausible, is not absurd. Against this, we could point out that we must not use too high a standard of what makes a theory scientific.

Even in the natural sciences, the most we can hope for is that if certain conditions obtain the theory would be undermined rather than disproved; we could always adopt desperate *ad hoc* devices to save a theory. So the fact that if full blooded splitting occurred, we could still save the non-reductionist view by adopting desperate, *ad hoc*, implausible devices (such as the fourth solution) does not show that the non-reductionist view is not a scientific one. The non-reductionist view is scientific in the sense of being falsifiable in the weak sense (i.e. it would be undermined if certain conditions occurred.)

It might be suggested that the non-reductionist view is not only falsifiable (in the sense discussed); it has already been undermined because splitting in the relevant sense has already occurred. If this is correct, then the non-reductionist view is like a scientific theory that has already been rendered implausible.

But is it true that splitting in the relevant sense has already occurred? The kind of splitting that Wiggins envisages has not occurred. Nor is there any reason to think that it is physically possible that it could occur. It is true that science has made enormous advances in transplanting various organs from one human being to another. It is also true that the two hemispheres of the brain are each capable of functioning even when the other is completely destroyed but it does not follow that they could each function simultaneously in different human bodies. For even if we could have brain transplants (which would be much more intricate than transplanting of hearts, kidneys, etc.) there is only one brain stem common to the two hemispheres, the brain stem cannot be split, and it is most unlikely that the hemisphere that was without the brain stem could ever be used to construct a live offshoot of the original person.

Swinburne says that the difficulty of splitting the brain stem is only a technical one and that though we may need to manufacture a new half-brain-stem such difficulties are mere technical ones.[8] How does he know this? Of course nor do I *know* that the difficulties are deeply impossible to surmount, but I would defend my defeasible conjecture by appealing to the doctrine of reasonable faith. If the splitting of persons is possible, then the non-reductionist view would be undermined. Since the non-reductionist view is in harmony with our subjective and practical views the onus is on the opponents of this view to show that it has been undermined.

However, for splitting to take place, it is not necessary to have two different bodies. Could there not be splitting of a person within the same body? Indeed some philosophers would argue that such splitting has already occurred. Let us then examine some of the cases of splitting that have already occurred and see whether they are sufficiently disturbing for the ordinary concept of the person.

Section 2: Some Actual Experiments in Brain-Splitting

Let us now turn to the actual experiments in brain splitting. In order to cure (or partially cure) epilepsy, surgeons have sometimes cut the bridge between the two hemispheres of the brain, known as the corpus callosum. As a result there appear to be two separate spheres of consciousness. Broadly speaking, the left hemisphere is connected with the right side of the body (e. g. the right hand, right eye, right ear, though not with the right nostril which is connected with the right hemisphere) and the right hemisphere with the left side (except for the left nostril which is connected to the right hemisphere). Even after the patient's corpus callosum has been severed, the two hemispheres broadly act in unison.[9] But in special test situations, where the input to one hemisphere is segragated from the input to the other hemisphere, the two hemispheres seem to have two spheres of consciousness, each unaware of what is happening in the other.

When input is sent to the left hemisphere (which is the dominant hemisphere and has the speech centres), the patient responds verbally, when input is sent to the right hemisphere, the patient does not respond verbally (since the right hemisphere is the minor one and cannot speak) but can respond manually and shows signs of following some language and some, though not all, instructions given to it. Thus Sperry tells us 'if the name of some object is flashed to the left visual field, like the word "eraser", for example, the subject is then able to search out an eraser from among a collection of objects using only touch with the left hand. If the subject is then asked what the item is after it has been selected correctly, his replies show that he does not know what he is holding in his left hand – as is the general rule for left hand stereognusis. This means of course that the talking hemisphere does not know the correct answer, and we concluded accordingly that the minor hemisphere must, in this situation, have read and understood the test word'.[10]

Sperry goes on to say that the minor hemisphere also shows 'emotional reactions as for example when a pin-up shot of a nude is interjected by surprise among a series of neutral geometric figures for the right and left fields at random. When the surprise nude appears on the left side the subject characteristically says that he or she saw nothing or just a flash of light. However the appearance of a sneaky grin and perhaps blushing and giggling on the next couple of trials or so belies the verbal contention of the speaking hemisphere. If asked what all the grinning is about, the subject's replies indicate that the conversant hemisphere has no idea at this stage what it was that had turned him on. Apparently, only the emotional effect gets across, as if the cognitive component of the process cannot be articulated through the brainstem'.[11]

Emotion is also evident on the minor side according to a study by Gordon and Sperry[12] involving olfaction. When odours are presented through the right nostril to the minor hemisphere the subject is unable to name the odor but can frequently tell whether it is pleasant or unpleasant. 'The subject may even grunt, make aversive reactions or exclamations like "phew!" to a strong unpleasant smell, but not be able to state verbally whether it is garlic, cheese, or some decayed matter. Again it appears that the affective component gets across to the speaking hemisphere, but not the more specific information. The presence of the specific information within the minor hemisphere is demonstrated by the subject's correct selection through left-hand stereognosis of corresponding objects associated with the given odor. The minor hemisphere also commonly triggers emotional reactions of displeasure in the course of ordinary testing. This is evidenced in the frowning, wincing, and negative head shaking in test situations where the minor hemisphere, knowing the correct answer but unable to speak, hears the major hemisphere making obvious verbal mistakes. The minor hemisphere seems to express genuine annoyance at the erroneous vocal responses of its better half.'[13]

Such observations have lead Sperry and others to postulate a 'conscious entity that is characteristically human and runs along in parallel with the dominant stream of consciousness in the major hemisphere'. But of course some people have been sceptical of the significance of such empirical findings. Excessive claims have been made on both sides. Some philosophers are convinced that there is a second person associated with the minor hemisphere and we should even try to liberate it, and respect its rights.

Sceptics, however, have denied all such claims. Scepticism in such cases has interesting parallels with scepticism with regard to the view that animals have minds and rights. Just as it used to be argued by Descartes and others that animals are automata, so too it has been argued that the right hemisphere is just an automaton. The next stage in the animal debate was for some of the sceptics to admit that animals had feelings and so were not just machines, but deny that they have a language and self-consciousness. Similarly, in the case of the right hemisphere, some of the sceptics, in the face of powerful evidence of the presence of emotions, admitted that the activities of the right hemisphere reflected feelings and that the right hemisphere could perform[14] many tasks better than the left one, but denied that there was any self-consciousness and made much of the fact that it could not speak. When further evidence was produced to show that animals have self-consciousness (for instance, it was pointed out that chimpanzees can recognise themselves in the mirror and so have a concept of themselves), it was replied 'Yes, but only a very primitive kind of self-consciousness'. Thus Eccles complained that they lacked the ability to have moral ideals, make life-plans and so on.

A parallel situation arose with the right hemisphere. There was evidence to show not just that there was consciousness but also self-consciousness. Thus Sperry got his patients, under test conditions, to evaluate photographs with their minor hemisphere. They had to do thumbs up to photos that they approved of and thumbs down to photos they disapproved of. In the case of one of Sperry's patients, the evaluative response from the right hemisphere was thumbs down for Hitler and Castro. The subject wavered when a photo of Nixon was shown (the date of the testing was around Watergate and the subjects may have been right wing Republicans). The subject was then shown a photo of himself, which evoked a thumbs down response, 'but in this case unlike the others, the response was accompanied by a distinct wide, sheepish, and (we think) self-conscious grin generated in the mute hemisphere.'[15]

Such experiments have encouraged Sperry and others to claim

that the minor hemisphere does reflect self-consciousness (for it can recognise itself) and reflect even moral capacties, for it can evaluate by means of thumbs up and thumbs down. But some of the sceptics, such as Eccles are still not very impressed. Thus Eccles complains that the minor hemisphere reflects only a very primitive kind of self-consciousness.

Animal lovers complain that animals have been denied personhood and moral rights by raising the cut off point higher and higher. First it was said animals do not have rights because they do not have consciousness. Next, it was granted they have consciousness. but they lacked self-consciousness. And now they are being denied rights because their self-consciousness is primitive and not sophisticated enough. The trouble with using such high standards is that some human beings too (such as idiots) won't qualify as rights holders either.

Similar points have been made with regard to the right hemi-sphere. Thus it has been said that if you deny that the right hemisphere is a person, and has human rights because it cannot speak, then you will have to deny that aphasics are persons and have human rights. And if primitive self-consciousness is not enough for persons and for human rights, then many children as well as many grown up human beings will have to be excluded too. One must not set the standards too high, unless one is willing to embrace scepticism with regard to other minds in general. Of course, scepticism with regard to other minds in general is notoriously difficult to refute. But once one admits the existence of other minds one must not use any higher standard for granting that the minor hemisphere reflects the workings of a mind (in the strong sense) than one does for granting that ordinary human beings have minds (in a strong sense). In many cases where people have had the 'major' hemisphere removed, the patients survive as full blooded persons. The 'minor' hemisphere in such cases reflects not just primitive self-consciousness but even sophisticated self-consciousness.

Should we then grant that there is more than one self or mind (in the strong sense) per human being? One should in accordance with the principle of reasonable faith resist such a conclusion as long as one honestly can. For it goes against so much of our practical and moral life. But of course if the case against the present conception of the person is overwhelming then honesty would demand that we recognise this. And if practical life demands the continuance of the old fashioned idea of the person, we could at best regard this as a practically necessary illusion. But is the case against the truth of the one person per human being view overwhelming?

Both the conservatives, i. e. those who are sceptics with regard to the existence of more than one self or mind (in the strong sense) per human being, and radicals (i. e. those who believe in the existence of more than one self person per human being) tend to make a common assumption, which seems to me to be a very dubious one. They both seem to think that if the minor hemisphere, in the test situations, does reflect the workings of a mind (in the strong sense) then the present views of the person will be undermined. That is why the conservatives are at such pains to show that the minor hemisphere acts in a mechanical manner, or that if it has consciousness (or self-consciousness) it is only at a very rudimentary level. The radicals are quick to point out that there is ample evidence to show that the minor hemisphere does at least sometimes reflect the workings of a mind in the strong sense. And on this point they are right. For though the minor hemisphere often acts in a mechanical manner, it does at least sometimes, as we have seen, exhibit a very human response. The conservatives think they have to deny this claim of the radicals. But in fact they do not.

The above-mentioned assumption that both the conservatives and the radicals make is in fact a false one. And it is misleading because it leads to a false dichotomy; either the minor hemisphere is a mere machine (or almost a machine!) or it reflects the workings of a second mind (in the strong sense). But there is a third possibility, namely that the minor hemisphere does sometimes reflect the workings of a mind (in the strong sense), but that it does not reflect the workings of a *second* mind (in the strong sense). There could be just one mind (in the strong sense); sometimes it acts through the minor hemisphere, sometimes through the major one. If the conservative view can be defended at all, it must I think be defended by means of exploring this third possibility. So let us now see if this strategy works.

It is probably true that some of the activities of the right hemisphere do reflect the workings of an inner life, but does it follow that this inner life is different from the main inner life of the subject? Experimenters in this area such as Sperry believe that emotions tend to be bilateralised 'Emotional effects triggered through one hemisphere as by lateral presentation of an offensive odor, embarrassing photo etc. tend to spread easily into the opposite hemisphere, presumably through intact brain stem routes and through feedback from peripheral changes. Vascular reactions like blushing and alterations in blood pressure. facial expressions, giggling, frowning, exclamations, and the like all help to bilateralise an emotion and to counteract attempts to establish concurrent sets on left and right sides."[16] In the case where the right hemisphere was shown a nude photo of a man, the patient's left hemisphere (i. e. the speaking hemisphere) knew she was embarrassed but did not know why. However in cases where the right hemisphere was given an unpleasant odor to smell the unpleasant smell tended to remain lateralised, confined to one hemisphere, and the patient would wince and grunt.[17]

Sperry's view seems to be that emotions from one hemisphere tend to normally spill over to the next one. On this view, there is normally a doubling of emotions, for an emotion such as embarrassment occurs first in one hemisphere and then spills over to the next. It would seem that on this view if the patient had only one hemisphere the total amount of embarrassment would be less, for there would be no spill over to the next hemisphere. So on this view if you torture a person under test conditions, the total suffering would be much greater than if the patient had one of the hemispheres removed before the torture!

Now I want to suggest that there is no need, as yet, to postulate a doubling of such emotions. It is true that the mind associated with the right hemisphere behaves in a much more human way than chimpanzees and apes do. But it does not follow that there is a separate inner life associated with the right hemisphere. Take the case where the right hemisphere is embarrassed when it is shown photos of naked men. Since the embarrassment is also something that the left hemisphere is aware of, why not postulate that there is only a single feeling of embarrassment. Even if the right hemisphere can, unlike the left one, tell us (manually, not verbally) why it is embarrasssed, it does not follow that there are two feelings of embarrassment. It could be the same feeling of embarrassment; it is just that the right hemisphere is not only embarrassed but also 'knows' the cause of it, whereas the left hemisphere only knows that it is embarrassed, not its cause.

It might be objected that this analysis will work at best only for those emotions where there is alleged doubling. But what about those emotions which are felt only by the mind associated with the right hemisphere; such as the case of the unpleasant smells Sperry refers to? And what about the perceptions that are had only by the right hemisphere, when the left hemisphere has quite different perceptions. Do not such perceptions imply an inner life too? So the perceptions of the right hemisphere would seem to belong to one stream of consciousness while the perceptions of the right hemisphere would belong to another.

Again, the right hemisphere knows things which the left hemisphere does not know and *vice versa*. For instance, the right hemisphere, unlike the left one, knows in the case we discussed earlier, why there is embarrassment. And Norman Geschwind says 'we constantly found that many confusions about the patient in our own minds as well as those of others resulted from failure to do the exact opposite of what the rule to look at the patient demanded i. e. from our failure to regard the patient as made up of connected parts rather than as an indissoluble whole. We were constantly dealing with questions such as "if he can speak normally and he knows what he's holding in his left hand why can't he tell you?" We had to point out that we could not say "the patient could speak normally" since that part of the patient which could speak normally was not the same part of the patient which "knew" (non-verbally) what was in the left hand'.[18] Geschwind goes on to conclude that human beings are made up of connected parts and that even in normal human beings total unity is lacking. It seems to me that Geschwind is right if he is talking about mind in the weak sense not being unified, but it does not follow that the mind in the strong sense is lacking in unity. Consider the following conjectures.

1. Each of the hemispheres from time to time reflects not only the workings of the mind in the weak sense, but also of the mind in the strong sense.

2. Sometimes one of the hemispheres reflects mind in the strong sense, while the other hemisphere at the very same time reflects a different mind (in the weak sense). The two minds are dissociated from each other.

3. Sometimes one of the hemispheres reflects mind in the strong sense while (at the very same time) the other hemisphere also reflects the workings of a mind in the strong sense. There are two possibilities here:

(a) The mind (in the strong sense) that the left hemisphere reflects is not dissociated from the mind (in the strong sense) that the right hemisphere reflects.

(b) The mind (in the strong sense) that the left hemisphere reflects is dissociated from the mind (in the strong sense) that the right hemisphere reflects. There are two minds (in the strong sense) at the very same time, dissociated from each other.

The conservative could grant each of the above, except 3(b). He could not grant 3(b), for that would go against the present view according to which there is only one mind (in the strong sense) per human being.

In some cases of alleged second stream of consciousness, it is possible to take the behaviourist or functionalist line and deny that there is a corresponding inner life. One does not have to be a full-blooded functionalist or behaviourist to grant that sometimes the corresponding inner life does not exist. I agree with Nagel that all non-phenomenological approaches such as behaviourism and functionalism in general fail because they miss out on an essential part of subjective experience, namely, what the experience is like from the agent's point of view. But we can admit that sometimes the non-phenomenological approach works, that there is no inner feeling. This may happen for instance in some of the cases when the patient acts unconsciously. Again there are cases of patients who suffer from blind sightedness. Such people can sometimes tell you all the details about an object such as an apple in front of them, its colour, size, shape and so forth (without touching it) and yet they do not have the accompanying visual experience that occurs in normal cases. Again, sometimes patients under general anaesthetic exhibit pain behaviour such as grimaces, grunts etc. without feeling pain. So the mere fact that the right hemisphere correctly makes certain perceptual judgments, or knowledge claims does not entail that there must be accompanying subjective experiences.

Nagel points out that the right hemisphere (under test situations) does not undertake the task in a dreamy fashion but shows enough alertness and awareness of what it is doing to justify the attribution of conscious control.

Even in normal life we sometimes do two activities, such as talking philosophy and driving a car simultaneously. Our mind in the strong sense may be engaged in the philosophical discussion whereas the driving may be done by the mind in the weak sense. That can be so even if the person is not driving in a dreamy fashion. One can sometime do activities well (and not in a dreamy fashion), and yet the accompanying of subjective experiences may be lacking, as the example of blind sightedness shows.

In the case of the right hemisphere being subjected to unpleasant smells that we referred to earlier, it is true that the patient claimed not to smell anything, but does it follow that the unpleasant smells must have existed in dissociation from the main stream of consciousness? Could it not be that though the patient made facial gestures that normally are accompanied by unpleasent feelings, in this case there were no unpleasant accompaniments, somewhat as in the anaesthetic case we discussed earlier?

Admittedly the activities of the right hemisphere under test conditions are not always like those of the automaton or of an anaesthetized patient. The conservative could admit this. He could grant that sometimes the right hemisphere does reflect an inner life. There was a case where the patient would attempt to hit his wife with his left hand and control himself from doing so with the right hand. One possibility is that the movements of the left hand were instances of automatism. The conservative could even grant another possibility, namely that they were not instances of automatism but actions reflecting the agent's inner life. For instance anger is a feeling that could be reflected through the behaviour of the left hand. It might be argued that the problem would only arise if the agent was not aware of the anger, for then we might be tempted to postulate that anger as a feeling existed at the very same time in dissociation from the main inner life of the agent.

In fact even if the agent could not identify the feeling of anger, it does not follow that the feeling was not part of the main stream of consciousness of the agent. Except in the case of very simple feelings (such as pain), to identify a feeling requires more than introspection. It requires a knowledge of the behavioural and/or social setting. For instance in order to know whether the unpleasant feeling one has is a feeling of guilt, or feeling of shame, or just an uncomfortable feeling, one needs to know something about the social and behavioural setting, the publicly observable context. To say this is not to say that such feelings are not part of the inner life of the agent. It does not commit one to the reductionist thesis about such feelings. It is just that without the relevant knowledge of the public context, one would not be able to identify the feeling; one could still have the feeling and even be able to describe the introspective features of the feeling. One could for instance say that the feeling is very intense, and unpleasant, without knowing whether it is a feeling of shame.

Geshwind discusses some of the philosophical implications of recent work on the human brain. He suggests that the person is not such a unity as we once thought. As I said earlier, my own opinion is that these studies do reflect the lack of unity of mind (in the weak sense) but do not show that the mind (in the strong sense) is lacking in unity, or that there is more than one such mind (in the strong sense).

Geshwind also claims that such studies show that introspection is not a very effective method of obtaining information about the patient's experiences. In my opinion, there is some truth in this, but one needs to be clear about the reasons for this. The reason is not that there are experiences which are dissociated from the dominant stream of consciousness that the agent is aware of. That could be so, but I am arguing that as yet the conservative can honestly resist such views, the evidence for such views is not compelling. The reason why introspection is especially fallible in the case of split brain patients could be that the patient under test conditions lacks the relevant knowledge of the public setting and so he cannot correctly identify the feeling, although he is aware of the phenomenological nature of the feeling.

When it is claimed by the radical that the 'minor' hemisphere has a separate inner life associated with it, the conservative could reply that there are alternative possibilities, such as the following, which should be explored:

Firstly, it may sometime happen that though the right hemisphere shows intelligent behaviour (e. g. relating means to ends) there is no inner feeling acccompanying its activites. One does not have to be a full-blooded behaviourist or functionalist to admit that sometime parts of the brain can perform intelligent operations without there being accompanying inner feelings.

Secondly, the conservative could grant that sometimes there is indeed an inner feeling associated with the activities of the right hemisphere, and the speaking hemisphere is aware of what the feeling is though he cannot tell what has caused it. In the example we considered earlier a subject knows that he is embarrassed but does not know what has caused it, the naked photos being shown to the right hemisphere under test conditions.

Thirdly, it sometimes happens that there is a feeling associated with the right hemisphere and the speaking hemisphere has the feeling, but cannot identify it because he is unaware of the surrounding publicly observable circumstances.

The conservative who admits to the second or third possibility need not grant that there is a separate inner life associated with the right hemisphere.

There is also a fourth point, related to the earlier ones, that the conservative should stress. This is the possiblity that the self (or mind in the strong sense) sometimes acts through the left hemisphere, sometimes through the right one. Even in ordinary life when we undertake two tasks simultaneously, such as discussing philosophy while driving a car, for a time the mind (in the strong sense) may be engaged in the philosophical conversation, while the driving is done fairly mechanically, reflecting the mind in the weak sense. Suddenly there may be an emergency, the driver may need to solve a traffic problem and his mind in the strong sense may concentrate on the driving, and he may still go on discussing philosophy, but do so quite mechanically. So when we undertake two tasks simultaneously, the mind in the strong sense can switch from one of the activities to another. We do not have to postulate two minds in the strong sense.

It might be objected that in the split brain case, unlike in the case of normal activity such as driving and discussing philosophy, the switching of the mind (in the strong sense) hypothesis is implausible, for the two brains are disconnected from each other and so how can the mind suddenly go from one part to another. One can answer this objection by pointing out that the two halves of the brain are not totally disconnected from each other, that for instance they have a common brain stem, and it has been shown that one hemisphere can send information to the other even when the corpus callosum is severed.

This fourth suggestion is similar to a suggestion made by Freud. Freud did not consider the problem of split brains, but the idea of switching of consciousness from one ongoing mental activity to another was used by Freud to reconcile the facts of multiple personality with the denial of co-consciousness. Some psychologists such as William James and McDougall were convinced that the facts of multiple personality establish beyond doubt not just alternating personalities, but also co-consciousness (which, in my jargon, would imply more than one mind in the strong sense). Freud argued that cases that were described as splitting of consciousness could be explained away; they were better understood as involving 'shifting of consciousness... oscillating between two different psychical complexes which become conscious and unconscious in alteration'.[19]

McDougall objected that Freud offers no good reason for rejecting co-conscious activity. McDougall was impressed by the following consideration: '... if the unity of the individual is given once for all in the unitary nature of the soul, how are we to understand the facts of increasing integration and the defects and lapses of integration that result in multiple personalities each leading its own mental life and struggling, in real conflicts of will, against its fellow for the use and control of the common organism?'[20]

I think McDougall's argument looks more impressive than it is. Once we distinguish two senses of mind, and correspondingly, two senses of unity of mind, we can point out that it is quite consistent to believe in the unity of consciousness (or of mind in the strong sense) and yet allow disunity and lack of integration of the mind in the weak sense. And while it is true that in the case of multiple personality, the personalities compete with each other for the running of the 'common organism', one can explain this by saying that the various minds (in the weak sense) compete with each other. Each of them from time to time attempts to take control of the common organism and its subjective world. Sometimes one succeeds, sometimes the other.

This does not of course mean that the self has to be completely passive, merely responding to the pressures of the various minds in the weak sense. McDougall accused Freud of implying that consciousness was passive and an epiphenomena. 'He consistently treats consciousness as though it were a lamp, a light or an illumination, suffusing the interior of a certain chamber; and he assumes that psychic processes may go on equally well either inside this chamber suffused with this light, or outside of it in the region he calls "the unconscious"; the illumination of the processes by the light which is consciousness making no more difference to them than the turning on or off of the lamp in an engine room makes to the running of the engine'.[21]

I do not know if Freud ever did treat consciousness as playing such a useless role. If he did he was inconsistent. For as McDougall points out Freud also regarded consciousness as playing an important role, the hidden processes of the unconscious were brought to light so that a cure could be brought about. It seem to me that the view of the switching of consciousness from one 'psychic process' to another, does not by itself imply that the consciousness makes no difference to the 'psychic process' that it attends to.

One of the problems about the view that there are two persons during split-brain experiments is that it seems to commit us to two persons even at other times. For the alternative view according to which the second person only comes into existence during the experiment but disappears once the experiment is over seems strange.

How can a person come in and out of existence? Of course this problem would disappear if we abandoned the present conception of a person. For instance if we embraced the reductionist view there would be nothing mysterious here. Persons could come in and out of existence just as states do. A state can be divided into two, and then be reunited again. There is nothing mysterious here about where the second state has gone, if we take the reductionist view of the state. But if we assume that the person or the state is an indivisible self or soul then the problem remains, where has the self or soul gone?

Nor will it do to take the line that the split brain experiments are irrelevant to our ordinary conception of the person because they deal with abnormal subjects. In fact if there are two selves in the case of abnormal subjects, this will lead us to revise our ideas of normal human beings as well. For though the subjects of these experiments are abnormal in the sense of being epileptic patients, they are not different from us in any relevant respect. There is every reason to think that if our corpus callosum was severed, the split brain experiments would yield very similar results with us as they do with the epileptic patients.

Those who are more impressed than I am by the results of the split-brain experiments might suggest that the contention that there are, even at normal times, two persons per human being is the most plausible one, in view of the experimental findings.[22] If there are two selves per human being all along, then one does not have the problem of how the second self comes in and out of existence. And it is a good compromise solution between the present system and the extreme radical view (e. g. the reductionist view) which would abandon the non-reductionist self view altogether. For the view that there are two persons per human being goes naturally with the view that there are two hemispheres of the brain each of which is capable of functioning at a human level, without the other. And the non-reductionist self view could be preserved. It is just that there would be two non-reductionist selves per human being.

But the two selves per human being view is far from established. Since there is no positive scientific evidence in favour of any non-reductionist selves, one can hardly admit that there is evidence in favour of two non-reductionist selves. We saw earlier that the view that there are two non-reductionist selves per human being goes against our subjective experience and our moral and practical experience. This is an important point against it since the chief reason for postulating the non-reductionist view is that it is presupposed by our subjective and practical experience.

On my view we do have evidence for the presence of consciousness. In chapter 2 I commended the expressive test of consciousness. But we do not have objective evidence for the view that there are non-reductionist selves; our reasons for postulating such selves are practical and subjective ones. The presence of consciousness is compatible with the reductionist view.

Evidence might turn up which would make us abandon the one self per human being view. For instance, earlier I considered the sort of evidence that that might convert us to the view that there are two selves per human being. But there is no *objective* evidence for the view that there are two *indivisible* selves, whose survival is a matter of all or nothing. We might find it reasonable to believe even that view, but that would be an act of faith.

The doctrine of reasonable faith is there to tell us when an act of faith is reasonable. There is also the constraint that we must not be arbitrary in our judgements. If the case for the existence of the second self is as good as the case for the existence of the first one, then it would be quite wrong to say that the first one is a non-reductionist self while the second one is not. In order to postulate two non-reductionist selves, we would need evidence to show not just that there are two selves during short periods, such as during split-brain experiments, but also during the intervening periods. For a non-reductionist self does not come in and out of existence. We saw earlier that such evidence was not forthcoming; indeed we have seen that even during split brain experiments there is no evidence of the existence of two selves.

If however such evidence were to turn up, one could abandon the non-reductionist view and still defend the two persons per human being view. One may, for instance, attempt to combine it with the reductionist view. On the reductionist view whether there is one person or two is a matter of convenience. If certain facts occurred then it might be more useful to bundle human beings into two persons per human being. The sorts of fact that might incline one to do this would be if there were simultaneously two separate streams of consciousness, each with its own unity. If the two streams did not merge one might claim that there were two persons per human being. If the streams did merge at times and then separated at times, we could adopt the reductionist view and claim that the second person comes in and out of existence. In the case of split brain patients it has been observed that the patient's behaviour (except during the experimental situation) tends to be fairly unified, and this would favour the view (assuming for the sake of this discussion that there is more than one stream of consciousness!) that the split in consciousness occurs at the time of the experimental situation, and after that the different streams merge into one.

Against the view that there is more than one person per human being (whether one combined it with the non-reductionist view or not) it may be objected that if there was more than one person we would expect some evidence of the existence of the second person, not just during the split brain experiments. One would expect, for instance, patients who have had their major hemisphere removed to tell us, when they have recovered their powers of communication, what it was like in the past to be a second person co-existing alongside another person. Yet such evidence is not forthcoming.

It might be replied that there is some evidence of a second person being there in the background; it comes not just from split brain experiments, but also at other times such as during hypnosis, self-deception, sub-conscious mental functioning, multiple personalities, automatic writing. Sometimes people complain that they felt that someone else was acting, moving their hands or speaking; they were just passive spectators.

But it seems to me that though such cases do point to the existence of more than one mind, they do not establish the existence of more than one mind in the strong sense. The conservative view would stress that in such cases the one person view could be defended by distinguishing two senses of mind, or in some cases by allowing the switching of consciousness from one mind to another.

The crucial test for whether there is more than one person would be if both hemispheres, under test conditions, can be made to respond in a human-like way, reflecting the simultaneous workings of two different minds in the strong sense. What sort of evidence would we need for the existence of a mind in the strong sense? The following is some of the relevant evidence: the expressions in the eye, the voice, the smile; we can at an intuitive level distinguish an expressive eye from a glazed look, a voice that reflects consciousness from one that sounds quite mechanical, a stroke of the hand that reveals consciousness from a mechanical touch. Of course this is a very rough test and often we go wrong. Sometimes a person may appear to be acting mechanically, but there may be consciousness going on. This is one reason why it would be helpful to observe a person over a period of time as well as to observe a large part of him at any given time.

Even apart from split brain cases, there have been cases of alleged second consciousness. Thus Hilgard tells us 'Estabrooks (1957) reported an experiment with a friend who was reading *Oil for the Lamps of China* while his right hand screened from view by passing it through a cloth curtain was engaged in automatic writing. The hand was not in awareness because of hypnotic procedures; it was also anaesthetized. However, when Estabrooks pricked the hand with a needle, it wrote a stream of profanity "that would have made a top sergeant blush with shame". This went on for five minutes, an attack on the hypnotist for having pricked him. The subject continued his reading calmly, "without the slightest idea that his good right hand was fighting a private war".' Here we do not have sufficient evidence of the workings of a second mind in the strong sense. Even a simple computer could be programmed so that when it is being damaged it emits print outs such as 'I am in pain. Stop hurting me'. The hand in the above example could simply be carrying out the instruction of part of the brain. Just as human behaviour is sometimes not accompanied by consciousness, so too with human writing, even when the writing is about alleged experiences. Similarly, in the case we mentioned earlier where the patient attacked with the left hand but tried to control himself with his right hand, the left hand could just have reflected the workings of a mind in the weak sense.

A similar analysis could be given of another case mentioned by Gazzaniga: A split brain patient was asked under test conditions to respond verbally to what was being shown exclusively to the right hemisphere. The patient at first guessed at a chance level, but after some time the scores improved when a second guess was allowed 'We soon caught on to the strategy the patient used. If a red light was flashed and the patient by chance guessed red, he would stick with that answer. If the flashed light was red, and the patient by chance guessed green, he would frown, shake his head and then say, "Oh no, I meant red".'[24] The patient who was speaking, would correct his first guess by observing the frown originating from activities of the right hemisphere. The frowning and shaking of the head by themselves are not sufficient to indicate consciousness. They can merely reflect the workings of the mind in the weak sense. Parts of the brain are regularly sending messages to other parts, somewhat as parts of the computer send messsags to other parts.

We must not of course use too high standards for the presence of consciousness. For we are here assuming that human beings in general have consciousness. The standards for the presence of the second consciousness must not be any higher than those for the presence of the first consciousness. But the standards are not being set too high. We are willing to allow that when we observe a person's face, his eyes, his smile, etc. often we can tell from the expression that he has consciousness at the time. But if we just observe a frown or shaking of the head, it is by itself not sufficient evidence. I am not of course saying that the minor hemisphere never reflects consciousness. In the case where the subject smiled and did thumbs down, there could have been good evidence. Some smiles can be quite revealing especially when accompanied by a hand gesture. No doubt in some circumstances a frown could be quite revealing of the presence of consciousness, especially if it is accompanied by appropriate expression in other parts of the face, such as the eyes. The larger the part of the person's body, especially his face, that can be observed, and the longer the time period of observation, the more evidence we can get for deciding whether or not to attribute consciousness.

Wittgenstein said 'only of a living human being and what resembles (behaves like) a living human being can one say: it has sensations; it sees; is blind; hears; is deaf; is conscious or unconscious'.[25] The relevant resemblance should be not only in the behaviour (which Wittgenstein stresses) but also in the structure of the brain, the expression of the eyes, in the voice and so forth.

One can use this resemblance test without being committed to Wittgenstein's anti-realism. Indeed I think this test is more plausible if it is combined with realisim with regard to other minds. For it is less open to the charge of chauvinism, the objection that we rule out forms of consciousness merely because the creatures who may have them are very different from us human beings.[26] For on the realist view the resemblance test is used to deal with the problem of evidence of consciousness. It does not rule out that creatures very different from us may have consciousness. It is just that since we assume that human beings have consciousness, the relevant resemblances with other creatures provide us with some evidence that they have consciousness.

In order to establish two selves (or minds in the strong sense) per person, the split brain experiments would have to be such that each of the experimenters (i. e. the one attempting to have a dialogue with the right hemisphere and the one attempting to have a dialogue with the left hemisphere) is in contact with a different self. But now there is one difficulty in the way of getting the relevant evidence regarding the existence of two selves. For it may be objected that the patient has only one face, so how can two different selves in the same body use the same face to express different emotions, feelings etc. So is it not in principle impossible for us to get evidence that the patient has two selves?

To answer this objection, we can point out that though the patient has just one face, there are several channels for expressing emotions. Thus he has two eyes, a mouth to smile and speak from, and two hands to reinforce facial expressions. So in the example where the patient (right hemisphere) did thumbs down and smiled at the sight of his own photo, one would like to know how the left hemisphere was behaving at that very time; was it showing signs of consciousness? Trevarthen tells me that the answer to this question is No.

Normally one can get the left hemisphere to speak, so one can try to tell whether there is consciousness from the voice (suppose the voice is very expressive), together perhaps with the expression in the right eye. But of course there is the problem that if the 'right hemisphere' is smiling then the mouth is partly under the control of the right hemisphere, and so how can it be used (without causing chaos) by the left hemisphere to speak through. But since there are two eyes, it should not be impossible for one eye to express one emotion and the other to express the opposite emotion. In fact it has been observed that the two profiles of a face (even of a normal person) often have different expressions at the same time. So in split brain experiments, it should not be impossible for the right hemisphere to express one set of emotions through the left profile, while the other side of the face expresses the opposite emotion.

The expressions of the face, the manner of speaking etc. can often enable us to tell that there is consciousness. It is more difficult to infer the lack of consciousness from the lack of expression, for it is possible for there to be consciousness without visible and obvious signs of it. Indeed, those such as William James who believe in the existence of several streams of consciousness simultaneously, would stress the existence of hidden consciousness. My own view is that when intellectual considerations leave it open whether or not there is a second stream of consciousness, we should assume that there is only one stream of consciousness. I would defend this by appealing to the principle of reasonable faith according to which when intellectual considerations leave an issue open, it is reasonable to take that view which squares with the rest of our moral and practical system. Of course, my view is consistent with the view that we must not deny objective facts. If good evidence turns up which shows there is a second stream of consciousness within a human being, we must not deny such evidence merely because it conflicts with our moral and practical views. Rather we may need to revise our moral and practical views. Our views regarding one stream of consciousness, the existence of free will, the non-reductionist self, are defeasible. They cannot be shown to be true. It is reasonable to believe in them because they square with the rest of our system of beliefs. But if and when evidence against them turns up, we must not ignore such evidence.

The present view of the person is a sort of conjecture which cannot be proved to be true, but which is scientific in the sense of being falsifiable. It is defeasible in that we assume it to be true until evidence against it makes it implausible to hold it. My view is that the evidence against it so far is not conclusive.

Colwyn Trevarthen, who has done some of the celebrated pioneering experiments with Sperry on the split brain patients, told me that what is remarkable about Sperry's findings is that there are two conscious streams, cut off from each other, each with its own memories, emotions etc. and each with a considerable degree of internal coherence and integration. But when I asked him what happens to the major hemisphere when the minor one shows signs of consciousness, he admitted that it tends to become mute and shows no signs of consciousness.[27]

This admission is consistent with my view that there is just one subjective consciousness, which switches from one mind (in the weak sense) to another. Such switching of consciousness does not undermine the traditional conception of the person. Nor is there anything unique in what is true about Sperry's findings. For cases of multiple personality have already made us familiar with alternating personality. Let us now turn to the evidence provided by the multiple personality cases.

NOTES

1. D. Wiggins, *Identity and Spatio-Temporal Continuity*, Blackwell. Oxford, 1967, p. 53.
2. See D. Wiggins, *Sameness and Substance*, Blackwell. Oxford, 1980, p. 166. The view that a person is a concrete universal is defended by T. Sprigge, 'Personal and Impersonal Identity', *Mind*, 1988.

3. See B. Williams, *Problems of the Self*, pp. 80–81.
4. A variant of the fourth solution would be to assert that there are several individuals in the same human being. See D. Lewis. 'Survival and Identity' in A. Rorty. ed. *The Identities of Persons.* Some of my discussion and objections to the fourth solution would apply *mutatis mutandis* to this variant also.
5. See *Equality, Liberty, and Perfectionism,* ch. 5 sec. 2.
6. On the view under consideration one would expect Brown before the split to show inter-personal conflict within 'himself', whereas his offshoots should be free of such conflict, since his offshoots unlike himself consist of only one self per human body. If it really did turn out to be the case that after the split, the offshoots seemed different from the old Brown in this respect. (i. e. had substantially less conflict) this would be some evidence in favour of the fourth solution.
7. See J. Shaffer, 'Personal Identity: The Implications of Brain Bisection and Brain Transplants', *The Journal of Medicine and Philosophy,* 1977 vol. 2 no 2.
8. R. Swinburne, 'The Structure of the Soul', in *Persons and Personality,* eds. A. Peacocke and G. Gillet, Blackwell, Oxford, 1967, p. 37. Of course Swinburne is not an opponent of the non-reductionist view but a notable defender of it. But he wrongly thinks that cases of fission, even if they were to occur, would not undermine the non-reductionist view.
9. Not always. Gazzaniga tells us of a patient who 'would sometimes find himself pulling his pants down with the one hand and pulling them up with the other. Once, he grabbed his wife with his left hand and shook her violently, while with the right trying to come to his wife's aid in bringing the left belligerent hand under control' M. S. Gazzinga, *The Bisected Brain,* Appleton-Century, Crofts, New York, 1970, p. 107.
10. R. Sperry, 'Hemisphere Deconnection and Unity in Conscious Awareness', *American Psychologist,* 1968, p. 731.
11. R. Sperry, ibid., p. 732.
12. H. W. Gordon and R. W. Sperry, 'Lateralization of Olfactory Perceptions in the Surgically Separated Hemispheres of Man', *Neuropsychologia,* 1969, p. 119.
13. R. Sperry, 'Hemisphere Deconnection and Unity in Conscious Awareness', *American Psychologist,* 23, 1968, p. 732.
14. To be sure, the brain or the brain hemisphere does not act, nor is it conscious or aware of anything, certainly not on my view. But in this chapter I sometimes use such language for the sake of brevity. To be accurate, one should say that the person connected with the brain or the hemisphere acts or is conscious, but it is difficult to describe the facts in a neutral and non-question begging way. For if the brain is

the person then it would be misleading to say that the person connected with the brain acts or is conscious; rather one should (on that view) say that the brain or the hemisphere who is the person acts or is conscious.

15. R. W. Sperry, 'Forebrain Commissurotomy and Conscious Awareness', *The Journal of Medicine and Philosophy*, 1977, p. 112.
16. R. W. Sperry, 'Lateral Specialization in the Surgically Separated Hemishpere' in F. O. Schmitt and F. G. Worden (eds.) *The Neurosciences*, M. I. T. Press, Cambridge, 1974, p. 8.
17. H. W. Gordon and R. W. Sperry, 'Lateralization of Olfactory Perception in the Surgically Separated Hemispheres of Man', *Neuropsychologia*, 1969, p. 119.
18. N. Geschwind, 'Disconnection Syndromes in Animals and Man', *Brain* 1965 p. 131.
19. Quoted by McDougall, *Outline of Abnormal Psychology*, Methuen, London, 1926, p. 523.
20. ibid. pp. 522-3.
21. ibid p. 524.
22. For a defense of the two persons view see R. Puccetti, 'Brain Bisection and Personal Identity', *British Journal of Philosophy of Science*, 1973, pp. 339-355.
23. E. Hilgard, *Divided Consciousness*, John Wiley and Sons, London 1977 pp. 200-1
24. M. S. Gazzaniga, *The Bisected Brain*, Appleton-Century, Crofts, New York, 1970, ch. 6, p. 107.
25. L. Wittgenstein, *Philosophical Investigations*, Blackwell, Oxford, 1953, para. 281.
26. See G. Sheridan, 'Can There Be Moral Subjects in a Physicalistic Universe?' *Philosophy and Phenomenological Research*, June 1983, pp. 425-447.
27. There are supposed to be cases where the two hemispheres are each 'aware' of different things. Thus in the key-ring experiments, 'key-ring' is flashed on the screen with 'key' appearing to the right hemisphere, and 'ring' to the left hemisphere. If asked to pick out the object seen, the right hand would pick out ring, and the left one would pick out key. The subject when asked what he saw, said he saw 'key' and showed no awareness of 'ring'. In this case there may well have been simultaneous activity of the two hemispheres, each cut off from the other. But in this case there is not sufficient evidence of a second simultaneous consciousness associated with the right hemisphere.

VI. *Multiple Personality*

In chapter 2 I distinguished two approaches to the study of multiple personality cases, the functionalist approach and the approach (which I favour) that stresses consciousness. On the consciousness view there is just one stream of consciousness per person. On the functionalist view there is one person per human being if the relevant behaviour, beliefs, desires etc. can be integrated into one rational system, in the way we saw in chapter 2; this view does not insist on one stream of consciousness per person for it can allow that there is splitting of consciousness, in split-brain cases and in multiple personality cases, without denying that there is only one person, as long as the potential for integration is there.

The functional view goes against our common-sense views and the first person perspective. From the first person egoistical perspective I cannot imagine myself splitting into two, even for temporary periods (as the functionalists would allow), with Haksar 1 enjoying a wonderful time and Haksar 2 suffering enormously. One can imagine such things happening from the outside, but not from the first person egoistical perspective. If such things started happening it would be rational to embrace reductionism and abandon egoistical concern in any strong sense.

If it is conceivable from a first person egoistical perspective that there will be splitting of my consciousness in the future, or that there has in the past been such splitting, then so too should it be conceivable that there is now another stream of consciousness that is mine, but which is not part of the main stream of consciousness. I appear to myself to be happy, but perhaps (unknown to my main stream) I am suffering enormously in another stream of consciousness ! The dentist example in chapter 2 shows that from an *egoistical* first person perspective this does not make sense. One may take the view (as some mystics do) that there is just one (cosmic) self running through us all and that if millions of people are suffering in the poor countries, then their suffering is my suffering. But this view abolishes any deep distinction between the egoistical and altruistic point of view.

Another respect in which the functionalist view goes against the common-sense view is that according to it a person's survival admits of degrees. For on that view a person consists of the system of preferences, dispositions, memories, beliefs etc. and as these change in degrees, so too does the person's survival admit of degrees. So the functionalist view seems to go more naturally with the reductionist view than with the non-reductionist view. Indeed Dennett, a leading functionalist, explicitly compares the human being to a large organisation which is made up of various parts in certain relations to each other.

Again, the functionalist system can be instantiated, not only by human beings but also by sub-groups within a human being,[2] by corporations, by groups of people, by robots etc. So on the functionalist view robots, corporations and other groups that instantiate rational systems will also be moral beings. Some functionalists[3] are prepared to accept such a consequence, but I think such a view is counter-intuitive. It is true that our legal system does grant legal rights to collectives or groups such as corporations, but we clearly do not regard them as possessing *fundamental* rights that can be used to evaluate social institutions and practices. If we abolish I.C.I. and set up a more efficient organisation have we commited anything akin to murder? If we abolish I.C.I. and then set up another very similar organisation, there does not even seem to be any deep truth regarding whether the new organisation is the same as the old one. Compare, if we kill an infant and replace it by a similar but more productive infant, we would have commited murder. In deciding whether or not to replace an organisation with another we take into account the interests of the relevant human beings. It is these individuals who are regarded as having subjectivity and fundamental rights. Corporations, robots etc. are not regarded as possessing subjectivity and fundamental rights merely because they instantiate functional systems.

We have seen several ways in which the functionalist view conflicts with our common-sense view. In chapter 4 I have contended that there is a defeasible presumption in favour of our common-sense views. I do not deny that if there is sufficient evidence against the common-sense view then that view can be rejected. But, as the best amongst the functionalists rightly admit, the functionalist views are in their infancy, at a very speculative stage, and their truth is by no means established.

So I shall assume that on our present view there is just one stream of consciousness per human person. The problem then is whether the multiple personality cases can be reconciled with the view that there is just one person (with one stream of consciousness) per human body.

One of the most fascinating and problematic of the multiple personality cases was that of Miss Beauchamp, where there were not only multiple personalities, but one of them, Sally, claimed to be a second co-conscious personality,[5] co-existing throughout along with the other characters in the same human body.

Morton Prince,[6] Miss Beachamp's psychiatrist tells us that there were several alternating personalities in the Beauchamp case. His problem as he saw it, was to find out which was the real Miss Beauchamp. It was the real Miss Beauchamp that he wanted to preserve; the others would become integrated with the real one or become extinct. Some of the personalities suffered from considerable anxieties that they might get extinguished and Morton Prince, who was treating them, even saw himself as committing psychic murder.

The several personalities saw themselves at loggerheads with each other, each with their own egoistic concerns and value systems. In this respect they appear different from split brain cases, where it is claimed that there is no clash of wills. There can be different, even disparate goals pursued by the two hemispheres; but there are not two wills for evaluating those goals. This is the view of Mackay and Mackay. According to them, an ideal demonstration of the existence of two wills would be if the two 'half systems' could be got to bargain with each other in the sense of trying to get each other to change each other's criteria for evaluating priorities or goals, as opposed to merely carrying out goals that conflict with the other's goals. Attempts to get the two half systems to bargain with each other in this sense have failed. During one such attempt where the two half-systems were made to play a bargaining game with each other, the patient commented 'Are you guys trying to make two people out of one?'[7]

In the case of multiple personalities, often the opposite fear appeared to predominate. The different alternative personalities felt themselves different from each other, had different goals and different values for evaluation of their goals. They could well have asked 'Are you trying to create one person out of all of us?'

A striking test would be to ask the two hemispheres (during split brain experiments) how each of them would react to hemispherectomy (i. e. the surgical removal of one of the hemispheres). If say the right hemisphere was diseased, the left hemisphere (or rather the person connected with it) may well be better off without the right hemisphere; but if there was a separate person connected with the right hemisphere then he should view such surgery as involving his death! In the multiple personality cases some of the personalities did see themselves as about to be extinguished by their psychiatrist. Bernard Williams implies that this fear was unjustified; he thinks that when Miss Beauchamp was cured, 'she spoke freely of herself as having been B1 and B4. These different states seem to her very largely differences of mood. She regrets them, but does not attempt to excuse them, because as she says "After all, it is always myself"'.[8]

What Williams omits to mention is that Sally Beauchamp never got integrated into the final Miss Beauchamp. She was squeezed and was asked by the psychiatrist to go back to where she came from, whatever that meant. Sally actually wrote a fascinating autobiography, describing not just what it was like to be an alternating personality but also what is was like to be a second co-conscious personality, existing at the very same time as the dominant personality. At times Sally was the dominant personality i. e. the personality in direct control of the body, but at other times she tells us she was merely a co-conscious personality, and she describes how she could read the thoughts of the dominant personality, though the latter could not read Sally's thoughts. She also describes how she moved parts of her body, not normally but by a sort of effort of will of the kind that might be involved in psycho-kinesis, where one wills to move an external object. This reflected the fact that she was not in direct control over the body. She also describes vividly the frustrations she felt when the dominant personality indulged in activities that she (Sally) did not like. Though Sally claimed to be aware of the dominant personality's thoughts and feelings, she did not regard these thoughts and feelings as her own, but as quite alien to her. While her movements of the body were akin to psycho-kinesis, her reading of the dominant personality's thoughts was akin to telepathy, where one person reads another's thoughts.

So does it follow that there were two persons? There is no doubt that at times Sally was the dominant personality, i. e. the person in control over the body, and that at these times she did show all the signs of a conscious person, not a robot or a machine. She would enter into inter-personal relationship with other persons including her psychiatrist. But this does not show that there were two persons in one human body at the very same time. The crucial evidence for the two persons view is Sally's autobiography where she claims to co-exist as a non-dominant personality while another person was in direct control of the body. But there is some room for scepticism with regard to her claims and their significance.

One possibility is that there was switching of consciousness. Even if we grant that Sally at times had consciousness even when she was the non-dominant personality, being frustrated by the actions of the dominant personality, it would not follow that there were two conscious minds existing simultaneously. For it could be that at times Sally was conscious, the dominant personaliy was not conscious. One can be dominant in the sense of directly controlling the actions of the human body, without reflecting a mind in the strong sense. Thus one sometimes runs in a mechanical way, while one's conscious thoughts are engaged not on the running but on something else. Of course there is very good evidence that from time to time when Sally was not dominant, another personality was not only dominant but also conscious. But what is the evidence for the view that Sally was not only non-dominant but also conscious at the very same time when another personality was not only dominant but also conscious?

Sally claimed that she could, when non-dominant, read the thoughts of the dominant personality not by observing the latter's behaviour but by some kind of telepathic mind reading. But even if Sally was conscious at the times when she read the mind of this other personality, does it follow that the mind that she read was also conscious at that time? If telepathy is possible, could not a conscious mind read the unconscious thoughts of another personality?

It is interesting to compare the multiple personality case with the case reported by Hilgard where a patient under local anaesthetic said that he felt no pain yet afterwards (under hypnosis) claimed to clearly remember having undergone pain when he was under local anaesthetic. Here too there are different possible explanations.

Firstly it may be suggested that his memory later on was not reliable. Perhaps, as he tries to relive the past scene, he imagines that since what would normally be associated with pain was present, (e. g. the causing of an incision) therefore pain must have been present. As Hume stressed when we come across an instance of a thing, the mind often makes a transition to the idea of what normally accompanies it. 'A man whose memory presents him with a lively image of the Red Sea, and the Desert, and Jerusalem, and Galilee, can never doubt of any miraculous events, which are related either by Moses or the evangelists. The lively idea of the places passes by an easy transition to the facts, which are supposed to have been related to them... '[9] Memory, even of ordinary people, often plays tricks on them. In the abnormal cases, such as those of multiple personality and of people who are made to recall under hypnosis, memory becomes even less reliable.

Secondly, it is possible that there was switching of consciousness. Even though the person later remembers correctly having undergone pain at the time of the local anaesthetic, the mind that at the time of the anaesthetic said that there was no pain was a mind in the weak sense, it was not really conscious. The conscious mind at that time was not dominant (in the sense that it did not have control over speech) and so though it felt pain at that time, it could not make its suffering known through speech. On this view, it is possible that what the local anaesthetic did in this case was to produce a sort of dissociation - the conscious mind ceased to be in control of the speech centres, but it suffered. This is a terrifying possiblity.

The third possibility is that there were two minds in the strong sense present simultaneously. One of them (the one that at the time of the local anaesthetic denied having the pain) did not suffer any pain, while the other (who later recalled suffering the pain) did suffer the pain at the time of the local anaesthetic.

Outside observers could, at the time when the local anaesthetic was in effect, have tried to see whether the patient that was claiming not to suffer pain showed signs of consciousness. If he was speaking in a mechanical way, this is something that should be observable to outsiders. So the second possibility is one that could be empirically checked. Ethically, of course, it is important to check, by observing the patient's manner of speech, etc. whether he was speaking mechanically when he denies suffering pain. For if he were speaking in a robot-like way, then it remains possible that if there is a mind in the strong sense, that mind could be suffering pain while it is dissociated from the speech centres.

But suppose that at the time of the local anaesthetic, the patient was observed to be talking in a conscious manner. Leaving aside the possibility that he may be lying when he says he feels no pain, we are still left with a choice between the first and third possibility. My own view is that we should try to defend the first possibility (as long as we honestly can) rather than embrace the third possibility. For the third possibility goes against much of our moral and practical life. According to the principle of reasonable faith we should only embrace it if the other possibilities are obviously implausible.

This discussion applies *mutatis mutandis* to the multiple personality case. Before we take the revolutionary view that there is more than one consciousness present simultaneously in a human being, we should make sure that the other possibilities have been ruled out.

There is also another ground of scepticism in the multiple personality cases such as that of Sally Beauchamp. C. D. Broad[10] considers the possibility that Sally may have made these fantastic claims because she was weak and suggestible. He rejects this possibility because Sally seemed to have a strong will of her own and be quite capable of rejecting suggestions that she did not like. But Broad goes on to point out that Sally may have liked the suggestion that she was co-conscious. For this would have satisfied her desire to appear as important and mysterious as possible. How tempting for Sally to accept a view that would imply that she was a mysterious being who was creating a revolution in medical and psychological thinking! Although Sally was not weak and suggestible, she could have been (rather like some hysterical persons whom she resembled) obstinate and suggestible, i.e. only accepted suggestions that she found palatable. Broad concludes that though the claims of people like Sally must be given some weight, we must regard these claims with great suspicion.

We saw in the last chapter that Hilgard mentions cases where the subject under local anaesthetic denies feeling any pain, yet at the very same time he writes with one of his hands that he is feeling intese pain. Wilkes[11] thinks that such cases show that we sometimes have two separate conscious personalities present at the same time. She uses the language test of consciousness. She thinks that the person who denies the pain and the individual who writes that he is in pain are each conscious because they each use language. But the language test of consciousness is clearly insufficient. For one can use language in a mechanical way without there being consciousness. The test that I favour (in chapter 2) is the expressive test of consciousness. And I am not at all convinced that the use of that test shows that there are cases of more than one conscious personality being present in a human body at at any one time.

The use of the language test of consciousness also leads Wilkes to say that in the Beauchamp case there was more than one conscious personality present at the very same time. Wilkes is impressed by the fact that Sally wrote her autobiography with B4's hand while B4 commented caustically upon what appeared before her. But if we use the expressive test of consciousness then it does not follow that we have two conscious minds present simultaneously.

It might be argued that if there is more than one person in a human body, the evidence for it is more likely to come from split brain experiments rather than from multiple personality ones (or from other cases where memory claims are involved). For in the multiple personality cases, the patient's memories can play tricks on him; whereas in the split brain experiments there is an opportunity for outside observers to try to observe more directly whether or not they are in contact with a separate consciousness at the same time.

But memory reports should not be discounted altogether. If we have independent evidence for the existence of two persons, for instance by observing split brain patients, then if these people make appropriate memory claims afterwards, this could reinforce our initial impression that there is than one person present.

One of the problems is this. Even if there is more than one consciousness at the same time, what view of the person would best accommodate such facts? Could one continue to believe in the non-reductionist view, with the difference that there may be more than one indivisible self per human being? Or should we abandon the non-reductionist view altogether and embrace the reductionist view?

In the split brain cases, the patients behave fairly normally in ordinary life when they are not being experimentally tested. In ordinary life, the inputs to the two hemispheres are very similar, and the patient behaves in a fairly unified way. So even if there are two consciousnesses at the time of the split brain experiments, there seems to be just one at other times. Moreover, as we saw earlier, even under test situations, the two hemispheres do not provide evidence for the existence of two wills. So it seems that even if evidence for the existence of two consciousnesses at the time of split brain experiments does turn up, one cannot infer that there are two persons (in the sense which implies two simple selves with free-will etc.) per human body. Rather we may have to adopt something like the reductionist view of persons so that splitting of persons during test situations becomes no more of a problem than does the splitting of nations.

If Sally Beauchamp's claims of co-consciousness are believed, do they provide better evidence for the view that there is more than one self per human body? Sally claims to have existed as a co-conscious personality over a long period, and so in her case there isn't the problem of how a second consciousness just comes in and out of existence. However when Sally was the dominant personality there does not seem to have been any other personality that was co-

conscious. B1 for instance, seemed to disappear completely at the times when Sally was dominant. And so the problem remains, how did B1 just come in and out of existence?[12] The reductionist view would of course dissolve this problem.

Wilkes is impressed by the fact that in the Beauchamp case, each of the personalities had completely different, but internally consistent and coherent characters, outlooks, tastes and habits. Wilkes also believes that each of the personalities satisfied the common conditions for personhood. Each was a rational system in the relevant sense, each knew at least one language, each was an object of moral treatment, each was treated as a moral agent by the psychiatrist, each was subject to praise and blame.

Now it is true that each was a person. The crucial point was whether 'they' were separate persons, or the same person. The mere fact that each of them was a person does not show that they were each separate persons. John Doe, the child and John Doe the old man each have different characters, goals, tastes, etc., they each satisfy the conditions of personhood; it does not follow that they are separate persons.

Wilkes also stresses the fact that the personalities had different egoistic fears and hopes. Thus both for B1 and for B4, B2's survival meant death. It was no consolation to them to be told that B2 claimed each of them as herself: 'consider the difficulty of persuading anyone that he continued to exist over a lengthy period of time of which he had no recollection, simply on the grounds that an individual, of whom he knew nothing directly, claimed to be him. Intuition is often a frail and unreliable tool to use in philosophy but when it comes to the fundamental and heartfelt claim "that's not me" we surely ought not to regard it lightly'.[13]

I agree with the importance of intuition in matters of personal identity. Indeed the non-reductionist view is not something that can be proved to be true; it is based on a sort of an intuition from a first person perspective. The view that each of us is separate person is also bolstered by the fact that we have different egoistic fears and hopes. So the fact that B1 and B4 do not identify with B2 is disturbing for the view that they are identical with B2. But it does not conclusively establish that they are not B2. Wilkes is not correct in saying that the case for regarding B2 as identical with B1 and B4 is *simply* that B2 regarded herself as identical with B1 and B4. In fact B2 had memories from the inside of what B1 and B4 did (even though B1 and B4 did not have memories of what B2 did) and accepted responsibility for what they did. Morton Prince, the psychiatrist of these personalities, claimed that B2 was a sort of fusion of B1 and B4, 'a harmonious combination of the two'. And though the egoistic fears of B1 and B4 are important data, one needs to make a distinction between being afraid that one's way of life does not survive and being afraid that one does not survive. On the reductionist view this distinction tends to vanish. For on that view one's survival consists of things like the survival of one's way of life. But on the non-reductionist view this is not so.

Often one wants to survive in what I called the combined sense, where there is persistence of my self, as well as persistence of my way of life. Suppose John Doe is now an amnesiac, and builds for himself a new way of life during his amnesia. He falls in love with a woman, and so forth. He may now be terrified at the prospect of recovering his memories of his past; for if he was treated and regained the memories of his past he may lose his present way of life. Perhaps he was married to a woman quite different from the woman he now loves. He may dread to lose his present way of life. It does not follow that he would not survive the treatment of his amnesia. Of course, the ordinary non-philosophical man does not make these fine distinctions. So too with B1 and B4, when they are afraid of B2 taking over, they do not really distinguish beween their way of life disappearing, and their disappearing.

Of course, Sally never got integrated into the 'real' Miss Beauchamp. And this presents a problem for the one person per human being view. But as we have seen, there are possible explanations which could explain or explain away Sally, consistently with the one person per human being view.

There is one other possibility that Morton Prince did not explore properly. This is the possibility that Sally was the 'real' Miss Beauchamp. Prince, as we have seen, was primarily concerned with trying to find out which was the real Miss Beauchamp. Actually he should have talked more accurately. For each of the personalities that in turn was dominant was real in a perfectly good sense of real. Each was there for everyone to observe, each as we have seen satisfied the conditions of personhood. The real problems facing Prince were two. Firstly how many *separate* persons were there? Secondly, which of the personalities should be preserved and which not? The second involves normative issues, about which of the personalities was more desirable as well as the factual issue of which of the personalities was most like the original Miss Beauchamp who existed before the onset of the pathological condition.

In fact Prince did not make these distinctions. He seemed to be searching for the real Miss Beauchamp and brought in normative considerations through the back door. Sally was not the real Miss Beauchamp, because she was too irresponsible, childish, devilish, etc. B1 was not the real one because she was too high minded and morbid. B4 was not the real one because she was bad tempered and wilful. B2 was the real one because she was healthy and integrated. 'Physically she was well. The neurasthenic had vanished in the twinkling of an eye. In place of pains, fatigue, and insomnia, she boasted of a joyous feeling of well-being, of freedom from every discomfort, of peaceful nights, and sleep free from disturbing dreams. She never heard nor saw hallucinations; she was free from impulsations, obsessions and aboulia.'[14]

It seems to me that such considerations may well be relevant to the problem regarding which of the personalities ought to be preserved, assuming that we do not want them all to be preserved. But such considerations are not relevant to finding out the real Miss Beauchamp. Personalities that were undesirable or unhealthy were no less real.

With regard to the problem of how many separate persons there were, the real problem for the one person per human being view was that Sally did not get integrated into the final Miss Beauchamp. But this could have been the fault of the psychiatrist. Prince was trying to squeeze out Sally. He did not seriously consider preserving Sally's personality. Yet it was only Sally who had 'memories' from the inside of the thoughts and/or actions of each of the other personalities. It is true that Sally did not identify with these other perosnalities and indeed was often trying to hurt some of the other personalities. But Prince could have tried to treat this alienation. Instead he encouraged Sally to feel alienated from the other personalities by his attempts to eliminate Sally. Because Sally's character did not appear morally desirable to Prince he did not strive to preserve her personality. Had he concentrated on preserving Sally and integrating her with the other personalities of whose thoughts and/or actions Sally had inside knowledge, Prince may have succeeded in creating a fusion of all the personalities. We shall never know for certain whether this conjecture is correct.

It might be suggested that even if such fusion was possible, it would not have shown that there was not more than one person to begin with. It may be that there were several persons to begin with and then as a result of the 'treatment', they were all fused into one. But on the indivisible self view, this suggestion will not work. For an indivisible self cannot fuse with another. Two simple selves could of course jointly constitute a compound; but in that case there would not be a true fusion.

One possibility is that in the multiple personality case we have a freak. There may be more than one indivisible self per person. It would not follow that we have to abandon the one person per human being view for normal people, unless it could be shown that even normal people can, under certain conditions, degenerate into multiple personality cases. It might just be possible that the world is divided into some abnormal cases where there is more than one indivisible self per person, and the rest. The existence of a few freaks then would not upset our normal view of personal identity. Although this is a theoretical possibility, the empirical facts seem to go against such a speculation. For in the actual multiple personality cases, before the onset of the illness, the people concerned seemed much like you and me. If they had the potential for several selves, then so do we. Or so it seems. Actually, Sally did claim that she was present as a second co-conscious person right from infancy?

It is even less plausible to treat the split brain cases as 'freaks'. For though the actual cases have involved epilepsy, the abnormality is irrelevant to whether or not there is more than one person per human body. It is not at all plausible to argue that epileptics are freaks and have more than one person per human body, while the rest of us have just one person per human body. For there is every reason to think that if the brains of ordinary people were split they would react under experimental conditions in a way that is similar to the way that the epileptic patients react.

I have tried to suggest strategies for preserving the one indivisible self per human being view. But I have also argued that this view is falsifiable or at least that it could be undermined if certain facts turned up. And we must not be dogmatic and assume that our ordinary view must be true. There may be more than one person per human being, and we should try to see if there is good evidence in favour of such a hypothesis. There are of course ethical limitations to the carrying out of split brain studies. For instance, it would not be right to prolong the split brain experiments over a continuous indefinite period with a view to testing the hypothesis that a second agent will emerge with a will of his own. And it may be that in multiple personality cases, the evidence for the view that there is more than one person would be better if we split their brains; for it *may* happen that one of the multiple personalities would manifest itself through one of the hemispheres while another one manifests itself at the very same time, through the other hemisphere. Outside observers could try to get in direct contact with more than one person over a long period of time.

But there are ethical limitations to such experiments. In cases of epilepsy splitting the brain was used because it was thought of as a partial cure for epilepsy. The knowledge that we gained from the experiments with split brain patients was a desirable by-product, but of course it would not by itself have justified the splitting of the brain. In the case of multiple personality, the splitting of the brain would not help to treat the patient and it would not be possible to justify it solely for the sake of advancement of knowledge.

Our conventional moral views, which are based on the one person per human being view, prevent us from getting possible evidence against the one person view. There is a sort of circle here, for if there are several persons per human being then multiple personality is not a pathological condition. Indeed if there are several persons per human being, then our conventional moral view of the person is involved in suppressing the growth and liberation of the non-dominant persons within a human being. We use the conventional moral views to forbid certain experiments, such as trying to turn the epileptics whose brains we have split into multiple personality cases by prolonging the split brain experiments over a long continous period of time. Yet such experiments might help to provide evidence against the one person per human being view and against our conventional moral views.

How then do we defend our present views in a scientific spirit? Are we doomed to be dogmatic and to prevent the collection of any evidence that might go against our current views? No, we are not. The view that there are ethical limitations to our collection of the relevant evidence does not imply that we should never look for evidence that goes against the conventional wisdom. Often the study of multiple personality cases as well as of the split brain cases does no harm to the patient. The increase in our knowledge can be a desirable by product of the study of many of these cases. Compare, it would be immoral to encourage the breakdown of families in order to study the effects upon the victims ; but it is all right to study the effects upon the victims if the family broke up due to other reasons.

In chapter 5 we saw that there were different possible solutions that might be offered to cope with the problem of splitting. That discussion applies *mutatis mutandis* to the problem posed by multiple personality cases. Which of the solutions we should adopt will depend upon what the facts turn out to be. Thus if we get evidence of co-consciousness, not just during split brain experiments, but also at other times, then we may well opt for the solution according to which there was more than one person all along. We saw earlier that the view that there were two simple selves per human being might tend to discredit the indivisible self view by undermining its practical basis. However, if the two selves view was confined to the freak cases, then the indivisible self view could be believed in for the ordinary cases; and though the simple self view would be difficult to operate in the freak cases (e. g. the problem of how many votes to give to such freaks) this would not undermine the whole system.

The trouble with granting the two selves view in the split brain cases (as well as in at least some of the multiple personality cases) is that they cannot be regarded as freaks in the relevant sense. Each of us could have our brains split and we would then react under test situations very much as the split brain patients have so far reacted. If it turned out that ordinary people could also 'degenerate' into multiple personality cases then the freak argument with regard to the multiple personality cases would not be able to rescue the practical basis of the indivisible self view if it were in danger of being undermined by the presence of more than one person in a human body.

We can imagine that there is more than one person per human being and that the different selves can be neatly divided and so each given their rights etc; thus if B1 inhabited the body on every odd day and B2 on every even day, then each could have a vote, B1 on an odd day and B2 on an even day. But in practice the multiple personality cases are much more messy.

If we do not get evidence of co-consciousness, if we get the evidence of one mind in the strong sense co-existing with other minds in the weak sense, then we could adopt the solution according to which we have a single person with a divided mind.

If we get evidence of co-consciousness only at certain times, but not at normal times, then it is difficult to adopt the view that there is more than one person all along; so we would still be left with the problem of how a second self comes in and out of existence. If the patients behave in a normal unified way at all times except under test situations, then the view that there are two full blooded persons is less plausible than the reductionist view that persons are like nations, so the splitting of persons at certain times and their fusion at other times would present no more of a problem than the splitting and fusion of nations.

So we see that the solution that we should adopt in the split brain cases and in the multiple personality cases should depend upon what facts we observe in these cases. I have tried to show that on the present findings we can retain the one (non-reductionist) person per human being view.

There are many psychiatrists nowadays who believe that major mental disorders such as schizophrenia and manic depression have a genetic component, which is not to deny that unfavourable environment may also contribute to the onset of the illness. Multiple personality is not discussed so much nowadays as it once was (though in the last decade there has been some revival of interest in it), but it is possible that it might turn out that there is a genetic component to the multiple personality cases also, which is not to deny that traumatic events, such as childhood abuse, contribute to the onset of the illness. If there is a genetic difference between the multiple personality cases and the normal population, could it not be that though people with multiple personalities have multiple selves, or the potential for them, the rest of us do not?

It might be objected that even if the multiple personality cases do have some special genetic component, it is difficult to think of them as multiple persons. For in some of the cases they seem quite normal before the onset of the illness as well as after the various personalities have been integrated. If we say that there are multiple persons only during the intervening periods, then there is the problem on the non-reductionist view about where these other persons were before the onset of the illness, as well as after the cure. That is one reason why it is best to preserve the one person per human being view as long as we honestly can.

Even if the multiple personality cases have a genetic component, this component may not be accompanied by the presence of a second person in such cases, but it might be that it is so accompanied. All this is speculation.[15] If we get substantial evidence that in such pathological cases one of the personalities never got integrated with the others, as

Sally never got integrated with the others in the Beauchamp case, this may reflect the fact that in some of these cases there was a second person, or it may simply reflect the fact that the treatment was not developed enough at that time. That there are two persons in such cases could be the most plausible hypothesis, if there was evidence of two different personalities being simultaneously conscious in the same human body. In my opinion such evidence has not been forthcoming. And so we can retain the one person per human being view by appealing to the idea of switching of the same consciousness from one personality to another.

NOTES

1. D. Dennett, *Brainstorms*, p. 152. Shoemaker is another leading functionalist who is a reductionist with regard to personal identity.
2. See D. Dennett, *Brainstorms*, chapter 9.
3. See W. Lycan, MIT Press, Cambridge Mass., 1987, *Consciousness*, chapter 3 and appendix on Machine Consciousness
4. See S. Shoemaker, *Personal Identity*, p. 101.
5. When we say that two experiences are co-conscious we sometimes mean that they both belong to the same consciousness. When we say that the two personalities are co-conscious we mean that they are each a seperate consciousness, embodied in the same human being.
6. M. Prince, *The Dissociation of a Personality*, O.U. P., Oxford, 1978.
7. D. M. and Valerie MacKay, 'Explicit Dialogue between Left and Right Half-Systems of Split-Brains', *Nature*, 1982 pp. 690-1.
8. B. Williams, *Problems of the Self*, p. 18.
9. D. Hume, *A Treatise of Human Nature*, ed. L. A. Selby-Bigge, Clarendon Press, Oxford, 1978, Book 1 Part 3 Sec. 9.
10. C. D. Broad, *Mind and Its Place in Nature*, Kegan Paul, London, 1937, pp. 428-9.
11. *Real People*, p. 108. However, in ch. 6 she argues against the whole concept of consciousness.
12. A similar problem was posed by Nagel in the split brain cases, *Mortal Questions*, p. 161.
13. K. Wilkes, 'Multiple Personality and Personal Identity', *British Journal of Philosophy of Science.*, 1981.
14. *Dissociation of Personality*, p. 518.
15. What would be most implausible would be to argue that the reductionist view applies to the multiple personality cases while the non-reductionist view applies to the normal population. For the multiple personality cases before and after their illness seem like the rest of us in the relevant respects.

VII. *Non-Reductionism and the Use of Imaginary Examples*

In the first section I shall defend the non-reductionist view against some of Parfit's criticisms; some of his arguments seem to rely on the use of imaginary examples. In the second section I shall examine the relevance of imaginary examples to discussions of personal identity.

Section 1: Parfit's arguments against the non-reductionist view. The non-reductionist view of the self cannot I think be proved to be true, nor can objective evidence[1] be brought to show that there are non-reductionist selves. My view is that it is reasonable to assume that there are such selves because their existence is presupposed by our subjective experience and by our practical and moral life. The belief in non-reductionist selves is not to be held dogmatically but as a defeasible conjecture.

Some philosophers think that we can actually prove that we are persistent non-reductionist selves. It has for instance been argued that if there was no such persistent entity, there would be no understanding; for in order to understand a sentence as a whole, each part of the sentence must be understood by the same entity. What are we to make of this argument? It is true that if one human being hears the earlier part of the sentence and another hears the later part of the sentence, then neither of them has heard or understood the sentence as a whole. But the relation between the earlier self and the later self of a human being could be more intimate than and different from the relation of one human being to another. For instance it could be that the earlier self passes on its experiences and properties to the later self, somewhat as one elastic ball passes on its properties to another such ball that it hits.

While some philosophers think (wrongly) that there is some proof or at least objective evidence in favour of the non-reductionist view, others think that there might have been such evidence. Parfit, for example, thinks that Cartesian dualism is the most plausible version of the non-reductionist view and he thinks that there might have been evidence in its favour, though in fact there is evidence against it.

I am not convinced that Cartesian dualism is the most plausible of the non-reductionist views, but it is one of the most popular and persuasive versions. So it is well worth discussing what the evidence against it is and if there might have been evidence in its favour. Some of this discussion would apply *mutatis mutandis* against other versions of the non-reductionist view.

Parfit argues that if people in this life claimed to remember things that happened in their previous lives, if on the basis of their apparent memories predictions were made and checked by anthropologists and if there is no other way in which we could explain how we know things had happpened long ago, then the simplest hypothesis might be to postulate that one is the same soul as the person whose life he remembers.[2] Actually, though these happenings, if they occurred, would provide evidence for the view that one has a soul which is the carrier of memories, they would not provide evidence for the view that one is identical to the soul. We saw in chapter 1 that people make a similar mistake with regard to our brains; they think that because there is evidence that the brain is the carrier of our memories, dispositions, etc., therefore we are identical to our brains.

Cartesian dualism assumes that I am the soul, rather than just that I am realised in the soul. In my view it is doubtful that any objective evidence could demonstrate that I am identical to a soul as opposed to being realised in the soul,[3] or as opposed to having the soul as an aspect of me. Consider the following possibility. Suppose that whenever a replica of a human being was created the original human being whose replica was created collapsed and became lifeless. We can imagine evidence which might show that it was impossible to create a replica unless the original human being 'died'. The best explanation of this might be that the soul of the original human being has to be transferred to the replica. We have assumed here that no physical part of the original human being was transferred to the replica, so the crucial link between the 'death' of the original and the creation of the replica must be the transference of something non-physical.

Such evidence, like the reincarnation evidence that Parfit asks us to consider, would at most show that the soul of the human being has transferred to another, but it would not show that the person is the soul. Such facts, like the facts in the reincarnation cases, could be consistent with some sort of dual-aspect theory; the soul which is transferred from the previous body to the present one, could be the inner aspect of the person who is transferred from the previous body to the present one. Such facts would also be consistent with the reductionist view that the person consists of his psychology; it could be that the person is realized in the soul which is the carrier of his psychology.

But now suppose we combine evidence in favour of reincarnation with evidence in favour of the Law of Karma. Suppose the people who are suffering now remember correctly the wicked deeds that they committed in the previous lives and that those who are prospering now remember correctly some of the saintly deeds they did in the previous lives; and suppose these memory claims were checked by anthropologists etc. and found to be accurate. If such extra-ordinary evidence in favour of the operation of the Law of Karma was forthcoming, then perhaps one would have some sort of moral evidence for the non-reductionist view of persons; for as I said earlier the reductionist view does not make sense of the Law of Karma, notwithstanding the Buddhists.[4] The evidence would not however demonstrate the truth of the non-reductionist view, it would at best establish a *prima facie* case for such a view. Such a case could be rebutted if it could be shown that the Law of Karma is set up by a fallible God who wrongly thought, like the Buddhists, that the law of Karma was morally compatible with the reductionist view. So the Law of Karma and the reductionist view might co-exist as a matter of fact even though they are morally incompatible.

Parfit says that even if there was good evidence for reincarnation, this would not conclusively verify the non-reductionist view. It would not show that the continued existence 'of these Egos is all or nothing'. But he thinks that there might have been evidence to support even this claim. 'There might have been various kinds or degrees of damage to a person's brain, which did not in any fundamental way alter this person, while other kinds or degrees of damage seemed to produce a completely new person, in no way psychologically continous with the original person. Something similar might have been true of the various kinds of mental illness. We might generally have reached the conclusion that these kinds of interference either did nothing at all to destroy psychological continuity or destroyed it completely.' In fact we find intermediate cases where psychological connectedness holds only in degrees, and Parfit thinks that these facts are inconsistent with the non-reductionist view according to which our survival is a matter of all or nothing.

Besides cases that involve divided minds and imaginary cases such as the combined spectrum (which I shall discuss shortly), Parfit's chief argument against the non-reductionist view is that there is no evidence that the carrier of psychological continuity is something whose existence must be all or nothing; and there is much evidence to show that the carrier of these states is the brain whose survival admits of degrees. He rightly points out that there are many actual cases where psychological connectedness holds only in degrees and the same holds of physical connectedness.

So Parfit believes that we actually have evidence against the non-reductionist view. In fact his argument is vitiated by the failure to make the distinction that defenders of the non-reductionist view could stress between the agent (or the self), whose survival does not admit of degrees, and his character, which does admit of degrees. We saw earlier that the person on the non-reductionist view could have had a very different character if he had been brought up differently and so the person or the self should not be equated with its character. The non-reductionist could grant that the brain is the carrier of memories and other psychological traits, he could even grant that the brain's survival admits of degrees, and yet he could say that the person is not his brain and so his survival does not admit of degrees.

One of the major arguments Parfit has against the non-reductionist view is the combined spectrum: 'At the near end of the spectrum is the normal case in which a future person would be fully continuous with me as I am now, both physically and psychologically. This person would be me in just the way that, in my actual life, it will be me who wakes up tomorrow. At the far end of the spectrum the resulting person would have no continuity with me as I now am, either physically or psychologically. In this case the scientists would destroy my brain and body, and then create out of new organic matter a perfect replica of... Greta Garbo. We can suppose that when Garbo was 30 a group of scientists recorded the states of all the cells in her brain and body'.[5]

Parfit says that at the near end of the spectrum his brain, body and mind would all be there; as one progresses towards the far end the proportion of his cells as opposed to the 'Garbo' cells will gradually get less and less, until one reaches the far end where there is nothing of the original Parfit left. He thinks that if such a replacement of cells was undertaken we would get a fusion of the personalities of Parfit and Garbo. As one moves along the spectrum towards the far end there will be more and more of Garbo characteristics in the fused personality and less and less of Parfit.

Actual cases of such fusion would present a problem for the non-reductionist view, at any rate for the simple version. But how can imaginary cases of such fusion (or fission for that matter) present a problem? Parfit thinks that cases of fusion and fission are physically possible. And I agree with him that if they are, then the non-reductionist view would be undermined. But I am not at all convinced that these cases are possible. Parfit admits that except for the cases at the near end, the cases in the combined spectrum are likely to remain technically impossible. But he says that they are 'only technically impossible'. How does he know this? Could the reason why they are likely to remain technically impossible not be that they are physically impossible? His argument for the view that these cases are only technically impossible is that our psychological features depend upon the states of the brain. But this is a weak argument. Even if our psychological features do depend upon the states of our brain, it does not follow that it is physically possible to create a fusion of two different people by mixing their brain cells. Nor does it follow that it is possible to produce replicas of brains or of parts of the brain.

The combined spectrum argument assumes that replicas of people can be created; for it assumes that it is physically possible to create a replica of Garbo's body and brain and mix parts of it with another body and then get a fusion of the two personalities. There is no evidence to show that it is physically possible to create viable replicas of people. And if it were possible to create such replicas, the non-reductionist view would be undermined anyway,[6] so the combined spectrum argument against the non-reductionist view would be rendered redundant. So the combined spectrum argument is based on an assumption, which in fact renders it false, and if true renders it redundant.

Parfit says that if we could carry out the combined spectrum operations, the results would be what he has described. It is not clear to me that this is so; the fusion could be a failure or a partial failure, so that there is a degenerate or abnormal or multiple personality, frequently alternating between Garbo and Parfit.[7] But even if there would be a proper fusion, it would not follow that it is physically possible to carry out these operations. The view that these operations are physically impossible is compatible with the truth of the hypothetical that if these operations could be carried out they would result in a proper fusion. Unless we assume that the cases appealed to in the combined spectrum are physically possible, the argument will not be able to undermine the non-reductionist view. Imaginary counter-examples cannot refute the non-reductionist view, any more than they can refute scientific theories. The fact that such counter-examples are imaginable only shows that the theory is falsifiable, which is a virtue of the theory.

Cases of fusion as well as cases of fission would, if they occurred, create great problems for the non-reductionist view. There are no good arguments to show that the fusion of the kind involved in the combined spectrum argument is possible. Some of his other arguments involve cases of fission (or splitting of a person's consciousness into two). and again, as we saw in chapters 5 and 6, there are no conclusive arguments to show that such cases are possible.

Parfit is too impressed by split brain experiments. Although he says at one point that the split brain cases present only a small part of his case against the non-reductionist view, in fact they play a vital role in his argument. For in these arguments he frequently appeals to imaginary cases of replicas, of fission and of fusion of persons. When confronted with the objection that these are only imaginary cases he replies that the impossibility is merely technical and not a deep one, for the essential features of the cases, the division of consciousness into separate streams, has already occurred several times. In chapter 6 I argue that if splitting of consciousness occurs this would indeed undermine the non-reductionist view, but I argue that such splitting has not been shown to be possible.

Section 2 : The Relevance of Imaginary Examples

Imaginary examples have been used both to defend and to criticize the non-reductionist view. In this section I shall try to examine what, if anything, they do succeed in showing. Philosophers, while discussing personal identity, often use examples such as the following:

(1) The person or self is not the brain or body because if we replaced his brain or body by another one and his psychology remained intact, he would have survived the loss of the original brain or body.

(2) The person or the self is not the soul (or subjective world) because if the soul (or subjective world) passes on its psychology to another soul (or subjective world) the person goes with the psychology, not with the soul (or subjective world).[8]

(3) The person or the self is not its psychology for if the same subjective consciousness persists in the same body such that the

human being remains conscious while its psychology is altered bit by bit, until the human being acquires a substantially new psychology from the one he started off with, the person or self would survive the dissolution of its psychology.[9]

(4) The person or self is not its psychology. For the same self from the time it came into existence could have developed a psychology that is substantially different from its present psychology.[10] For instance, a psychopath might have had a very different psychology now, had he had a good environment since birth.

Philosophers often use the first two illustrations to show that personal identity goes with psychological continuity and psychological connectedness rather than with brain or soul identity or identity of the same subjective world. The third example has been used to show the opposite, viz: that personal identity does not go with psychological connectedness. One needs to be very careful with the use of imaginary examples. The most that these examples show is that it is logically possible for there to be persons that are neither brains nor souls nor subjective worlds. But imaginary examples cannot be used to refute views about the actual nature of existing persons.

Things would be quite different if these were real examples rather than imaginary ones. The fourth illustration is a real one and the argument there is a good one. If the examples in the first two cases were real ones, the argument there would also be a good one. If in fact all our psychological characteristics could be passed on from one subjective world to another, and from one brain to another, we would need to become reductionists and abandon our view that we are subjective worlds or that we are brains. It does not follow that we should now abandon such beliefs. The fourth example is only a counter-example to the view that the non-reductionist self is to to be analysed in terms of its psychology. If we give up the non-reductionist view, the fourth example ceases to be a counter example to the view that I am my psychology. For on the reductionist view there is no deep truth to my existence beyond my psychology and if I had been brought up differently, there would have been a different psychology and hence a different person from what there is now.

That actual, not merely imaginary, counter-examples are needed to refute theories about personal identity is an obvious point, yet it has been neglected even by outstanding philosophers. For instance, Nagel[11] thinks that his view that he is a brain commits him to the view that if replicas could be created he would not survive in his replica, for the replica would have a different brain. Reductionists such as Shoemaker have argued rightly that we would survive in our replicas even when we are not identical to our replicas. But they wrongly criticize non-reductionists on the grounds that it must involve a denial of this view. These reductionists and some non-reductionists such as Nagel make a common assumption which is false, viz: the assumption that non-reductionism involves a denial of the view that if replicas could be created we would survive in our replicas. This assumption is wrong. For non-reductionism need only assert that fission, and the creation of replicas etc, are not possible. It could and should grant that if such things were shown to be possible, we should become reductionists and agree that we would live through our fission and survive in our replicas or in our offshoots just as much as (or as little) as we did before there was branching.[12]

Nagel has made his non-reductionist view that we are brains look unneccessarily vulnerable by taking it to imply the denial of the view that we would survive in our replicas. It might be thought that the creation of replicas is compatible with the non-reductionist view that we are brains or that we are subjective worlds; for the creation of the replica involves the creation of a new self. But this suggestion will not work. For consider a case where a surgeon gradually replaces parts of my body (including the brain) with new parts, eventually replacing all the parts of the old body with the new one, the psychology remaining the same. In this case it would be odd to deny that the old person does survive. And this would be so even if with all the old parts another person was created, both the persons having the same degree of psychological connectedness with the original person. In that case what has happened to the original person?

The best answer would be that the original person survives in both the existing persons, without being identical with either of them; such talk of survival without identity would involve abandonment of the non-reductionist view. And if one allows that in this sort of case the person survives without identity, it would be odd to deny that the person survives in his replica even when he also continues to survive in his original body. And this again would involve the abandonment of the non-reductionist view where survival goes only with identity.[13]

To be accurate, the existence of a replica by chance or by a miracle is compatible with the non-reductionist view. For instance, if God by some miracle could create a replica of me, it would not follow that I would survive in that replica in the way that I would in my own body.

For it could be that God had created a new self. It would not follow that it is physically possible to produce replicas by replacing parts of me by new ones until all the old parts are replaced by new ones in the way required by the argument in the previous paragraph. But if it is physically possible to produce replicas, then the non-reductionist view would be undermined. For if cases of replicas were physically possible, then so too would cases of fission. And if cases of fission are physically possible then the non-reductionist view would be undermined. We would then have to be content with the view that there is reductionist survival without identity.

Parfit and Shoemaker both use imaginary examples in their attempt to undermine the non-reductionist view. But while Parfit believes (wrongly!) that these cases are physically possible and that what is essential to them has already occurred, Shoemaker believes (rightly) that these examples are purely imaginary and that they do not occur.[14] Parfit is I think wrong about the facts, but Shoemaker is wrong about the inference he draws from purely imaginary cases. Shoemaker grants that one's initial reaction is a non-reductionist view; he grants that it is natural to make Swinburne's assumption that 'when I want to survive, it is essential to the satisfaction of my want that I, the very person who is now wanting this should exist in the future'.[15] But he thinks that reflection on the fission cases and on cases where replicas of us are created would convince us that we would survive in our offshoots and replicas and convert us to the reductionist view according to which what really matters is psychological continuity. In cases of fission neither of the persons after the fission is identical with the person who existed before the fission. If identity is what matters then the person would not have survived the fission. But a person clearly would survive such fission. The future offshoots will remember their past and be motivated by the old person's intentions and desires. So Shoemaker concludes that we would clearly live through our fission and that our present reflective view is that identity is not what ultimately matters. There are two mistakes here. Firstly he implies that it is not necessary for his argument to show that such imaginary cases can in fact occur. Secondly, it is a mistake to think that our present reflective view is the reductionist view.

In fact, reflection on such imaginary cases only helps to reveal that we believe that identity is what ultimately matters. For it is because we believe in the non-reductionist view that we would find cases of fission so baffling, if they were to occur; on the reductionist view splitting of persons would be no more baffling than the splitting of nations. If fission were shown to be possible, then reductionist survival would be what ultimately matters. This is consistent with the view that since fission has not been shown to be possible, it is reasonable to believe in non-reductionist survival.

Can we preserve both Swinburne's natural assumption which does seem to have intuitive plausibility and Shoemaker's claim that we would live through our fission which also seems to harmonise with common-sense. Some people would say that the two views are inconsistent with each other and the fact that they each harmonise with common-sense only shows how unreliable comon-sense is as a guide in such matters.

Some non-reductionists would say that if fission occurs we would survive in one of our offshoots though we cannot tell which; I do not find such a solution plausible. For if fission did take place it would be difficult to deny that the person survives in each of his offshoots.[16] My own solution for preserving both Swinburne's natural assumption and the view that we would live through our fission, is as follows: there are two kinds of survival, reductionist survival and non-reductionist survival. Non-reductionist survival is a deeper form of survival and our present views of personal identity presuppose such survival. I am not convinced by those who argue that our present traditional view of personal identity is based on an error. In my view though we cannot show our present views to be correct, they are presupposed by much of our civilised life and subjective experience. They are falsifiable and have not been shown to be false. It seems reasonable to adhere to such traditional practices unless and until they are shown to be false.

If fission is shown to be possible then it would be reasonable to abandon the non-reductionist view, if that were psychologically possible, and perhaps to believe in the reductionist view. We should then admit that one would live through one's fission. For if fission is possible and a person only survives in a reductionist sense, then even before a person splits he was only enjoying reductionist survival.[17] So of course a person lives through fission in the sense that he continues to survive in the reductionist sense. This is compatible with the view that since fission has not occurred we should continue to adhere to the non-reductionist view and to make Swinburne's natural assumption. The non-reductionist need not deny that if fission were possible, we would live through our fission; rather he would deny that fission is metaphysically possible.

I have argued that purely imaginary cases cannot be used to undermine the non-reductionist view. But it might be suggested that there is a difference between normative theses and factual theses with regard to the relevance of imaginary cases. A scientific theory cannot be refuted by imaginary counter-examples, but an ultimately normative thesis should be able to deal even with imaginary cases. The thesis that we are non-reductionist selves is a factual thesis but it is a normative thesis that what ultimately matters in survival is not the persistence of such a self but psychological connectedness.

What are we to make of this suggestion? It is true that in normative matters it is sometimes permissible to appeal to imaginary examples. If a white person approves of the persecution of blacks, it is relevant to ask him to imagine himself as black and consider whether he should be persecuted if he were black. It is no objection to to say that he could not be black, that if 'he' were black he would have a different genetic make up and so would be a different person. Even though it is physically impossible for them to become the other person, we often ask people to put themselves imaginatively in other people's shoes, so that they can see things from the other person's point of view and from an impartial standpoint. Moralists often appeal to hypothetical or imaginary persons, such as an impartial spectator, or people in the Rawlsian original position, in order to achieve a fair perspective. But to grant the value of such imaginary experiments is not to deny the importance of what in fact happens even in deciding ultimately normative issues.

Of course in the case of non-ultimate values, factual views are relevant. Suppose the only ultimate principle is that we should promote the greatest happiness of the of the greatest number. The subordinate principle that one accepts, such as the principle that promiscuous sex is wrong, might depend upon the relevant facts. But cannot even what ultimately matters depend upon the facts? One's view of what ultimately matters could vary with whether one believes that God exists or the soul exists. It seems reasonable to believe that if we are souls and if God exists, then what ultimately matters is the union of one's soul with God, but if God does not exist and if there is no immortality then what ultimately matters is happiness on earth. Similarly it would be consistent to take the line that if persons are persistent indivisible selves then what ultimately matters for personal survival involves the survival of indivisible selves, along with the survival of other things such as one's memories and dispositions;

whereas if there are no persistent selves than what ultimately matters is not the survival of the persistent self but the survival of one's memories and dispositions.

Imaginary examples can be and have been used to reveal our preferences and beliefs regarding personal identity[18] as well as in other areas. For instance, imagine two worlds where there is equal amount of happiness but in one world there is more knowledge. If we are indifferent between the two worlds this suggests that we regard happiness as an intrinsic good but not knowledge. If we prefer the world with more knowledge this suggests that we regard knowledge also as an intrinsic good.

Though imaginary examples can sometimes reveal our beliefs about personal identity, they cannot verify or falsify them. But one has to be careful in seeing what they reveal. They do not reveal that we believe in reductionist survival. At most they reveal that if fission etc. were possible then reductionist survival would be what matters. Though imaginary examples cannot show our beliefs about personal identity to be false, they can show that they are not immune to revision. Imaginary counter examples can show that our beliefs are falsifiable. Real life counter-examples will have to be brought in to be show that they are false.

If anything, the imaginary examples tend to favour the non-reductionist view. For, though they do not verify or falsify our beliefs, consideration of them does, as we have seen, reveal that we believe in the non-reductionist view. If we also accept that there is a presumption in favour of what we are inclined to believe (see chapter 4) then the discussion of imaginary examples helps to support the view that we should continue to adhere to the non-reductionist view until and unless real life counter-examples have undermined it.

In the next three chapters I shall concentrate on working out some of the practical and moral implications of the reductionist view. This will enable us to see how deep seated and widespread the non-reductionist view is.

NOTES

1. Objective evidence is here contrasted with subjective evidence as well as with 'evidence' derived from moral and practical considerations.
2. Peter Geach objects to the view that we can imagine evidence in favour of reincarnation. 'If on growing up the Oxford baby reveals knowledge of what we should ordinarily say only Hitler can have

known, does that establish a presumption that the child is Hitler? Not
at all... might not several children simultaneously satisfy the criteria
for being Hitler?' *God and the Soul*, Routledge and Kegan Paul,
London, 1969, p. 24. Bernard Williams makes a similar point in
Problems of the Self, Cambridge University Press, Cambridge, 1973, p.
19, where he argues against the psychological criterion of personal
identity on the grounds that it could not distinguish between numerical identity and qualitative similarity. It seems to me that if several
children simultaneously satisfy the criteria for being Hitler, this would
indeed destroy the presumption that any of them is Hitler. But the
fact that a presumption can be defeated in some circumstances, does
not show that it was not reasonable to make the presumption. Some
presumptions do not get defeated, not because no circumstances are
imaginable where they would get defeated, but because circumstances
that would defeat the presumption do not occur. A scientific theory
does not get refuted merely because conditions are imaginable where
it would get refuted. As long as the reincarnation cases are in fact
one-one there is a presumption of identity. If such cases became one-
many (e.g. several children could rememeber from the inside what
Hitler did) we may abandon the non-reductionist view and talk of
Hitler surviving in these children though he is not identical with any
of them. Imaginary cases of several Hitlers can be used to show that
psychological connectedness and psychological continuity cannot
provide logically sufficient conditions of personal identity. But they
cannot be used to argue against the defeasible conjecture that psychological continuity and connectedness can be used as evidence of
personal identity, as they are on the non-reductionist view. Actual
cases of branching would be needed to show that this conjecture was
false.

3. See S. Shoemaker, Critical Notice of *Reasons and Persons, Mind*, 1986,
    pp. 443-53
4. See ch. 4 sec. 3.
5. *Reasons and Persons*, p. 236-7.
6. See ch. 7 sec. 2.
7. G. Madell, 'Derek Parfit and Greta Garbo', *Analysis*, 1985.
8. I do not necessarily imply that the view that I am a soul is the same
    as the view that I am a subjective world. indeed one may want to
    combine the view that I am a subjective world with some sort of
    double-aspect theory; rather that similar arguments can be used with
    'souls' as with 'subjective worlds'.
9. See C. McGinn, *The Character of Mind*, Oxford University Press,
    Oxford, 1982, p. 111.
10. See T. Nagel, *A View From Nowhere.* , p. 38.
11. *A View From Nowhere*, p. 44.

12. Non-reductionists can, without abandoning their views, grant that there is reductionist survival. Those who have stressed reductionist survival have tended to deny the non-reductionist view, but there is no reason why those who believe in the deeper form of survival cannot grant that there is a shallower form of survival which is there whether or not there is a deeper form of survival.
13. For a similar argument, see D. Parfit, *Reasons and Persons*, Appendix D.
14. S. Shoemaker, *Personal Identity*, p. 120.
15. *Personal Identity*, p. 119.
16. See ch. 5.
17. Some philosophers maintain that the view that persons are divisible is compatible with the non-reductionist view; it is only actual division of a person that is incompatible with the non-reductionist survival. This position is quite implausible.

    The view that a person enjoys non-reductionist survival until the time of splitting, but only reductionist survival after it, is untenable. For it involves the view that one does not live through splitting, or that one goes in for some kind of reduced or shallower form of survial after splitting. How can double success involve destruction or even partial destruction? Such considerations suggest that it is not just actual splitting that is incompatible with the non-reductionist view; the view that the self is divisible is also incompatible with the non-reductionist survival. If we are divisible selves then we do not enjoy non-reductionist survival, but only enjoy reductionist survival, even though we do not in fact split.
18. See *Reasons and Persons*, p. 200.

VIII. *Egoistical Concern Without an Ego*

In this chapter, I shall discuss whether the reductionist view of persons is compatible with the rationality of egoistical concern and of the pursuit of personal salvation. We saw in the introduction that Parfit has a moderate view and an extreme view regarding the compatibility of the reductionist view with our moral and practical life. With regard to egoistical concern, he thinks that it is defensible to maintain the extreme view according to which our egoistical concern is incompatible with the reductionist view. Indeed, some of the arguments that I use in this chapter in favour of the extreme view are quite similar to his. But, unlike me, he also believes that the moderate view regarding the compatibility of the reductionist view with the rationality of egoistical concern is also defensible. In my view, the case for the extreme view is powerful enough to undermine the case for the moderate view.

Section 1: Psychological Connectedness and Egoistical Concern
Following Sidgwick, one could ask the reductionist why the welfare of the future self should provide the earlier self with a reason for egoistical concern. 'Granted that the Ego is merely a system of coherent phenomena, that the permanent "I" is not a fact but a fiction, as Hume and his followers maintain: why then should one part of the series of feelings into which the Ego is resolved be concerned with another part of the same series, any more than with any other series?'[1]

But could we not ask the non-reductionist a similar question? Even if there is non-reductionist survival, even if there is a permanent 'Ego', why should I have egoistical concern for the future welfare of the Ego? One could reply that since I am the Ego, as long as this Ego exists, its welfare does provide me with a reason for egoistical concern. Perhaps one could take a sceptical line and deny the rationality of egoistical concern altogether. But given that it makes sense to have egoistical concern for my present welfare, it follows that it makes sense to have egoistical concern for my future welfare; for as there is a permanent (and simple) I or Ego, just as much of 'me' will be there in the future as there is now.

I do not deny that if reductionism is true, we may still have egoistical desires for our psycho-physical organism and even that such desires may promote some desirable utilitarian ends by helping to preserve human beings. What I do deny is that reductionist survival by itself (i.e. apart from the existence of corresponding desires) provides us with a reason for full-blooded egoistical concern.

I contend, largely for the reasons given by Parfit, that physical continuity is not even part of what matters on the reductionist view.[2] If this is so, the continuance of my psycho-physical organism does not by itself (i.e. apart from the existence of the corresponding desires) provide me with a reason for egoistical concern. I shall also argue, as against Parfit that psychological connectedness by itself does not provide us with a reason for egoistical concern, except perhaps in some very attenuated or trivial sense. Since neither physical continuity nor psychological connectedness nor a combination of the two[3] by itself provides us with a reason for egoistical concern, it follows that on the reductionist view, nothing by itself provides us with a reason for egoistical concern.

If fission or the creation of replicas were to occur, I would get converted to the reductionist view of persons, but not to the view that reductionist survival by itself (i. e. apart from the existence of current desires) provides me with a reason for egoistical concern.

Parfit claims that in some ways I can be better off if I undergo fission. I might want to be both a novelist and a philosopher. Ordinarily I will not have time to be both but if I undergo fission one of my offshoots could be a novelist, the other a philosopher.

There is the objection that this won't fulfil my egoistical ambitions, if my identity is destroyed. My egoistical ambition is that I should be a successful novelist. This ambition won't be fulfilled if I cease to exist and my offshoot writes a novel. Parfit replies that this objection assumes that there is a real question whether I shall be one of the resulting people, or the other or neither. He says this assumption is false. On the reductionist view, there are not different possibilities regarding what really happens. What really happens is given by the fact of fission. It is then up to us to choose the best description of what has happened. According to Parfit the best description is that neither of the offshoots will be me. We could give a different description, we could say that I shall be the resulting novelist, but of course there is no moral or rational significance in how we choose to describe the case. I cannot fulfil my ambition by calling the resulting person me.

I agree that on the reductionist view there is not a real question whether an offshoot is me. The real question is not whether one can survive one's fission, for clearly there is something absurd in the view that one survives until the time of fission but not afterwards. One clearly would live through one's fission.[4] The question is whether, if the reductionist view is the correct view, one survives in any deep sense, even before there is fission. The objection is that personal survival in any deep sense which provides a reason for egoistical concern is incompatible with the reductionist view.

Can one distinguish one's egoistic concerns from one's non-egoistic concerns without resorting to the notion of personal identity? Some reductionists think we can, for they think that what is ultimately important is survival, not personal identity. Parfit argues that what we value are the various relations between ourselves and others, whom and what we love, our ambitions, achievements, commitments, emotions, memories and so forth. But this still leaves the problem of distinguishing what we value from an egoistical point of view from what we value from an altruistic point of view. I have many projects, concerns etc. Some of these are altruistic ones, others are egoistical ones. Can this distinction be sustained on the reductionist view?

It might be argued that I can distinguish my egoistical concerns from my altruistic concerns in the following way: my egoistical concerns have selves that are psychologically connected with me (and are related to me from the inside, as it were) as their object, while non-egoistical concerns have others as their objects. This reply assumes rather than proves that my survival consists of psychological connectedness. A sceptic could say that I do not survive in my replica even though the replica will be psychologically connected with me; Parfit does not have a knock down argument against such a sceptic. But he maintains that though he cannot prove his position to be true, his position is a defensible and coherent one.

Even though talk of survival in terms of psychological connectedness involves a departure from our existing sense of survival (where survival presupposes personal identity and is a matter of all or nothing) could we not reconstruct the notion of survival in the way recommended by Parfit? It seems to me that the real question is whether such survival is relevant for our moral and prudential concerns. Can such survival provide a reason for egoistical concern? Is such survival relevant for purposes of distributive justice and for judgements of compensation and desert? I shall discuss these questions in this and in the following chapters.

There is a distinction between concern for my survival and concern for the projects and aims that I have and value. This distinction remains even though one of the reasons I want to survive is in order to fulfil the projects that I have. We could also distinguish among my projects and aims between the egoistical ones (i. e. those that have me and possibly my offshoots as their object) and the rest. Even after my death some of my altruistic projects can be carried out by others. The same is true of some of my egoistical projects. I may want good reputation and fame. After I die my friends may be able to do a lot to increase my posthumous reputation and fame by writing in my defence and so forth. Since some of my egoistical concerns can be promoted even after my death, it is reasonable for me now to be egoistically concerned for human beings who will look after my interests after my death. I do not have to think that I will survive in them, it will suffice that they will be promoting my interests. So even if I should be egoistically concerned with my replica, it does not follow that I shall survive in my replica.

We can now distinguish between primary egoistical concern which involves my survival from secondary egoistical concern which does not involve my survival. I can be egoistically concerned in the secondary sense with what my agent does for my interests after my death. One striking difference between the two cases is that in the case of secondary egoistical concern I egoistically care for the suffering of the agent only to the extent that it intereferes with the carrying out of the relevant projects, aims etc.[5] In the case of primary egoistical concern I care in an egoistical way about the pain that I apprehend and anticipate having in the future.[6] We can imagine a world where we only had primary egoistical concerns but no secondary egoistical concerns – in such a world people do not care about their posthumous reputations, interests and so forth. But we can't imagine a world where there was secondary egoistical concern but no primary egoistical concern. So secondary egoistical concern is parasitic on the primary one.

One can perhaps imagine a world where I care for my projects, plans etc. without caring, except in an instrumental sense, for the person who has these projects. But will such concern be egoistical? For such concern to be egoistical it is not enough that I should care for these projects but also that I should care for them because they promote my interests or bolster my ego. If I am concerned with the promotion of these projects because they promote the welfare of humanity, why is this egoistical concern?

No doubt one could still have egoistical desires if the reductionist view is true. But I suspect such desires are not rational, except in the instrumental sense. Instrumentally, one may justify my egoistical desires on the grounds that they help the survival of my psycho-physical organism. But there is no intrinsic rationality to such desires. Indeed, they are irrational, if the reductionist view is true, to the extent that they assume falsely that the non-reductionist view is correct. Later in this chapter, I shall argue that the reductionist view cannot justify the reflexive element in the phenomenology of egoistical concern.

On the reductionist view, ordinary survival is not any better than survival in one's replica. Even if this is so, it does not follow that on the reductionist view I should have egoistical concern for my replica. For it may be, as the Buddhists would argue, that it is not rational to have egoistical concern at all on the reductionist view, neither for my replica nor in the ordinary cases. Might not the replica example be used as a *reductio ad absurdum* of the view that there is personal survival on the reductionist view?

It is true that on the reductionist view my future self could carry out my projects but why does this provide any reason for primary egoistical concern? True, the future self can finish my unfinished projects but as Parfit is aware, such concern is like concern for someone who can in various ways act on my behalf. This can be seen most clearly in the case of my replica. Thus if I am writing a book and love a woman, then I can have a special interest in the survival of my replica for he can finish my book and the woman can continue to receive the love. One can hand over one's projects and one's woman to one's replica as one hands over a baton in a relay race. But why should I have any primary egoistical concern for the suffering of the replica?

There is this difference that the replica will have memories (from the inside) of what my life was like, and will also remember (from the inside) what my intentions were, and so the replica could carry out my intentions in a different way from the way an ordinary agent would. Such facts may explain why I may feel closer to my replica than to an ordinary agent. But even if as a result I care more for the future suffering of the replica than of the agent, it is not clear that this concern is more like egoistical concern. It could be that I have more sympathy for the suffering of someone who is closer to me. In fact in some cases one may feel greater sympathy for the agent's future suffering, for instance if the agent is my child, while the replica is someone who has not yet come into existence. The important point is that one would not anticipate or apprehend the sufferings of the replica in the way that one does one's own suffering. This can be seen most clearly if one were to create the replica oneself and continue to exist along with the replica. My concern for the replica will be felt as altruistic concern in a way in which my concern for the person who continues to survive in my body will not.

Parfit says that if the reductionist view is true, then ordinary survival is no better than survival in the replica. But to this it could be replied that as a result of evolution we have an egoistical concern for our psycho-physical organisms and not for the replica. On the reductionist view, we can take our egoistical concern as a brute datum and try to match our ideas of personal survival to it. If we feel egoistical concern for the future of our psychological organism but not for our replica, this is one reason (according to individual ascriptivism) for ascribing our survival to the former but not to the latter. Even Parfit admits (while discussing tele-transportation) that we do tend to identify ourselves with our psycho-physical organism in a way in which we do not with our replica. But he thinks that this is irrational; we should try to decondition ourselves from such prejudices.

But now Parfit is on the horns of a dilemma. If reductionism is true, either we should decondition ourselves in which case we should adopt the extreme Buddhists sage-like stance, rise above our desires and abandon egoistic concern. Or one regards oneself as a creature of desire (in the way that Hume does) and in that event we should regard the fact that we specially care for our psycho-physical organism in a way in which we don't for our replica as a brute datum. I shall come back to this problem later.

Parfit believes that it is defensible to contend that psychological connectedness *by itself* provides us with a reason for egoistical concern. And he points out that my concern for the future (on the reductionist view) corresponds to the degree of connectedness between me now and my future self. Since connectedness is nearly always weaker over longer periods, I can rationally care less about my future.[7]

If we grant that psychological connectedness by itself provides us with a reason for egoistical concern, then it will follow that we should have egoistical concern for our replica. But Parfit's argument for the view that psychological connectedness by itself provides us with a reason for egoistical concern is a weak one. He argues by elimination. He shows that physical continuity by itself does not provide a reason for egoistical concern. For if I lost all psychological connectedness I would not worry in an egoistical way about the fate of the future self who lives in the body continuous with mine.[8]

Those who have stressed the physical criteria of survival have to face the problem that a person would survive even if large parts of his body are replaced. Is it then that enough of the brain must continue if I am to survive? But why is the brain so crucial? Is it not because it is the carrier of psychological connectedness (and continuity)? But in that case if a duplicate brain could replace the existing one, provided there was psychological connectedness one should survive. If bits of my brain were replaced by replicas of these bits, and the psychological traits remained unaffected, there would be survival. If the whole of the brain (or even whole of the body) were destroyed at once, and a replica created then there would be survival, if the psychological features remained unaffected. For the difference between replacing the brain (or the body) bit by bit, and replacing it all at once is not important. And if the replica was created and the original was not destroyed, then too there is survival (though identity is lost). For it is difficult to deny that there is survival in this case while admitting that there is survival in the case where the original was destroyed.[9]

Some such considerations have led Parfit to the view what matters in survival is psychological connectedness and that we would survive not only in our offshoots that are physically continuous with us but even in our replicas. Physical continuity is not even part of what fundamentally matters for egoistical concern.

It has been objected that Parfit's views are implausible in the case of certain people, such as ballet dancers and boxers, for whom the body has great importance. But such objections are based on a misunderstanding. Parfit does not deny the importance of the body. Indeed psychological characteristics are often expressed through the body. But such considerations only show that we need we need a certain type of body, not a particular body. If a boxer could have another body qualitatively identical to his present one, but numerically different from it, why should he (assuming he survives) be any worse off as a boxer?

A non-reductionist might reply that I do not only want that my aims and projects should be fulfilled. It is essential for my egoistical desire for survival that I should continue to exist. And if some physical part of me is essential for my continuing to exist, then it does matter for personal survival that that part should continue to exist. But if one abandons the non-reductionist view then the force of this reply will be undermined.

Parfit's argument against the view that I am my brain (as well as against other versions of the physicalist criterion of personal identity) are better against the reductionist version of the view that I am my brain (or body) than against the non-reductionist version. I believe this partly for the reason given in the previous paragraph. And partly because I think the earlier argument that we just discussed, where we compare the creation of a replica with the bit by bit transfer of another brain, works better against the reductionist version than against the non-reductionist version of the physicalist criterion. Parfit thinks this argument works against Nagel's non-reductionist view that I am my brain. As I said in chapter 7, Nagel has made his view unnecessarily vulnerable by denying that one would survive in one's replica. He would then have to face the absurd consequence that we would not survive in the replica but we would survive in the bit by bit transfer case.

In my view the non-reductionist who wants to defend the view that I am my brain should say that things such as the bit by bit transfer of another brain and the creation of replicas are not possible. If it turns out that such things are possible, he should then abandon his views and embrace the reductionist view; if such things turn out to be possible then one could use the replica case and the bit by bit transfer case to show that the view that I am my brain is not plausible. I think one can make a good case for the view, on Parfit's line, that if one becomes a reductionist, the psychological version is the more plausible version.

Parfit has not succeeded in showing that psychological connectedness by itself provides grounds for primary egoistical concern. For if he is right (as I think he is) in his view that, at any rate on the on the reductionist view, physical continuity by itself does not provide grounds for (primary) egoistical concern, and even if he is right in his view that physical continuity is not even part of what fundamentally matters from the egoistical point of view, it would not follow that psychological connectedness by itself provides a reason for (primary) egoistical concern. For it could be (as I suspect is the case) that on the reductionist view nothing by itself provides us with a reason for egoistical concern.

What is possible is to combine reductionism with the existence of egoistical desires.[10] We have egoistical concern for our psycho-physical organism. This is not to say that the survival of my organism by itself provides me with a reason for egoistical concern; but simply that I am so constructed (as a result of evolution) that I have a strong desire to care for and identify with my psycho-physical organism. The view that the existence of my organism by itself provides me with a reason for egoistical concern would imply that I would have such a reason even if I did not have the desire to care for my organism. Compare; some philosophers believe that if another person is suffering and if I can relieve this suffering without much trouble, then there is a reason for me to relieve his suffering, quite apart from any desire that I may have to relieve his suffering.[11]

Even if I did not have the corresponding desires, it is plausible to argue that the existence of my psycho-physical organism would provide me with a reason for concern. It does not follow that such concern would be egoistical concern.

Being creatures of evolution, we have a strong desire to look after our psycho-physical organisms. Moreover, the concern for the future suffering of our organism is felt as egoistical concern, for we apprehend the future suffering of our organism as falling on us in the future. So there clearly is a sense in which we care egoistically for our psycho-physical organism. And as a matter of fact most of us would not feel the same way towards our replica. Parfit grants this is the case, but thinks this attitude is irrational. He thinks that physical continuity is only important if and when it is necessary for psychological connectedness. Its importance lies in bringing about its effect, which is psychological connectedness. If and when the effect can be brought about without the normal cause, we should not miss the normal cause.

But from the evolutionary point of view, our egoistic concern is for the psycho-physical organism. Parfit wants us to reflect upon such allegedly hard facts about human desires. He thinks that upon reflection we will realize that there is no relevant difference between the case where we survive in our normal bodies and the case of the replica.

But we must not reflect half-heartedly. Either we just accept our desires as a brute fact and forget about reflection, and at that level there is a difference between our psycho-physical organism and the replica. Or we reflect thoroughly and in that case we shall realize (for the reasons given in this chapter) that the reductionist view, at any rate of the Parfit variety, is not compatible with our egoistical hopes and fears. Indeed, Parfit's argument, that on the reductionist view ordinary survival is little better than survival in a replica, can probably be reconstructed to provide a *reductio ad absurdum* of the view that reductionist survival provides a reason for (primary) egoistical concern.

Parfit asks us to imagine the following case. I can go to Mars by a spaceship, preserving my brain and body. This would involve ordinary survival. Alternatively, there is teletransportation which involves the destruction of my brain and body on earth and the creation of a replica of mine on Mars, which involves the creation out of new matter of a brain and body exactly like mine. Before the destruction of my brain and body, the exact states of all my cells were recorded. The replica was created with the help of this information.

Parfit rightly thinks that judged from the standpoint of non-reductionist view, ordinary survival on the reductionist view is little better than being destroyed and having a replica. He concludes from this that it would be irrational to pay much more for a conventional spaceship journey. But it would be wrong to infer from this that psychological connectedness by itself provides us with a reason for egoistical concern. Judged from the standpoint of the non-reductionist view, ordinary reductionist survival is indeed no better the being destroyed and having a replica; but that is because in neither case is there genuine survival of the kind that provides a reason for (primary) egoistical concern.

Judged from the point of view of Humean-rationality, i. e. rationality that is primarily concerned with the satisfaction of our desires, there is a difference between ordinary survival where we identify with our future selves and survival in a replica where we do not so identify. If one tries to improve upon Humean rationality by using our reflective powers, then we shall be driven to the Buddhist conclusion that on the reductionist view nothing by itself (i. e. apart from the existence of desires) provides a reason for egoistical concern.

Can Parfit properly distinguish what we value from an egoistical point of view from what we value in general? According to him my survival is determined by the survival of the psychological features that I have. This clearly implies that my altruistic aims and goals also constitute my survival. For my altruistic goals are mine in the sense that these goals are mine, part of my psychology, even though I am not the object of these goals. If psychological connectedness by itself provides me with a reason for egoistical concern, then since my altruistic aims are also part of my psychology, their presence too could provide me with a reason for egoistical concern. But this is odd. I can be very concerned now about my altruistic aims and goals in the future, but such concern is not egoistical concern. Not all my fundamental concerns are egoistical concerns. I might value above all the welfare of humanity. It does not follow that the welfare of humanity provides me with a reason for egoistical concern.

It might be replied that on any view it is difficult to distinguish one's egoistical concerns from altruistic ones. Thus, if I have altruistic aims such as the welfare of humanity, I may still have an egoistical interest in achieving my aims which include my altruistic aims. Egoistical concern is a second order notion that takes our aims as given and is concerned with their satisfaction.

But this is not the whole story. My egoistical concern is not just with promoting and satisfying my aims; it is also concerned with doing so in order to promote the interests of my self. The interest of my self does not wholly consist in satisfying the aims of the self; some of my aims (including some of my altruistic aims) may be quite destructive of my self-interest, as when I aim to sacrifice myself for the sake of other people. A no-self view which regards egoistical concern as derivative from one's aims and preferences is unable to sustain the *rationality* of the distinction between egoistional concern and altruistic concern. Whereas if one believes in the self, then one can make the distinction, by pointing out that egoistical concern is motivated primarily by the interest of one self, while altruistic concern is concerned with promoting the interests of other selves. This does not show that the existence of the self is necessary to mark the distinction. It could suffice that we believe in the self. But if our belief is false, then though we may continue to make the distinction between egoistical and altruistic concern, we shall be carrying on with an illusion.

Some Humeans would regard such an illusion as a psychologically necessary illusion. Buddhists would regard the illusion as something from which we should try to decondition ourselves. Parfit too wants to base our morality and practical life on truths, not errors, yet he thinks that it is not irrational to retain egoistical concern. For he thinks that it is defensible to argue that egoistical concern as a whole does not rest on an illusion, though he thinks that the view that we should care equally for all parts of our future does rest on the non-reductionist view, which is false. On his view, once we adopt the reductionist view, we could, without any irrationality, have more egoistical concern for our future selves in the near future than in the remote future.

On the reductionist view, if I want to survive in the future I should preserve my psychology and my values but many of us would not place such high value on such survival. In many cases I have certain aims and goals that I value highly, what I want is to fulfil these goals, rather than to preserve them indefinitely. In many cases once one's goals have been achieved one moves on to other goals. In some cases even when we do not achieve our goals, we may want to move on to other goals. Those who value reductionist survival highly would be involved in an attempt at freezing their psychology and values. If this is what survival is, why value it so highly? If this is what survival is, is it not rational to adopt the Buddhist approach, and abandon egoistical concern? This would be consistent with retaining concern for our aims, values, commitments etc.

Our attitudes towards our children also shows that we do not value reductionist survival all that much. Thus if we love our children, we should want them to develop their nature and wonderful potential; we should not want them to retain their present views and aims indefinitely. In pathological cases the child remains mentally a child even when he is an adult. The pathological case survives in the reductionist sense much longer than the normal child does. But we would think that if the child who is a pathological case could be cured, then it would be in his interest to become like a normal child who will develop and mature when he grows up.

Perhaps reductionists should use survival in some broader sense, to include not just one's actual projects, aims, dispositions, etc, but one's potential ones too. So that when a child grows and evolves into adulthood and some of his potential is realised, he has in a sense not altered so much, it is just that some of the characteristics that were there in potential form are now there in actual form. I shall discuss this suggestion in chapter 10, section 2.

In the case of many aims and goals, commitment to them involves a long term undertaking. But even here in some cases, what one wants done can be achieved by other people. Thus if I want to contribute to the welfare of humanity, why worry much about my survival rather than the survival of others who are more fitted to achieve such a goal. Do I worry about my extinction only to the extent that other human beings cannot in fact fulfil my goals, aims, commitments as well as I could?[12] Do I not also worry about my extinction even when other human beings could fulfil my goals? In some cases they may fulfil my goals better than I can e.g. when I am old and decrepit and my fellow workers are young and vigorous. I may be sad at the prospect of death not because others cannot fulfil my aims but because I love life!

To be sure, survival on the reductionist view also involves survival of one's memories, and other character traits. But it is not clear why such survival should provide a reason for primary egoistical concern. When memories of my present experiences are preserved in the future, it does not follow that the present experiences themselves are preserved in the future or that I am preserved in the future. Even after a human being dies, the memory of his present conduct can be preserved by other people. The difference is that my future self remembers from the inside, it remembers what is was like to have that experience. Such inside knowledge is lost when I die. But why get egoistically worked up about the loss of such knowledge of my present experiences? Parfit himself sees the force of similar considerations in his section on liberation from the self which I discuss later in this chapter.

Parfit claims that nothing is lost if my body is destroyed and an exact replica is created. But why not create a superior of mine rather than a replica, the superior being a person who shares some of my fundamental goals but can achieve them much better than I can? Or why not create several partial replicas, so that the different replicas can pursue different goals with much greater efficiency due to a division of labour. Is it that I have a desire that the several goals should be pursued by one character with the relevant memories and dispositions? If such a desire is to count as (primary) egoistical desire is it not essential to add that I should be that character?

Non-reductionists could admit that in many cases what is important from the egoistical point of view is not just that my various goals should be pursued, not just that they should be pursued by one character, but that I should be that character. But on the reductionist view where identity is not ultimately important, such sentiments are based on an illusion. It would follow that (primary) egoistical concern too is based on an illusion. The reductionist cannot account for what is distinctive about such concern. The Buddhist view, which regards egoistical concern as based on an illusion, is more plausible than Parfit's moderate view.

On the reductionist view what fundamentally matters for personal survival is psychological connectedness. There are degrees of survival corresponding to degrees of psychological connectedness. As my aims and goals change, I survive less and less in the future. But as Parfit rightly points out out, not all goals and aims have equal importance. I value some goals very highly, other goals I value less highly, and some of my goals I value negatively. Thus I may be ashamed of some of my goal-directed activities such as going to drunken orgies. This normative view involves a kind of personal ascriptivism. For how far I survive in a future self will depend partly upon how far I value some of the psychological traits that persist. On this view the extent of my egoistical concern now about suffering of my future self will depend partly on my attitude now, not just my attitude towards the suffering but towards the psychological traits of my future self. On this view I can get less concerned now about the suffering of my future self, not just by adopting a philosophical attitude towards such suffering, but by adopting a critical attitude towards some of my goals that will persist in the future self.

Individual ascriptivism and reductionism go naturally with the view that egoistical concern is part of the determinant of whether I survive. If the extent to which I now identify with my future goals (by being being proud or ashamed of them) determines the extent to which I survive in the future, it is arbitrary not to allow that the extent to which to which I identify now, by having egoistical concern, with my future suffering and pleasures also determines the extent to which I shall survive. Having egoistical concern for my suffering (and happiness) in the future is at least as good a way of identifying with my future self, as taking a positive normative stance towards the goals of my future self.

If the above argument is correct, then there is yet another problem for the view that psychological connectedness (which constitutes survival) by itself provides us with a reason for egoistical concern. For on the reductionist view the truth would seem to be that it is my concern that helps to determine my survival (or psychological connectedness), rather than that my survival provides me with a reason for concern. Perhaps it could be replied that both views are correct, that egoistical concern partly determines personal survival, yet there are other determinants of survival, and to the extent that survival is determined by these other factors, psychological connectedness by itself can provide a reason for egoistical concern.

But what are these determinants? Presumably, they are memories, dispositions, intentions and so forth. But not all memories, intentions and dispositions count for the same. Some are more important than others. So normative considerations come in here too. Moreover, bare memories, even memories from the inside, do not seem enough to constitute survival. On the non-reductionist view they are evidence of the persistence of a permanent ego or self. On the reductionist view, suppose one remembers from the inside something that was done by a personality in the past, but one does not identify with it, as sometimes happens in the multiple personality cases; then such rememberings, by themselves, do not provide one with a reason for believing that the person whose actions are being remembered has survived in one to any substantial degree. Reductionist survival requires identification, either with the person concerned or at least with his values or with his joys and his suffering, or with his remembered conduct. Since this is so, it is trivially true that one is concerned about the interests of the future selves with which one identifies. Since on the reductionist view it is our egoistical concern which determines whether we survive, reductionist survival does not provide us with any reason for egoistical concern.

It might be suggested that one could give a non-ascriptive, value-free sense of survival. But I do not see how a reductionist can succeed in doing this. For it would be absurd to be democratic and give equal weight to all memories, dispositions and projects, however trivial. A non-reductionist could provide a value-free sense of survival. For if survival is explained in terms of persistence of the same permanent self or ego, and since survival on this view does not admit of degrees, we do not need norms or values to deal with the problem regarding what weight to give different factors in measuring the degree of survival. Since on the non-reductionist view, survival can be explained without appealing to our values and identifications, it will not be circular to claim that our survival can provide a reason for egoistical concern. Nor is this a trivial truth. It is a controversial claim which could be challenged by the sceptic. For a sceptic who admits that I am a permanent self but denies that I have a special reason for being concerned about my present pains merely because they are my pains, could deny that I have a special reason for being concerned with my future pains.

Section 2: Reductionism, Egoistical Concern and Groups
Philosophers have drawn different practical conclusions from the

reductionist view. Broadly we may distinguish three sorts of reactions.

Firstly there is the radical liberating reaction of the Buddhists who stressed that since there is no substantial ego, egoism is irrational. And once one realizes this truth, not just intellectually but also emotionally, one will cease to live a selfish life and become serene and detached and sage-like.

Secondly there is the conservative reaction of philosophers such as Hume and Shoemaker. On their view practical life remains and should remain much the same as before. Philosophical reflection has little power to change human nature.

Thirdly there is the moderate reaction, found in Parfit's book, which adopts a position between the radical one and the conservative one. Parfit stresses some of the liberating effects of giving up the non-reductionist view. He thinks that on the reductionist view there would still be a difference between his life and the life of others, but the difference would become less. The wall between him and others is removed. When he believed the non-reductionist view the air he breathed was stuffy, life seemed like a glass tunnel at the end of which there was darkness. Now he lives in the open air, and death has lost some of its terror. Indeed terror has lost some of its terror.

Parfit cares less about his death because, on the reductionist view, death means only that there will be no experiences that will be 'connected to my present experiences by chains of such direct connections as those involved in experience memory or in the carrying out of an earlier intention'. There will remain other experiences that will be less directly related to my present experiences. There will be memories of my life, and there may be thought and actions that are influenced by my thoughts and ideas and advice.[13]

The prospect of terror becomes less terrifying. For suppose I have to face some torture in the future or some suffering, then I can reflect on the fact that all that this means is that there will be suffering that will be related in certain ways to my present experiences. The reductionist does not regard the view that the person suffering will be me as a deep truth.

Such considerations can be used to liberate ourselves not only from the fear of distant suffering but even from the fear of suffering in the immediate future. Parfit is aware of this. Indeed the example he gives is of an immediate operation that he is about to undergo.

Should we then not go further and argue not just (as Parfit does) that the reductionist view is partly liberating but that it wholly liberating from egoistical concerns? What reason is there for stopping midway and not going all the way with the extreme Buddhist view and abandon egoism altogether? Parfit points out that the liberating effects that he discusses are only partly liberating because they only briefly stun our natural egoistical concern for the future. Buddhists would claim, as against Parfit, that human beings can decondition themselves to a greater extent. Be that as it may, Parfit is confronted with the dilemma that I pointed out earlier. One either adopts a Humean view and argues that one cannot decondition oneself or an extreme Buddhist view.

To be accurate, there are positions in between such as the moderate version of the Humean view which claims that philosophical reflection can partly decondition us.[14] We can argue that to the extent that we can't decondition ourselves we are conservative Humeans, to the extent that we can decondition ourselves we should go in the direction of abandoning egoistical concern. But Parfit's view that psychological connectedness by itself provides us with a reason for egoistical concern, implies that even if we could decondition ourselves from our brute desires, psychological connectedness would provide us with a reason for egoistic concern. His excellent section on 'Liberation of the Self' has arguments which can be extended to undermine his view that psychological connectedness by itself provides us with a reason for egoistic concern. For his arguments in that section can be extended to show that we should abandon egoistic concern to the extent that we can, whereas his view that psychological connectedness by itself provides us with a reason for egoistic concern, implies that we should have egoistical concern even when we can decondition ourselves from our desiring nature.

The arguments that Parfit advances for the liberation of the self can be used not just to liberate ourselves from the fear of pain and death in the more remote future but even to liberate ourselves from pain and death in the near future. Thus if I am to be tortured tomorrow I could say that (on the reductionist view) all this implies is that there will be a lot of suffering tomorrow which will be related in certain ways to my present experiences. As Parfit would say 'Does this matter all that much?' Why not go even further and ask: Does it matter at all from the (primary) egoistical point of view? As long as the suffering does not interfere with the implementation of my projects, why is such suffering a reason for egoistical concern?

Of course to the extent that we are conditioned creatures we shall worry in an egoistical way about such suffering. And to the extent that we can give a justification of such conditioning (e. g. that it helps in the survival of human beings) the existence of egoistical concern with regard to our future selves is instrumentally rational, even on a reductionist view. But this sort of instrumental (or means-ends) justification is quite different from the view that psychological connectedness by itself provides us with a reason for *egoistical* concern.

Some would say that egoistical concern has survival value and that it is not desirable to eliminate it completely, as some Buddhist sages would have us do. It might be replied that even if human beings do not have egoistical concern for their future selves, they would still survive and even flourish, for they could have sympathetic concern for their future selves and moral concern. So egoistical concern is redundant. Against this it could be pointed out that there is a limit to which our altruistic sympathies can be relied upon to look after our future selves. Self-love is in general a stronger passion than sympathy (and the desire to do what is moral) and is in general a more reliable method of looking after the interests of our future selves (especially in the more distant future, for our sympathy is less easily awakened by individuals who are far away in space or in time). If I apprehend that I might be tortured in the future, I am much more likely to try to avoid it, than if I look at things in an altruistic way (or moral way) and sympathise with the self who will be tortured. Indeed on some views sympathy is parasitic on self-love in the sense that I sympathise with others because I imagine what it would be like for me to be in their condition. If I did not have self-love such imagination would not move me to sympathise with others.

On the reductionst view egoistical concern would be there as a brute datum. And it might also be justified in instrumental terms (i.e. that it fulfils a useful role in our survival and flourishing) but none of this would show that there is an intrinsic fittingness between any form of reductionist survival (such as psychological connectedness) and egoistical concern.

Of course, talk of survival in some sense is compatible with the reductionist view. We can talk of survival of cars, nations, machines and many other things without presupposing that they survive in some deep non-reductionist sense. Cars don't have selves, and yet survive, So too individual human beings could be said to survive even if they had no self or ego. But this sense of survival by itself does not provide a reason for egoistical concern. We can talk of the survival of a nation and of its welfare but not of its egoistical concern, unless we believe that a nation has a self or an ego.

Take a group of people travelling in a bus. This group is interested in its survival in the sense that the people travelling want to survive as individuals. Let us call such survival, survival of the group qua individuals. One could also talk of survival of this group in a second sense, so that if the group were to break up and the individuals go their separate ways, the group would not survive. Let us call such survival, survival of the group qua group. Many are not interested in surviving in this second sense. Some are. Nations are usually interested in surviving in this sense.

When we talk of survival of a group qua group, we do not (at least not normally) talk of egoistical concern. We talk of Britain's interests, even of Britain's acting in its self-interest; but we do not talk of Britain's egoistical concern. This is not because Britain has a self but no ego!

Even when groups of persons are concerned about the survival of the group qua group, such concern does not lead to egoistical concern on the part of the group. It may lead to egoistical concern on the part of individuals who comprise the group. Thus a person may see himself very much as part of a group, such that the group's survival is essential to his own flourishing; so he has egoistical concern. But the group of persons qua group does not have egoistical concerns.

If individual persons are groups (as they are on the bundle theory of the self), can the group that constitutes a person have egoistical concerns any more than Britain can have egoistical concerns? True, the British have egoistical concern on the old fashioned theory of persons, in the sense that individual Britons have egoistical concerns. But in the case of persons, if the bundle theory is correct, the group or bundle consists of individual items of experience. And how can individual items of experience have egoistical concerns? Parfit thinks that at any given time I have egoistical concern. Perhaps he thinks that at any given time it is the set of experiences of a person at that time that has egoistical concern.

In one of his articles Parfit says 'It would be barbarous to speak of the interests of me now.'[15] But he thinks that one can (on the reductionist view) talk of my present point of view. Even if he is right about this, it does not follow that the reductionist can rationally distinguish my present egoistical concerns (or point view) from my present altruistic concerns (or point of view).

There is not anything it is like to be a group or a bundle. There is not anything it is like to be Britain, though there is something it is like to be John Smith. We do sometimes talk of a group's emotions, but these terms can be cashed in terms of the emotions of its members in certain relation to each other. A group does not have concern for its survival except in the sense that its members who are individuals have concern for the survival of the group in one or both of the senses of a group's survival that we distinguished earlier. But now if a person is really a group, then it too would be a bundle, a mere logical construct, and it would not have concerns. It could not have concerns in the sense that its members have concerns, for individual items of experience do not have concerns. If the bundle theory is correct then there is not anything it is like to be a person. Parfit allows that there are persons who have emotions, commit acts etc. but on his theory this is merely a manner of speaking; a person does not have emotions in any but a trivial sense. So how can a person have a reason for egoistical concern?

If the reductionist theory is correct, and emotion is itself a part of the bundle, egoistical concern exists but there is no subject of this concern (in any deep sense). Neither the persons nor any set of present experiences can be subjects of such concerns (in any deep sense) for there is no subject (except as a manner of speaking). On the reductionist theory, talk of persons is convenient, but it is eliminable. All truths can be stated without talking of persons. But how can the view that reductionist survival (e.g. in the form of psychological connectedness) by itself provides persons with a reason for egoistical concern, be stated without the language of persons?

The Humean view of rationality, where rationality is concerned with serving our passions, is compatible with the bundle theory of the self. Even if individual items of experience are the ultimate constituents of the world, we can distinguish behaviour that serves the passions from behaviour that does not. If my passion is for an apple, going up a pear tree (rather than an apple tree) is not a rational way of satisfying my passion. But if one appeals to rationality in some stronger sense, such as the Kantian sense where Reason can provide us with grounds for action, quite apart from the existence of corresponding desires, then it is persons who are subject to Reason.

Parfit has a problem that he is not aware of. He follows Hume's bundle theory of the self, but also appeals to a view of rationality that goes beyond Humean rationality. He would need to show that a bundle of experiences, a mere logical construct, can be subject to Reason. He might argue that groups such as nations are not persons yet they are subject to Reason. The suffering of the Third World provides America with a reason for action, quite apart from the existence of American desires to alleviate such suffering. But is this not because America consists of individual persons in certain relations to each other, living in a certain territory? Ultimately it is such persons who are subject to Reason. From the fact that a group of persons (on the non-reductionist theory of persons) can be subject to Reason, it does follow that persons themselves would be subject to Reason if persons were groups of items of experience.

It might be suggested that on the reductionist theory, it is not the bundle that is subject to Reason, but individual items of experience that are subject to Reason. But how can this be? An important feature of egoistical concern, unlike altruistic concern is that it is reflexive. The individual agent who is the subject of concern is also (at least part of) the object of concern. This difference from altruistic concern is reflected in the phenomenology of egoistical concern; since it is directed at onself, egoistical concern feels quite different from altruistic concern. Can the relevant difference be preserved on the reductionist view?

The reductionist view cannot justify the reflexive element in the phenomenology of egoistical concern.[16] On the reductionist view the agent or the person who has egoistical concern is eliminable; we use the language of persons because it is convenient, but it is only a manner of speaking. All truths can be stated without the use of terms like person, agent, subject of experience. But how do we state the truth that a person has egoistical fear or that a person has a reason for egoistical fear about some future suffering that will be inflicted upon him?

Is it that on the reductionist view the egoistical concern is felt (or should be felt) by an item of experience? But in that case for there to be phenomenological similarity to the old fashioned egoistical concern (i.e. egoistical concern on the non-reductionist view) the item of experience should feel concern for itself in the future. But that is impossible, for on the reductionist view an item of experience will not normally last into the future, and its concern would be for other items of experience. So the concern won't be reflexive. Or is it that on the reductionist view, the bundle of experiences feels concern for itself? But this is impossible. A bundle is not the sort of thing that can feel concern, let alone concern for itself; there is not anything it is like to be a bundle. On the bundle theory an item of experience qua member of the bundle can feel concern for another member of the same bundle, so does this not capature the reflexive element in egoistical concern? No, because such concern is, in its phenomenology, more akin to altruistic concern than to old fashioned egoistical concern. For qua member of a group, such as a nation, family or club, I can feel concern for other members of the group; this does not make the concern egoistical. For a group does not experience concern, its members do. Britain does not experience egoistical concern, for it does not experience anything. Individual Britons, when they act as Britons, can feel concern for fellow Britons, but such concern is not egoistical.[17] Similarly, if the bundle theory is correct, even when individual members of the bundle, qua members of the bundle, feel concern for other members of the same bundle, this does not make the concern egoistical in its flavour.

A reductionist could mark the distinction between egoistical concern and altruistic concern in the following way. Egoistical concern is there when an item of experience is concerned with another item of experience (or set of such items) because it is psychologically related to it; whereas altruistic concern is there when it is concerned for an item of experience (or set of experiences) that is not so related to it. But the phenomenological quality of egoistical concern and altruistic concern won't be very different here. A reductionist might argue that the former will be more intense, but this is not always so. One sometimes feels more intense concern for the suffering of one's children than for one's own suffering.

The crucial phenomenological distinction between old fashioned egoistical concern and altruistic concern is that in the former case the subject of experience can project himself forward into the future and anticipate the future suffering as something that will fall upon him. The subject of experience here is not eliminable.

The reductionist view cannot justify (primary) egoistical concern, but it is compatible with an explanation of how the belief in the non-reductionist view causes us to have the illusion of an ego, and hence of egoistical concern. The Buddhists did not, any more than Parfit, deny the existence of egoistical concern, but they thought, unlike the moderate Parfit, that such concern is based on an illusion. I believe in this respect they were right about the implications of the reductionist view.

The reductionists may also try to justify egoistical concern in the sense that they could try to show that egoistical concern (though it is based on an illusion) fulfils a useful rule by helping us to survive. The Buddhists thought that far from being useful, belief in the ego is the cause of our sorrows.

Some reductionists such as Mackie[18] have thought that our egoistical concern fulfils a useful role in helping human beings to survive and flourish. Mackie fails to realize that on the reductionist view egoistical concern is based on an illusion, even if belief in it has useful effects.

Section 3: Reductionism and the quest for Nirvana

One can distinguish two senses of ego (or self) - the empirical ego (or self) and the metaphysical ego (or self). We say of pompous people that they have big egos. Many of us believe that human beings would be better off if they did not have such big egos; self-centredness is self-destructive. According to the paradox of hedonism if you chase after happiness you won't find it. There is a similar paradox of the self, if you remain obsessed with your empirical self, with your petty goals, ambitions etc. you will destroy yourself. Sages such as Krishnamurti tell us how to dissolve the ego; then there is joy, understanding, love, a sense of wholeness. This is a profound truth. But it is wrong to infer that this involves a denial or dissolution of the metaphysical ego (or self).

The metaphysical ego or self is not something that is different from the person, it is the person on the non-reductionist view. The view that the self is primary is the same as the view that persons (in the non-reductionist sense) are primary in the sense explained in chapter 1. It is compatible to hold that persons are irreducibly primary and to admit that we should dissolve our empirical egos.

One of the profound insights of some of the great religious teachers is that one must die in order to live. It implies that one must surrender one's self-centred existence, one's petty egoistical aims, jealousies, materialistic goals, and care more for others. It is when we cease to be egoistical that we achieve not just happiness but a sense of wholeness and union with others.

It might at first sight be thought that this view goes more naturally with the reductionist view rather than the non-reductionist view. For the reductionist view allows a person to die and be succeeded by another while the same human body persists. When there is sufficient break in psychological connectedness, one person gives way to another. On the non-reductionist view the same person persists in spite of a change of personality, so how can we die in order to live on such a view?

But this involves a superficial understanding of the doctrine of dying in order to live. The doctrine does not tell me to die so that another person lives (a view which is perhaps compatible with the reductionist view) but to die so that I might live. What dies is my empirical ego, my selfish life style; but I remain. This view presupposes a distinction between my empirical ego and my metaphysical or true self. The person (in the sense of the metaphysical self) can persist even though the empirical ego has dissolved; indeed it could start to flourish when the empirical ego has dissolved.

On the reductionist view there is no such distinction.[19] The destruction of my empirical self involves my destruction. The way for me to preserve myself is to perpetuate my empirical ego. What a dismal prospect! Although Parfit points out some liberating effects of his doctrine, his moderate version of reductionism has the curiously depressing consequence, that the way to survive involves the freezing of one's psychology.

Perhaps one should not be surprised to find the reductionist view to be both depressing and liberating. The fact that survival on such a view is such a depressing prospect, provides one with the one reason for trying to liberate oneself. The Buddhists in this respect seem more consistent than the moderate Parfit. For they think that we should liberate ourselves as much as we can from our conditioned nature. Parfit on the other hand thinks that egoistical concern is not irrational. But even the Buddhists are involved in the paradox that they cannot explain why I should concern myself with my liberation. Nor, as we have seen in chapter 4, can they explain why the Law of Karma is just.

In Mahayana Buddhism, the Buddhisattva works for the salvation of everyone rather than for his own. He postpones entry into Nirvana until he has helped to save others. Indeed, there is the paradox that the Buddhisattva cannot enter Nirvana before saving others; for if he were to, that would be a selfish act and he would not be a Buddhisattva. But if he is selfless, then again he cannot enter Nirvana, for he must wait till he has helped all the others.[20]

One way out of this paradox would be for everyone to enter Nirvana together; but this would involve waiting till the last human being has been saved. It seems to me that a quicker way out of this paradox could be that the Buddhisattva enters Nirvana, but not as a result of an act of his. The Buddha was supposed to have had a choice regarding whether or not to enter Nirvana. But suppose some enlightened souls have no choice; suppose as a result of enlightenment they automatically enter Nirvana. This would not involve a selfish act, since it would not be a proper act.

It might be suggested that the problem of why, if there is no permanent self, I should seek my enlightenment rather than other people's, can be answered as follows. If I experience sorrow, I have a direct reason for trying to remove it; one's sorrow by itself is, almost by definition, something one wants to remove. Admittedly even other people's sorrow provides me with a reason for helping them. But if I am ignorant of my nature and consequently full of sorrow, I cannot help others in their quest for self-knowledge and enlightenment. I first need to attain enlightenment, only then can I tell others how to achieve it.

This reply is not foolproof. Cannot a psychotherapist treat others even when he does know how to treat himself? Cannot a tennis coach teach his pupil to become a great tennis player, even though he (the coach) cannot train himself to become so good? Even in the sphere of knowledge, cannot someone like Socrates act as a midwife and help others to attain knowledge even when the midwife himself does not have the knowledge?

Perhaps, spiritual enlightenment is different in that one needs to attain it before one can help others to do so. For it requires not only understanding but the emotional transformation that goes along with it. Only the truly enlightened soul, by achieving the peace that passeth understanding can communicate this to others. If so the Buddhists may be able to explain and to some extent even justify why an ignorant person should first pursue his own enlightenment.

Moreover, it might be argued that even if the reductionist view of persons is correct, people in fact have egoistical desires, and so they would still be interested in getting rid of their own sorrow. Since liberation involves the getting rid of sorrow, even a reductionist view of the self could explain why we should care for our liberation. So concern for one's liberation does not presuppose the non-reductionist view.

But if one's object is to get rid of one's sorrow, why not kill oneself rather than seek liberation through meditation and other high minded practices? The traditional Buddhists had an easy answer, for they did not think that suicide put an end to the cycle of birth, death and rebirth; but those who do not believe in reincarnation would have to give another answer. If I commit suicide and cease to exist I avoid suffering, but there is no positive happiness or joy; whereas true liberation offers not just the conquest of sorrow, but also the presence of joy, peace, bliss and so forth. But unless one adopts the non-reductionist view of the self, in what way can I be said to survive liberation? It might be replied that I do not have to survive in some deep metaphysical sense; John Smith survives in the sense that his psycho-physical organism survives. Each human being has (as a result of evolution) concern for the welfare of his psycho-physical organism; and if the enlightenment makes the human being very happy and joyful, then is he not very well off?

Even if, following Parfit, one allows some sort of reductionist survival in this life, how can a human being survive into Nirvana? Nirvana comes at the end of one's cycle of birth and rebirth, and nothing of his earthly characteristics survive in the state of Nirvana; so how does he survive in that state? From the point of view of the human being, how is Nirvana any better than suicide that is not followed by his rebirth? And how is it better from any other point of view? Is it that as each human being 'enters' Nirvana, though he ceases to exist, there is more joy in the state of Nirvana. So we have a sort of utilitarian vulgarisation of Nirvana. It is better if millions of people 'enter' Nirvana, for though none of them survives such entry, there is more and more total joy. The Buddhisattva is supposed to be very self-less; having attained enlightenment in this life, he postpones being in the wonderful state of Nirvana, for the sake of others. But this only makes sense if he could survive into Nirvana. If he does not, then how is his postponement of Nirvana any more of an act of self-sacrifice than his postponement of his suicide that is not followed by his rebirth? It might be pointed out that as long as he lives as a human being his life is full of sorrow, and so he is suffering all this sorrow for the sake of others. But even though he has not achieved final enlightment the Buddhisattva has achived substantial enlightenment in this life, and so why should there be so much sorrow in his life after his state of enlightenment and before his ascent into Nirvana?

Why then should we care for Nirvana if we won't be there to enjoy it? If we believed in the non-reductionist theory of personal identity, then we could claim that we have a persistent self that will survive the entry into Nirvana. And then the quest for Nirvana would make more sense.

Buddhists and Parfit have denied the separateness of persons because they believe in the no-self view. But some mystics have denied the separateness of persons by claiming that during mystical experience we experience unity with each other and indeed with the whole universe. Sceptics point out that such experiences do not prove the existence of a cosmic self running through us all; our experience of being one with the universe may be based on an illusion.

But then so too could the experiences of those who believe in simple selves separate from each other be based on an illusion. True, from the first person perspective we each think of our survival as an all or nothing matter. But why are such intuitions any more accurate than the mystic's intuition about the oneness of all life? As for the practical argument, it is true that much of our practical life presupposes the non-reductionist view according to which each human being is a separate self;[21] but then does not the mystic's way of life presuppose the cosmic self view? The answer is no, not necessarily.

It is important to stress that not all mystics deny the existence of separate selves; only the monists and the no-self theorists do. There are many others, such as Ramanuja who stress that the separate selves remain separate even when they experience union with nature and with the cosmos, somewhat as lovers remain separate though they enjoy ecstasy and union with each other.

According to the paradox of hedonism, if you want to enjoy happiness, you are not going to succeed if you go straight for it. Pleasure or happiness comes as a by-product of many of our non-hedonistic pursuits. I would suggest there is a similar paradox of mysticism and salvation. If one is obsessed with the liberation of one's soul, such craving will prevent one from achieving liberation; one will remain a slave of desires and remain quite miserable. In order to get out of this paradox, some have suggested that we must regard the separate persons view as illusory. But this suggestion creates more problems than it solves. So we should consider another way out, viz. we admit that we each have separate metaphysical selves, but we should cease to be obsessed with ourselves.

Neither the no-self view nor the cosmic self view can properly explain why I should care for my salvation. For on neither view would I survive the attainment of Nirvana or Moksha (which involves some sort of merger, with the Universe). In Indian Philosophy, the case of the individual merging with the cosmic self is compared to a drop of water merging in the ocean; the drop of water does survive the merger, and I also survive my merger with the cosmic self. Parfit's and Shoemaker's view of survival without identity was implicit in such discussions. But in this chapter we have seen the problems of relating egoistical concern with such attenuated survival.[22] In the case of Nirvana and Moksha, there are additional problems for such a view; for psychological connectedness disappears as a result of, if not before, such a merger, so in what sense can the previous person be said to survive in the cosmic consciousness? Even if the stuff (material or immaterial) out of which he is made survives in the cosmic consciousness, it would not follow that the former person survives; compare even if the stuff out of which a statue is made survives the break up of the statue, it would not follow that the statue survives.

There is also the problem that on the reductionist view, it is not at all clear why Nirvana or indeed any collection of *momentary* joyous states is a substantial good (from any point of view) if there is no persistent individual who enjoys it. In chapter 10 I argue that on the reductionist view it is difficult to show why the prevention of suffering and the promotion of joy are important goals. Such problems also arise for the reductionist version of the cosmic-self view but not for the non-reductionist version of the cosmic-self view. For on the latter view there is a persistent entity that suffers, is joyous etc. over a period of time. Though none of the versions of the cosmic-self view can properly explain why I should care primarily for my salvation, the non-reductionist version can explain why we should work for the salvation of all. For if we are all manifestations of the cosmic-self, then the cosmic self will be better off if people in general are better off. The egoistic view that I should work primarily for my salvation assumes the view that we each have a separate non-reductionist self.

NOTES

1. H. Sidgwick, *Methods of Ethics*, Macmillan, London, 1907, p. 419.
2. See *Reasons and Persons*, chapter 13, and appendix D. On some of the plausible versions of the non-reductionist view too, physical continuity is not what fundamentally matters. It is at best evidence of what fundamentally matters. However, if one combines the view that I am my brain with the non-reductionist view, then continuity of the brain would be what fundamentally matters.
3. The combination of the two does not by itself provide a reason for egoistical concern if Parfit is right in his view that physical continuity is not even part of what fundamentally matters on the reductionist

186   *Egoistical Concern Without an Ego*

view.

4. See chapter 7.
5. J. Perry, 'The Importance of Being Identical' in A. Rorty ed. , *The Identities of Persons*, University of California Press, Berkeley, 1976.
6. D. Parfit, *Reasons and Persons*, p. 312
7. *Reasons and Persons*, p. 313.
8. Critics of the psychological criteria point out that one cares now in an egoistical way about the tortures that will be inflicted on the future self that lives on in one's body after one has lost one's memory. Defenders of the psychological criterion could reply that even though one survives as an amnesiac, one does not survive a total and irreversible breakdown of all psychological connectedness, not just of memory but of all psychological dispositions. It is not all obvious that we should care in an egoistical way about the sufferings a future self that lives on in one's body with a totally different psychological make up. One of the counter-intuitive features of the psychological criterion (as well as of other reductionist views) is that according to it, personal survival admits of degrees. On that view even if one survives as an amnesiac, one survives to a lesser degree. So we should from en egoistical point of view cares less now about the sufferings of oneself when one becomes an amnesiac. If I am to undergo torture tomorrow, does the prospect of this torture become less terrifying if I am told that I shall be given an injection that makes me an amnesiac before I am tortured?
9. *Reasons and Persons*, p. 474.
10. See J. L. Mackie, *Problems from Locke*, Clarendon Press, Oxford, 1976, p. 197.
11. See. T. Nagel, *The Possibility of Altruism*, Clarendon Press, Oxford, 1976, 1970.
12. It is true that sometimes our desire to survive can diminish as a result of the knowledge that someone else can do our work. Russell said that Wittgenstein 'makes me less anxious to live, because I feel he should do the work I should do, and do it better'. B. McGuinness, *Wittgenstein: A Life*, Penguin Books, 1990, p. 103.
13. *Reasons and Persons*, p. 281.
14. In 'The Sceptic' Hume allows philosophical reflection to have some influence on our practice. But he thinks this influence is limited; and he thinks it is a vain hope that such reflection should have beneficial but no evil effects on our practical conduct. See D. Hume, *Essays*, Oxford University Press, Oxford, 1963, part 1, essay 18.
15. D. Parfit, 'Lewis, Perry and What Matters' in *The Identities of Persons*, ed. A. Rorty, p. 99.
16. One might use a similar argument to show that pride and shame cannot be justified on the reductionist view. For pride and shame also

involve a reflexive element. True, one can be proud or ashamed of people other than oneself, but these other people must be connected to oneself. See T. Penelhum, 'Self-Identity and Self-Regard' in *The Identities of Persons*, ed. A Rorty.

This view could be challenged. For it could be suggested that reductionism is consistent with the requirement that one is connected with another human being or group. I can be proud of my country but not of your country, because even if reductionism is true I am connected to my country in a way in which I am not connected to yours.

17. Unless, one personifies Britain, such that there is one soul running through all Britons; if a Briton believed this he could then feel egoistical concern for a fellow Briton, since he regards himself as identical with the other. But this example again illustrates the view that egoistical concern, since it is reflexive, presupposes a belief in identity.

18. J. L. Mackie, *Ethics*, Penguin Books, 1977, pp. 78, 82, 191-2.

19. To be accurate, the empiricist or reductionist view of the self can allow a part of my character to be destroyed, so that the rest of it can flourish. But on this view the destruction of even part of the character does involve my partial death. Parfit (*Reasons and Persons*, p. 299) would add that if I have a low opinion of the part of the character that I try to get rid of, then only a small part of me is being de-stroyed. But I find this version of the normative view rather extreme. Surely on the empiricist or reductionist view of the self the extent to which I identify with a part of my character, is also an important determinant of how much it is a part of me. And so if I identify with a part of my character that I have a low opinion of, then that part of the character could be as much a part of me as the high minded side of my character is. Sometimes we identify with a part of our charac-ter, by having a high opinion of that part but there are other ways of identifying - e.g. I may have a lot of egoistical concern about further-ing the ambitious side of my character, even though I do not have a high opinion of these characteristics of mine.

20. See A. Danto, *Mysticism and Morality*, Basic Books, London, 1972.

21. On the non-reductionist view a person is separate from another person; but I do not agree with Parfit in his claim that the ordinary view implies that persons are separate from their experiences.

22. See also D. Wiggins, 'Concern to Survive', *Midwest Studies in Philosophy*, Vol 4, 1979, pp. 417-22.

IX. *Persons, Justice and Desert*

In this chapter I shall examine how far ideas of distributive justice, retributive justice and compensation can be reconciled with the reductionist view of persons.

Section 1: Parfit and Distributive Justice

One of the standard criticisms of utilitarianism is that it neglects the separateness of persons. According to total utilitarianism, an action is right if it maximises total welfare. According to average utilitarianism an action is right if it maximises average utility. Each of these versions of utilitarianism has been criticised for neglecting considerations of fair distribution of welfare, except as a means for increasing utility. If and when utility can be promoted by slavery, then slavery is fair and just, according to utilitarians. Utilitarianism can lead to unfairness to individual persons, for it neglects the difference between persons. From a utilitarian point of view there is no difference in principle between inflicting hardship on a child for his own future wellbeing, and inflicting hardship on a child for the future welfare of another human being (or human beings). No doubt in the case where hardships are inflicted on a child in order to benefit someone else, the child himself may suffer in the future, as a result of the earlier hardships. But such undesirable side effects could sometimes be offset by beneficial and good effects, enjoyed by the other human being (or human beings) who benefited from the child's sacrifice.

If persons are logical constructions, if the real units are the items of experience rather than persons, then the objection that utilitarianism neglects the difference between persons loses much, if not all of its force.[1] Even if, like Shoemaker, one is not a reductionist with regard to persons but only with regard to personal identity, the distinction between persons becomes less important. For on the reductionist view (in its psychological version) personal identity can be analysed in terms of non-branching psychological continuity and connectedness. What is ultimately important is personal survival, personal identity only has derivative importance. The present self survives less and less with the passage of time. So different parts of a person's life can be treated as if they were different persons. On this view there is less unity to the human being's life and so the boundaries between different people become less important. My future self in the remote future may not be closer to me psychologically than some other human beings are. The difference between inflicting hardship on a child for his own future well being rather than for the well being of another human being becomes less important.

It might be replied that even if the non-reductionist view is false, it is (as reductionists like Parfit admit) the commonly held view. So in fact many (though not all) human beings do regard their lives as possessing a unity. They do identify egoistically with their future selves, in a way in which they do not with others. They feel guilt for their own past misdeeds in a way in which they do not for the misdeeds of others. Since people regard themselves as separate individuals, on the individual ascriptivist view this tends to make them separate individuals. Society also regards them as separate individuals, and so on the social ascriptivist view, this tends to make them separate individuals.

In fact some people (such as young children and some Buddhist sages) do not regard their lives as having a strong unity. Some of the Buddhist sages do try to lead lives that are in harmony with the reductionist view (in its psychological version); they may decondition themselves and cease to regard their lives as possessing a unity. Some of these sages are said to retain complete equanimity in the face of impending disaster, and in some cases they even watch their own torture with complete detachment. One strange consequence would be that in the reductionist sense of survival such people hardly survive over time whereas lesser mortals who regard their own lives as possessing a unity over time, continue to survive over time. To many people such a consequence would be a *reductio ad absurdum* of reductionist views; but the Buddhists would not find such a consequence disturbing, for they do not regard such survival as something that we should value. If survival is not such a good and even death is not such an evil, then what is so terrible about murder? Is it that people in fact regard their lives as possessing a unity and a great value and as long as this is so, murder is terrible? So the more people get emancipated from such prejudices the less terrible murder becomes!

Even if it is the case that people normally regard their lives as possessing a unity, it would not follow that on the reductionist view of the self utilitarianism would need to be qualified out of respect for rights of individual persons. Compare: suppose groups of people such as nations or other associations regard themselves as possessing a unity in some strong sense, it would not follow that such groups are the ultimate moral units. A nation's existence can depend upon whether its members regard it as a nation; if people feel a sense of unity, then this can help to create the nation, but this would not make the nation an ultimate moral unit that qualifies utilitarianism. The existence of the nation could of course have considerable intrinsic value, just as the existence of works of art can. But this admission is consistent with unqualified utilitarianism. For utilitarianism is concerned with maximising the creation of intrinsic value and minimising the amount of intrinsic disvalue.

One of the criticisms of utilitarianism is that it makes people replaceable. If some people could be replaced by better producers of utility, then utilitarianism could sanction the replacement of such people provided the good utilitarian effects more than outweighed the undersirable side effects. A doctrine of fundamental human rights qualifies utilitarianism so that such replacements would not be permitted. But if the reductionist view is correct, this would tend to undermine the doctrine of fundamental human rights that are independent of utility. Why, for instance, should the future selves of existing individuals have priority over the future selves of non-existant human beings? And unless they have such priority how can we rule out replacement policies?[3]

Admittedly, even if the reductionist view of persons is correct, a human being will in fact care a lot about his future selves. If one tried to replace existing adult human beings with other ones, the existing ones will suffer enormous fears of apprehension. But the existence of such fears could be taken into account by utilitarians in reaching their decision about whether such policies will in fact promote utility. When the desirable utilitarian effects of replacement policy outweigh the undersirable ones, will there be any non-utilitarian constraints on such a policy? Later I shall consider the possibility that there may be a doctrine of fundamental human rights which allows for the fact that within a human being one self gradually gives way to another.

Parfit's view is that utilitarianism needs to be qualified by certain principles of distributive justice. This is a view that is held by many liberals, including myself. We believe that without such principles of justice, it would be morally permissible to sacrifice the individual for the sake of utility. What is controversial about Parfit's view is that he believes that even on the reductionist view of the self, utilitarianism would need to be qualified in this manner. Parfit does however allow that reductionism would imply certain changes in our common sense morality. Thus he thinks that the scope of the principles of justice would alter. On the non-reductionist view each human being counts as a separate individual for the purposes of distributive justice. On the reductionist view, we shall have to worry about fair distribution even between different phases of an individual human being's life. The size of the units over which the distributive principles operate will be of smaller duration.

On the non-reductionist view it is not unfair to impose hardships on a child if, as a result, he (the same individual) benefits later on as as an adult; but on the (Parfit's) reductionist view when there are few connections between the young child and his later self, the benefit that occurs to the later self is like a benefit that occurs to another person; it may then be unfair to impose hardships on the child.

The reductionist view regards sub-divisions within lives rather like divisions between lives; in this way the scope of the distributive principles of justice are widened. But Parfit also believes that the reductionist view would involve giving these principles less weight. This last conclusion would seem to follow from the fact that reductionist survival is less deep than non-reductionist survival. If individuals do not survive in any deep sense then it could not be so bad to sacrifice them in order to promote utility.

Parfit takes seriously the idea that in his view we should widen the scope of distributive principles to treat each item of experience as a separate unit deserving of respect and consideration. The egalitarian principle of justice which asks us to concentrate on the plight of the worst off individuals, when combined with Parfit's reductionist view, would imply negative utilitarianism.[4] For negative utiltarianism also asks us to concentrate on the removal of suffering. But here Parfit commends negative utilitarianism not as the main principle of morals, but rather as a principle of justice which carries some weight qualifying the main principle of (positive) utility.

Parfit argues that though concentrated and prolonged suffering is bad on any view of personal identity, on the non-reductionist view there is a further moral reason to give priority to preventing suffering. He quotes me in support of the view that on the reductionist view non-utilitarian distributive principles should have less weight: '... if Parfit's theory is correct, if there are no persistent individuals (except in a trivial sense) why should we get so worked up about suffering in the world? Suffering would still be real, but how much worse it is when (intrinsically) the very same individual keeps suffering on and on.'

This quotation does not succeed in showing why on the reductionist view, principles of justice should carry any weight as qualifying principles. Even if suffering would still be an evil, ordinary utilitarianism too can allow for this. So how does the above quotation support Parfit's moderate view that it is defensible to argue that we should give some weight to distributive principles as qualifying the principle of utility?

Parfit shows some sympathy for the view that the principle of equality should aim at equality not between different lives but between the experiences that people are having at each particular time. On this view there can only be simultaneous compensation; for instance 'when the pain of exposing my face to a freezing wind is fully compensated by the sight of the sublime view from the mountain I have climbed'. Parfit then sympathetically considers the suggestion that perhaps there cannot even be simultaneous compensation. The unity of consciousness at a particular time is no more a deep fact than is psychological continuity over time. If there cannot even be simultaneous compensation then 'our *concern* would be to make better not the worst set of experiences, but the worst members of such sets, and these are more likely to be intense pains, or other kinds of extreme suffering'.[5] One problem with this view is that our concern for suffering must extend over a period of time and so cannot apply to discrete and momentary items of experience, not even to a set of such momentary experiences at a certain time.

A variant of the reductionist version that can avoid this problem is the following: items of experience are not discrete momentary units but form a continuous flow, more like a river than a bundle. This version can harmonise better with the requirement that our suffering must be over a period of time. So it can be reconciled with utilitarian ethics more plausibly than Parfit's version can be. To be an object of our concern, suffering must last for some time, for if suffering could be broken up into momentary items of experience, none of them could involve any substantial evil. But must suffering have an owner? Even if an owner is not required to show that suffering is an evil[6] it is probably required to bolster a theory of fundamental human rights that provides moral constraints on utilitarianism. If there is only a flow of experiences it is not clear why we should give any weight to non-utilitarian rights based principles of distributive justice.

Parfit allows talk of owners or subjects of experience, but only as a manner of speaking. But there are variants of reductionist theory (even in its psychological version) that allow the existence of owners. Thus, Sydney Shoemaker admits that experiences do not exist in themselves but are adjectival on subjects or persons. But the subject or person is here understood as a functional system. Any particular experience is understood as playing a purely causal role in the workings of such a system. No doubt a functional system can have an impressive unity, items within it can be intimately connected in a way in which they are not with items within other functional systems, so it is not arbitrary to lump them together within each functional system. But I do not think the functionalist approach captures the subjective element. There is not anything it is like to be a functional system, nor is there anything it is like for a functional system to suffer; if suffering just consists in certain outputs or in causing certain outputs, such as shrieks, following certain inputs, such as thrashings, what is so evil about suffering? If a person is a functional system, why is he an ultimate moral unit for purposes of distributive justice any more than groups such as G.E.C. or I.C.I. are? Such groups too can in some cases have an impressive unity within themselves.[7]

One might believe that there really are persons or selves (not just as a manner of speaking) and that within the life of a human being one self (or person) gradually gives way to another. One might for instance believe that I am my brain (or partly my brain and partly my psychology) and as my brain cells fade away and as my psychology changes, I change into another person within the same human body. Some such metaphysical view might go along with Parfit's view that the scope of the principles of distributive justice and of the doctrine of fundamental human rights should widen to include several persons within the life of a single human being. The complex version of the non-reductionist view might have some such implications. It might be suggested that similar implications follow from the reductionist version which stresses that a person consists of his psychology and that as the psychology changes one person gives way to another.

But there are problems with such views. How do we tell during the life span of a human being when exactly one person (or person-phase) ends and another begins. And unless we can answer such questions, how can we apply principles of distributive justice (or the doctrine of rights) to the various persons concerned? Whether we have a new person will depend not just upon changes in the brain (and/or changes in psychology) but also on how much weight we attach to the different changes. For Innokenty, when he met his wife after a substantial interval, his wife was no longer the same person as the 'blonde girl with the curls hanging down to her shoulders, the girl he had known in the tenth grade'. But it is quite possible that to some others who attach less weight to girlish looks, the two were the same person. Such considerations would show that on the view under consideration it is in principle (and not just in practice) difficult to decide objectively when one person ends and another begins. Perhaps there is no objective answer to such a question, and if so how can distributive justice apply to such persons?

There is also the problem that if we judge whether a person survives by an appeal to other people's point of view, we are not treating him as an end in himself. Perhaps the way out of this difficulty is to take the view that in order to treat the person as an end in himself, we must appeal to the person's own point of view. To the extent that we appeal to a person's own point of view, we can again get strange results. Sometimes an old man identifies himself with his young self in the past, another day he may be more impressed with the changes that have taken place in his personality. How do we decide whether he is the same person as his younger self for purposes of distributive justice?

Yet we would need to answer such questions if we are to apply the view under consideration. For instance, normally we give priority to younger men over older men with regard to the allocation of scarce medical resources, such as spare kidneys. This is partly on social grounds, the young have more to contribute to society in the future, but partly on the grounds of distributive justice; the old have already had a long life, unlike the young. But this last argument will be undermined if the old man is a different person from his younger self in the past. If the old are different persons from their young predecessors, then from an egalitarian point of view, they need to be pampered a lot, for they are having a much more miserable life than the younger members of society; and it is no use telling them that they have already had a good time when they were young, for on the view under consideration, they are not the same persons as their young predecessors. However, if we take an ascriptivist view, then whether the old man is the survivor of his young predecessor will depend upon one's (or his) point of view and values; and as such points of view alter, the relevant judgement of identity or survival could alter. This would make it impossible to apply principles of distributive justice.

The complex view, at any rate in the reductionist version, has to face another insoluble problem if it attempts to apply a rights based approach to persons or to person phases. On the reductionist view persons and person stages are logical constructions and logical constructions such as groups (e. g. corporations) do not, as we have seen,[8] have ultimate or fundamental rights; for similar reasons, they do not have deserts in any deep sense.

One might be able to apply rights based morality (as well as other parts of our non-utilitarian morality) even though persons were logical constructs made up of person phases, if person phases were not themselves logical constructs but were basic particulars, and if each person phase was a separate unit from its predecessor and its successor. But there is no good reason to think that such conditions are fulfilled in real life.

I have argued that if the reductionist theory (at any rate of the Parfit variety) is correct, one important objection to utilitarianism will be undermined. But one may still adhere to non-utilitarian moral constraints, not because persons are separate and sacred individuals, but because philosophical reflection does not alter one's emotional reactions substantially. As a matter of brute fact, people may continue to feel revulsion at the thought of sacrificing an individual for the sake of mere utilitarian considerations. Non-utilitarian constraints that are based on such brute emotional reactions are liable to disappear or change in different societies. Thus there are societies where a particular group may be regarded as the moral unit. Just as in the case of retributive justice there are societies which believe in collective retribution, so also in the case of distributive justice one could believe in a group rather than the individual human being as the ultimate moral unit.

But if one believes, as one does on the non-reductionist view, that quite apart from people's attitudes, human beings are separate and sacred, then we can use this idea to criticize societies which sacrifice the individual for the interests of a group or of utility, even when the society in question does not believe that individuals are separate units. The reductionst view will not be able to question the descent into collectivism. It can at best point to a feeling of revulsion that some people have towards the sacrifice of an individual.

Section 2: Reductionism, Punishment and Groups
Even if (non-utilitarian) principles of distributive justice would be

undermined (or partly undermined) if the reductionist view of persons were correct, may not principles of retributive justice still apply? Hume thought that the bundle theory of the self and retributive punishment were compatible, and Parfit too thinks that it is defensible to argue that the reductionist theory is compatible with old fashioned ideas of desert. Hume and Adam Smith also thought that our retributive instincts serve the utilitarian goal in the long run; whereas Parfit thinks that desert based principles are partly discrepant with the utilitarian goal.

Let us first examine Hume's argument to show that the bundle theory and retributive principles are compatible. Hume and Adam Smith thought that we praise characters who contribute to the peace and security of human society; when we come across characters who contribute to public detriment and insecurity we blame and punish them. The object of retributive punishment are conscious individuals. Actions are temporary and persisting, and they only render a person criminal when they reflect a criminal chracter. Even if an action causes great harm, the person who does it is not answerable for it unless the action proceeds from something that is durable and constant. 'Men are not blamed for such actions as they perform ignorantly and casually. Why? But because the principles of these actions are only momentary and terminate in them alone. Men are less blamed for such actions as they perform hastily and unpremeditatively than for such as proceed from deliberation. For what reason? But because a hasty temper, though a constant cause or principle in the mind, operates only by intervals and infects not the whole character. Again, repentance wipes off every crime if attended with a reformation of life and manners. How is this to be accounted for? But by asserting that actions render a person criminal merely as they are proofs of criminal principles in the mind; and when by an alteration of their principles they cease to be just proofs, they likewise cease to be a criminal.'[9]

Parfit (in his moderate version) has similar views to Hume. According to Parfit a criminal, whose crime reflects his criminal character at the time of the crime, deserves less and less punishment in the future as less and less of his criminal character survives with the passage of time. Parfit, Mackie, Hume and the Buddhists all believe in the error theory with regard to much of our practical and moral life. For they think the non–reductionist view is presupposed by our psychology and by much of our practical and normal life. But Hume was a conservative in moral and practical life. Since he did not think that we could change our psychology substantially, and since for him our moral life is based on our psychology, it follows that in his view our practical and moral life is doomed to be irrational. Parfit, Mackie and the Buddhists, unlike Hume, are revisionists to different degrees and think that we can and should try to reconstruct our moral and practical life in such a way as to bring it into harmony with the true view of the self, and indeed with the true view of all of reality.

Hume, unlike these revisionists, kept his metaphysical (or anti-metaphysical) views in a separate compartment from his views on our moral and practical life. So much so that when it comes to discussing our practical and moral life, he forgets the implications of his metaphysical views for the rationality of our practical life. For instance, if Hume is right in denying the existence of the self in any deep sense, then the pursuit of self-love becomes irrational.[10] The Buddhists had seen that this follows, but Hume did not see this, perhaps because he tended to forget his metaphysical (or anti-metaphysical) views when it came to discussing our practical life.

When it comes to punishment Hume seems to forget (if he ever properly realised!) that in his view, the error theory pervades our practical life. Thus he thinks that our resentment is directed against the evil character that a criminal has, and when the criminal reforms our resentment is no longer directed at him; for the criminal is his character, and when his criminal character has disappeared, there is nothing durable in him which has survived the change of character and which can be the object of our resentment. When only some good elements of his character have survived the changes, those elements cannot be the object of our resentment.

But according to Hume's error theory we are doomed to believe that people have a permanent self that survives changes in character. So why do we not direct resentment against the criminal's self that we believe continues to exist even after he has reformed? So Hume's meta-philosophical views about the limited influence of philosophical speculation on our practical life implies that our practical life should be more irrational than Hume thinks it is in the sphere of punishment. In the case of punishment (as we saw in the previous paragraph) he thinks that our current practices are based on the working out of the bundle theory of the self. The existence of this match between the true 'metaphysics' (i. e. the no-self view) and our practices is irreconcilable with Hume's views about the limited influence of philosophical speculation upon practice.

Parfit too, though he believes in the error theory (i. e. that a false view of personal identity permeates our practical and moral life), seems to allow that the true view of personal identity does in fact permeate some of our existing practices. Thus he thinks that the reductionist view of the self is presuposed by some of the Statutes of Limitations which do not allow punishment for a past crime after a certain period of time has elapsed. Again he gives examples from literature to bolster his view that human beings sometimes assume the reductionist view in their dealings with their beloved. But by and large Parfit's view is that the non-reductionist view permeates our existing moral and practical life. Unlike Hume he wants to reform our practical and moral life so as to bring it into conformity with the true view of reality. Unlike the Buddhists, he thinks that it is defensible to argue that this can be done without a complete overhaul of our practical life.

Can one reconcile desert-based views with the reductionist view? If the ultimate units are the items of experience, why do the later items deserve punishment for the crimes of the earlier ones? It might be useful to punish people even if the bundle theory is correct, but that is not to say that they deserve punishment.[11] Since there is no agent in any deep sense (for all talk of agency and personhood is eliminable) it is not clear who deserves punishment. Is it the individual item of experience? Or is it the whole bundle?

Hume does not have to face some of these objections; unlike Parfit, Hume does not think it defensible to claim that there is an intrinsic fittingness (i. e. apart from human sentiments) between a person's crime and the punishment of his future self that is psychologically connected to him. Again, unlike Parfit, Hume does not think that psychological continuity and connectedness by itself (i. e. apart from the existence of the of the relevant human sentiments) provides one with a reason for special concern. For Hume, Reason by itself can neither discover moral truths, nor provide us with a reason for action.

So Parfit has to face some special problems, which do not arise for Hume. On the reductionist view statements about persons and person-phases are logical constructions out of statements about items of experience; persons and person phases are eliminable. So the statement that it is intrinsically fitting that a person or a person phase deserves punishment for the crimes that he committed earlier must be shown to be eliminable; just as the statement that his future welfare provides a person now with a Reason for special concern must also be shown to be eliminable. So Parfit would have to show that it is defensible to claim that it is intrinsically fitting that items of experience be punished for the crimes committed by earlier items of experience; and that the welfare of some future items of experience, by itself (i. e. apart from the existence of relevant desires) provide present items of experience with Reason for action.

Hume does not have to face such problems. He adopts something like a social ascriptivist view of desert. People in fact will regard criminals as blameworthy and deserving of punishment as long as the character from which the crime flowed persists. He considers the objection that if determinism is true then our crimes are a result of a chain of causes ultimately beyond our control. If God is the ultimate author of the chain of causes that has led to a person's character being the way it is, why blame the person for his character? Hume's answer was to appeal to the brute fact that human beings feel resentment at an evil action that stems from an evil character, and the resentment does not disappear (or even get less) if we reflect upon the fact that the character itself was caused by factors outside our control, that the character we have is itself a matter of luck.

But this conservative answer is not open to modern liberal-egalitarians like Parfit. For Parfit thinks that we can and should reform our moral and practical system, and that our moral sentiments and dispositions are not a brute fact about us. Problems of moral luck are much more acute for the liberal egalitarian than for the conservative. For the conservative it may be a person's bad luck that he has got a certain criminal inheritance, but he nonetheless should suffer the consequences such as punishment. Some people are lucky in that they have better natural assets, such as intelligence and good health, others are less well endowed. On the conservative view, such unequal distribution of natural assets are not inherently unjust. But on the liberal-egalitarian view this is not so, people with disadvantages (whether these were a result of heriditary or environment) should be compensated, so as to bring them up the level of others. So why should the later self deserve to be punished for the crimes of the earlier one, any more than the son deserves to be punished for the crimes of the father? Is it not its bad luck that it is in a certain relationship to a past self?

It might be that the later self identifies itself with a certain past self but then so do members of a family sometimes identify themselves with each other. Would it follow that they deserve punishment for each other's crimes? On Parfit's theory, there is no survival in any deep sense, even in the short run. So why should a later set of experiences suffer for the 'deeds' of the earlier one? True, the criminal survives in some attenuated sense, but does such attenuated survival suffice for the view that there is an intrinsic fittingness between the crime committed earlier and the punishment inflicted later? In some attenuated sense a person also survives in his disciples, in his children and so forth, but do they deserve punishment for his misdeeds? Is the view that a criminal's future self in the near future deserves more punishment for the crime than does his later self in the more remote future (when the psychological connectedness would have weakened further) any more plausible than the view that a tyrant's son deserves greater punishment for the tyrant's crime than his grandson does?

Instead of treating these problems as constituting a *reduction ad absurdum* of the Humean view of punishment, one might try to defend the Humean view of punishment by modifying and extending it to include collective responsibility. Just as social ascriptivism can commend a system, where the later selves of some criminals deserve punishment, so also social ascriptivism can commend a system where other human beings related to the criminal in the appropriate way deserve punishment for his crime. There are societies where the son is said to deserve punishment for the crimes of the father.

But this way out is not open to those who want to defend judgements of desert as having intrinsic fittingness (quite apart from human sentiments), or to those who are liberal egalitarians. On the liberal egalitarian view too one might sometimes transfer liability, though not guilt. If the son has inherited his father's capital, it seems reasonable that he should be liable to meet his father's debts. Since the Germans after the 2nd World War inherited the assets of the previous generation, it seems reasonable to ask them to make reparations for the damage done by the previous generation (provided the liabilities do not exceed the assets). But this does not show that they are morally blameworthy or deserving of punishment.

Of course, often when a wicked criminal is deservedly punished severely, the rest of his family suffers even though they are innocent. But we do not regard those innocent members as deserving of suffering, though we might sometimes regard such suffering as an inevitable consequence of the deserved punishment of the criminal. Indeed, the egalitarian should try to minimise the suffering of the innocent members of the criminal's family, e.g. by providing them with welfare services.

If the reductionist theory of the self is correct, the punishment of the later self for the crimes of the earlier one would seem like the punishment of one individual for the crimes of another. And since the liberal egalitarian regards the latter as unfair and unjust, should he not also regard the former as equally abhorrent? On the moderate version of Parfit's views, if the reductionist view is correct, non–utilitarian principles (such as those concerned with desert) will have reduced weight and changed scope. As the psychological connectedness weakens, the later self deserves less punishment for the crimes of the earlier one. But may we not take a more radical line and argue that if the reductionist view is correct, then the non–utilitarian principles (such as desert) will have no weight? For the basic units of morality will be items of experience, and items of experience do not have any inherent right to distributive justice, nor is it intrinsically fitting that they should suffer for .the crimes committed by earlier items of experience. Indeed, an attempt to reward, punish or compensate a later item seems doomed to fail. For instance, if one puts John Smith in jail, then we create a different set of experiences, from what would have existed if he had not been punished. It is not as if there were a set of experiences out there in the future, which we can punish or reward.

Perhaps, we could introduce the idea of quasi-punishment. Quasi-punishment involves punishing an individual by punishing another with whom he identifies in the relevant ways. So we can try to quasi-punish the present self of the criminal for his crime by punishing his successive selves. One way to see collective punishment is the following: when we punish the son for the crime of the father our main justification is to inflict quasi-punishment on the father. The trouble with such a system is that it involves the infliction of suffering on innocent people. And it is important to realise that people do not cease to be innocent merely because they identify with the guilty. Nor do later stages of a person cease to be innocent merely because they identify with an earlier stage that was guilty.

Parfit endorses Wiggins' view that a malefactor cannot escape responsibility by contriving his own fission. This view seems to imply that in cases of fission, each of the offshoots deserves to be punished for the crime of the original person. I agree that it is absurd to try to escape one's criminal deserts by contriving one's fission. But there could be different explanations of this. Firstly, it could be (as Parfit and Wiggins assume) that one deserved to be punished before the occurrence of the fission and after its occurrence. Secondly, it could be that since fission is possible, the non-reductionist view is false and one does not survive in any deep sense even before the fission and so one does not deserve (in any strong sense) to be punished for one's crimes even before fission occurred. So on this scenario too it is false to say that a criminal could escape his just deserts by contriving his own fission. The occurrence of fission would provide evidence that he was not the sort of person (even before fission occurred) who had criminal deserts in any deep sense.[12]

It is worth stressing that the non-reductionist theory does not involve the absurd consequence that a person survives until the time of fission but dies with fission or that he escapes responsibility for them by contriving his fission. On my view the occurrence of fission (or the possibility of its occurrence) would undermine the non-reductionist view and would show that the person was not in any deep sense responsible even before fission took place. This is compatible with the suggestion that human beings do survive in some attenuated sense (before and after fission) and that one might be able to construct some theory of desert compatible with such attenuated survival. We do talk of collectives such as football teams as being deserving of winning or losing; and so if persons are like collectives they too may be said to deserve things in some weak sense.[13]

Desert in the full-blooded moral sense is a natural or pre-social notion in the sense that it can be used to evaluate social institutions and practices.[14] People sometimes appeal to such a sense of desert, for instance when they try to justify the institution of punishment on the grounds that morally wicked people deserve to suffer. However, those who are sceptical of the existence of desert in this strong sense, may still use desert in some weak non-natural sense. Thus, one might justify a sport such as cricket on social grounds. Once, a sport has come into existence, one may be able to make desert judgements in some weak sense. For instance, one might argue that though rain deprived cricket team A of victory, team A deserved to win for it displayed the relevant skills to a higher degree than the opponents. Even if the reductionist view is correct, this would not undermine the claim that team A displayed greater skill. So some desert judgements *in the weak sense* are compatible with the reductionist view.

A utilitarian theory of punishment can be more easily reconciled with the reductionist theory of the self than the (full-blooded) desert theory can be.[15] There can sometimes be a utilitarian case for punishing collectives. Punishing corporations, for instance, can help to deter anti-social activities by the same or similar corporations in the future. Punishing families of the criminal (however deplorable on other grounds) may also help to deter crime. Even if individual persons are like groups, it may be useful to punish the later self for the crimes of the earlier self. It may be that the Buddhist sage who has deconditioned himself from a belief in a permanent ego and the life style that goes with it, will not have any special concern for what happens to his future 'selves'. But such a sage is hardly the typical criminal. The ordinary criminal will be deterred by the thought that his later self will be punished, even when the later self no longer has criminal tendencies. Moreover, punishing a criminal (even after he has reformed) can help to deter other criminals in the future.

There is an even stronger utilitarian case for punishing criminals who retain their criminal tendencies. For in such cases there is the consideration that in addition to deterring others, punishment prevents them from committing crimes while they are in jail, and helps to deter them from committing crimes when they come out of jail.

I do not deny that one may continue to operate non–utilitarian punishment even if the reductionist view of the person is the correct one. We have seen that Hume advocated such a system. But we have also seen that from a cosmic point of view there is nothing intrinsically fitting about such punishment. It is just that human sentiments may be such that we would want to continue to inflict retributive punishment even if the reductionist view is true. Hume argued that as a matter of brute fact we do feel resentment against the criminal, as long as his criminal character is still there. We also saw that such a rationale could be extended to cover cases of collective responsibility. It may sometimes be, as a matter of brute fact, that people are prepared to inflict retributive punishment upon sons for the crimes of their fathers. A belief in the bundle theory does tend to reduce our inhibitions against such vicarious punishment. For the bundle theory denies the significance of the difference between persons. If we are willing to punish the later self for a crime committed by an earlier self, what is so wrong with punishing a son for the crime of his father?[16]

It may be replied that Hume is only willing to punish the later self as long as the later self still has the criminal characteristics of the earlier self that committed the crime. But then why not have a system where we punish sons for the crimes of their father only when the sons share the father's nature? On the non-reductionist view, the mere fact that the son has inherited the father's criminal tendencies provides no reason for punishing the son for the father's crime; we must only punish the son if and when he commits his own crime. If the son exercises self-control and does not commit a crime, he should not be punished, even though he shares his father's criminal nature. These views will be undermined if we accept the reductionist views.

Section 3: Compensation

In the case of compensation, Parfit commends the view that there cannot be compensation over time. He uses this view to argue for his version of negative utilitarianism which is a principle of distributive justice which concentrates not on removing the suffering of the worst off human beings, but on making 'better the... worst experiences that occur.' Instead of showing respect for persons, Parfit wants us to show concern for the worst set of experiences that occur at any time. To many people, such consequences would constitute a *reductio ad absurdum* of his views. We respect and show concern and sympathy for individuals but can we show concern for an individual experience at a particular time or even for a set of experiences at a particular time?

Parfit suggests that if there is suffering due to a freezing wind, we should provide simultaneous compensation, for instance by providing a sublime view of the sunset at that very time. It seems to me that we cannot compensate an item of experience or even a set of experiences at a given time. We can prevent an item of experience or set of experiences from coming into existence, and have instead another item of existence (or set of experiences), e.g. one that has less net suffering as a result of the presence of the sublime view. Such a policy may be justified to the extent that it promotes utility. But it cannot be justified on grounds of distributive justice or on any other rights based grounds. For the item of experience (or items of experience) that is prevented from coming into existence is not numerically the same as the item of experience (or items of experience) that has replaced it. An experience of suffering does not remain the same in the two cases, for the presence of the sublime view makes the experience of suffering different from what it would have been if there had been no sublime view.

It follows from such considerations that compensation of the individual only makes sense if the individual lives through such compensation. So how can there be compensation in the case of momentary items of experience? In the next chapter I shall consider the suggestion that there may be quasi-compensation in such cases.

Parfit considers an objection made by Temkin that if a reductionist denies compensation over time he should also deny simultaneous compensation. For the unity of consciousness at one time is not a deeper fact than psychological continuity over time. He concludes that if there cannot even be simultaneous compensation 'our concern would be to make better not the worst set of experiences, but the worst members of such sets, and these are more likely to be intense pains or other kinds of extreme suffering'.[17]

Now as we saw earlier we cannot make better a particular pain at a particular time. What we can do is to prevent it from coming into existence. Also, we can try to reduce a pain that has begun, in the sense that we can try to reduce its duration and its intensity while it lasts. But it is absurd to apply rights-based talk of distributive justice to momentary items of experience.

What is very curious is that Parfit is sceptical of talk of compensation over time, yet he claims that it is defensible to talk of desert over time. To be consistent one should grant that if a person does not survive over time for purposes of compensation, then neither does he survive over time for purposes of desert;[18] and since it is impossible (legally) to punish a criminal at the time he commits a crime, therefore (on the reductionist theory) it cannot ever be intrinsically fitting that he should be punished. On the reductionist theory, simultaneous punishment makes no more sense than simultaneous compensation, nor is deserved punishment over time less problematic than deserved compensation over time. Indeed something like quasi-compensation, which we discuss in the next chapter, is easier to justify than quasi-punishment. For the trouble with the latter is, as we have seen, that it involves the suffering of the innocent.

The next chapter will discuss further some of the issues raised in this one.

NOTES

1. Again, if there is a cosmic self running through us all, then we are not separate in the relevant sense. Believers in the cosmic self such as S. Radhakrishan (*Eastern Religions and Western Thought*, Clarendon Press, Oxford, 1939) and Sprigge stress that the cosmic self view tends to make us care for all sentient beings. The Advaita view 'Tat Tvam Asi' or 'That art Thou' enables us to see ourselves in other people, and so care for others.
It is true that this view undermines the distinction between the

egoistic point of view and the altruistic. It encouages us to care for everything in the Universe. But it would also encourage one to sacrifice an individual human being for the sake of the aggregate. As long as there is no conflict between an individual human being's interests and the interests of others, there is no problem. But when there is a conflict the cosmic self view, like the bundle theory, since it denies the separateness of persons, would not be able to distinguish between imposing hardship on a child for the sake of his future welfare and imposing hardship on the child for the sake of the future welfare of other human beings.

The problem of evil (i.e. the problem why a just God allows so much suffering in this world) may become easier to solve if there is a cosmic self of which we are all different aspects. On the separate self view, when an innocent separate self suffers a lot in his lifetime, one cannot deny the unfairness of such suffering by pointing out that others are enjoying themselves. But on the cosmic self view one can argue that looked at from the point of view of the cosmic self, the suffering of a particular human being is compensated by the happiness of others. Of course this argument will only get off the ground if there is more happiness than suffering in the world as a whole. If there is more suffering than happiness in the world, then the fact that there is the same cosmic self that keeps suffering on and on, from the beginning of time till the end of time, makes things even worse. For at least on the separate self view the suffering of a particular human being will not go on for an indefinite period (unless perhaps one believes in immortality).

2. See my *Equality, Liberty and Perfectionism*, ch. 8.
3. For similar reasons the cosmic self view cannot rule out replacement policies. Sprigge stresses that different manifestations of the cosmic self add to the variety and splendour in the universe. The cosmic self view, in the version he favours, treats variety and splendour in the Universe as a good. The cosmic self flourishes when different manifestations of it flourish in their different ways. But even if one grants this, I do not see how the cosmic self view can show why we should not replace some individuals by new individuals, when there is not enough room for both sets of individuals. No doubt by getting rid of some individuals, we suffer some deprivations, but why would not such deprivations sometimes be offset by the flourishing of the new set of individuals? Replacement policies may sometimes promote greater variety and splendour! The adverse side effects of such policies can sometimes be minimised. For instance, in an overpopulated poor country why not go in for a policy of permitting infanticide with the consent of parents? Utilitarians sometimes argue that such policies will coarsen our dispositions and and that will be bad; some

utilitarians stress the bad effects of such coarsening, while others such as Sprigge stress the fact that such coarsening is intrinsically evil as it lowers the quality of the experiences of those who who acquire such dispositions. But there are many strong measures that involve such risks, such as wars and severe punishment, yet there can sometimes be a utilitarian case for undertaking such activities. See my *Equality, Liberty and Perfectionism*, ch. 8.

4. *Reasons and Persons*, p. 345
5. *Reasons and Persons*, p. 521, italic mine.
6. Though, as the earlier quotation from my book shows the presence of a persistent owner does enhance the evil of suffering.
7. Similar criticisms can be made of other versions of the reductionist view. Thus if a person is a concrete universal in what sense can such a universal suffer? On the reductionist view the person does not suffer, items of suffering are parts of the bundle. In the next chapter I argue that this view cannot fully explain why it is wrong for there to be persistent suffering in the life of the same human being.
8. See ch. 6.
9. David Hume, *An Enquiry Concerning the Human Understanding*, (ed. L. A. Selby-Bigge, 2nd edition) section 8, part 2, p. 98
10. John Mackie (*Hume's Moral Theory*, Routledge and Kegan Paul, London, 1980, p. 160) thinks that Hume is quite consistent in denying the self in the strong Cartesian sense, and in using the notion of self as a bundle in his discussion of sympathy, pride etc.
11. See my *Equality, Liberty and Perfectionism*, p. 115.
12. See ch. 7.
13. See chapter 10, section 2.
14. See, J. Feinberg, *Doing and Deserving*, Princeton University Press, Princeton, 1970, and B. Barry, *Political Arguments*, Routledge and Kegan Paul, London, 1967, chapter 6, section 4.
15. See my *Equality, Liberty and Perfectionism*, chapter 7, section 2.
16. See my *Equality, Liberty and Perfectionism*, chapter 7, section 2.
17. *Reasons and Persons*, p. 521.
18. And if he does not survive then how can his survival provide him with a reason for egoistical concern?

X. Conclusion

Section 1: Suffering and the Reductionist View

There are several different versions of the reductionist view. There is the psychological version which we have discussed. Then there is the physicalist version which stresses that personal identity consists of the persistence of physical characteristics and there is the version which stresses the importance of both physical and psychological characteristics. We saw in chapter 8 that the psychological version is the most plausible version of the reductionist view. We also saw in the last chapter that there are sub-divisions of the psychological version.

Reductionists who think that the behaviourists and functionalists cannot account for our subjective experience have to face the problem of how the various experiences are related to each other. There is the atomistic view (which Hume believed in[1]) according to which the ultimate units are the various momentary items of experience. Each of the conscious experiences of a human being are separate units from the experiences of the next moment. There is no deep unity between our experiences over time, the experiences are linked to each other in various ways through resemblance, causation, memory, etc, but they remain separate and distinct units. There are two versions of the atomistic view. According to the extreme version even at a given moment of time the various experiences that a human being has are discrete experiences; the sound I hear now is a separate item of experience from the colour that I see now. The moderate version takes a holistic view regarding all of one's experiences occuring at the same time. All my experiences now form one unit of experience, unless there is splitting of consciousness. But the moderate view is, like the extreme view, atomistic with regard to one's experiences over time, my experience now is quite distinct from the ones that succeed it.

Then there is the version according to which my experiences now and some of the succeeding ones form a continuous flow. William James[2] believed in some such stream of consciousness version. This version too is a version of reductionism for it is the experiences that are the ultimate reality, there is no further fact such as the self which has these experiences. Let us call this the river version of the reductionist view.

Now there are certain problems that arise with the reductionist view in the moral sphere. Can it account for what is evil about suffering? If it cannot, how can it be reconciled with any civilized morality? Even if it can account for the evil of suffering, can it be reconciled with rights-based theories that stress the importance of distributive considerations, quite apart from consideration of total utility? Of course, if one is convinced of the truth of the reductionist view then one might abandon rights-based theories rather than deny reductionism. But I have yet to come across a decisive argument in favour of the truth of reductionism. Until one does so, it would be foolish to abandon our cherished moral practices.

One of the problems facing the reductionist view in the moral sphere is that one sympathises with the individual who suffers, not with the experiences. When you are sorrowful I sympathise with you, not with the sorrows. If experiences are the basic units, we would have to show concern for the welfare of these small units not with the people who have the experiences. Next, there is the problem that arises from the fact that the terrible thing about suffering is that it lasts for a substantial time. If there is 'suffering' that lasts a moment this is hardly an evil, however intense the experience. Yet, if the atomistic view is the correct one then the suffering of the individual would break down into lots of atomic units, each of which consists of only momentary unpleasentness. On the non-reductionist view one can see what is so evil about suffering, for the same individual keeps suffering on and on.

The atomistic version is the most vulnerable to these criticisms. Can the river version answer such objections? It might be argued that the commonsense view that one sympathises with the individual who has the experiences rather than with the experiences themselves needs to be revised. We could follow Adam Smith[3] and say that we sympathise with your sorrows. If there is a stream of suffering going on and on then this is an evil whether or not there is an owner who undergoes it. Perhaps it is just lack of imagination that prevents us from sympathising with ownerless suffering.

There remains the problem regarding the duration of ownerless suffering. This is particularly important from the point of view of distributive justice. What is the moral unit for the purposes of distributive justice, compensation, etc? If we give priority to the removal of the worst cases of suffering, we need to identify such cases. We need to know not only the intensity of the suffering but also its duration. For what makes suffering a really great evil is the combination of intensity and duration. Suppose, John Smith has a night of dreamless sleep. Is his suffering before his sleep part of a different moral unit from his suffering after his sleep? Even on the river version they are separate experiences; though they are intimately related and the later experiences would not have occured without the earlier ones.

On the old fashioned view of the self, it is the same individual that suffers before the sleep as the one who suffers after the sleep. Indeed all his suffering throughout his life is counted as part of one moral unit. But on the no-ownership view (as well as on the complex version of the non-reductionist view) we are left with the problem of deciding how long the duration of the suffering is, when one suffering ends and another begins. We have seen that on the atomistic view our experiences break down into momentary units. Who cares about momentary unpleasent experiences? Even on the river view, the river of experiences breaks down into lots and lots of rivulets of experiences. Since the duration of each of these rivulets is not long,[4] suffering, however intense it is, ceases to be anything like as evil as it would be if its duration were much longer, other things such as intensity remaining the same.

In reply, reductionists could point out that the various rivulets could merge into one big river by identifying and appropriating their predecessors. When a person wakes up, he identifies with his previous experiences, unless he is in a pathological state. So the duration of his experiences gets extended for substantial periods. William James said that one's present consciousness incorporates its predecessors by recalling them with warmth and intimacy. It incorporates them by saying 'Thou art mine'. It might be objected that identification or appropriation requires an agent or person who does the identifying or appropriating. But reductionists would deny that this is essential. They would maintain that identification or appropriation is an item within the flow of experiences.

In the case of the extreme version of the atomistic view, the act of identification or appropriation would be a separate item from other contemporary experiences, such as suffering. So how can an item of suffering now identify with past or future items of experience? It might be thought that on the moderate version of the atomistic view the act of identification or appropriation is part of the present set of experiences and so this problem would not be so acute. But there is the complication that one identifies with suffering over a period of time, not with momentary items of experience, not even with momentary sets of experiences. Both the act of identification and the object of one's concern that one identifies with lasts for some time.

The atomistic version, especially the extreme version, is more vulnerable to such criticisms than the river version. But there is one problem which is there even for the river version. Identification can occur even across individuals. Individuals can identify with other individuals and groups. Should these larger groups then be treated as the moral unit? If reductionism is true the moral units appear to be the items of experience, each of which last either for a moment or for a short duration. If these items can merge into larger units by identification, then so too can these larger units merge by identification into still larger units such as the family or tribe or nation. Some people care more for the suffering of their children than for their own future suffering.

Let us consider two families the Singhs and the Browns. The Singhs have suffered much more in general than the Browns, but suppose John Brown suffers more than Balbir Singh. Which of them should get priority? On the individualistic view John Brown should, for he has suffered more. Of course the suffering of the Singh family may have caused Balbir to suffer more, especially if he identifies with them. His consciousness of their suffering may increase the intensity of his own. Even if he does not identify with them, there may have been ways in which their suffering, caused him to suffer more than he otherwise would have. Deprivations suffered by generations of the Singh family may have adversely affected Balbir also. But if inspite of taking such factors into account we find that John's plight is worse, should not John get priority?

The fact that the Singh family has suffered for generations may be relevant in other ways too. Perhaps they identify with each other so closely that if we did not relieve the suffering of Balbir, his relations will suffer on account of him; whereas if we relieved his suffering they may regard this as some sort of quasi-compensation for the injuries that were inflicted on them in the past. So it may be argued that taking everyone's interests into account we should give priority to relieving Balbir's suffering even though John is suffering more than him. This conclusion will become less plausible the greater the extent to which John's suffering exceeds that of Balbir. Be that as it may, the fact that the Singh family has suffered so much, for say the last hundred years, is not quite so bad as it would be if the same individual had suffered for a hundred years. This is because the family is a complex unit and its suffering is undergone by different individuals. From the point of view of distributive justice, it seems better that the suffering is shared between different individuals, even though they identify with each other, than if it were borne by the same individual. The point here is not that the total suffering is likely to be less if it is so shared. That may well be the case and it would be one reason why such sharing would be less evil than if the suffering were undergone by the same individual. Quite apart from considerations of total suffering, the fact that it is the same individual that keeps suffering on and on is something terrible from the point of view of distributive justice.

This discussion is relevant to groups such as races. Certain races, such as the blacks, have suffered a lot during the course of history. Should we give priority to a person X if he is a member of such a group and identifies with it, over Y, who is worse off than X but who belongs to and identifies with a group that is better off than X's group? There is also the problem that, in fact, a person belongs to several groups. Which is the relevant one for purposes of distributive justice, reverse discrimination, etc. ? Suppose X's family has been worse off than Y's family has, but that Y's race has suffered more than X's race has. Should we go by the extent to which the individual identifies with the group or by the extent to which the group identifies with the individual or by the extent to which the deprivations of the group have damaged the relevant individual? These criteria may not always give the same result. It could be argued that on the individualistic view it is the last consideration that is the most ultimate. We shall however see in the next section that identification can be relevant for quasi-compensation; one can sometimes quasi-compensate members of a group by giving special consideration to other members of the group with whom they identify.

Sometimes reverse discriminatiion is justified because the individual person being given preferential treatment has had a raw deal in the past. But sometimes one may give preferential treatment to an individual because, even though he has been well off in the past, the group to which he belongs has as a whole had a raw deal. Consider, for instance, giving preferential treatment to a black man who has been to Eton. Giving such prefential treatment may be justified to the extent that it helps other members of the oppressed minority to which he belongs. For instance, if giving him an important job helps badly off blacks (who identify with him) by improving their morale and self image. The extent to which these others identify with him is important.

If one regards the individual, not the group, as the moral unit, one can still attach importance to groups as a means towards the promotion of the interests of the worst off. Some people, such as Plato, treat the group as the moral individual. On that view the group becomes much more important vis-a-vis the individual.

On the non-reductionist view of the individual self what makes suffering especially evil from a distributive point of view is that the individual is the same individual throughout, quite apart from whether he believes himself the same or identifies with the selves that suffered earlier. Consider a pathological case where the individual suffers from very severe loss of memories (except for very short term memory) and so cannot identify with his earlier selves; and suppose he has suffered a lot throughout his long life.[5] Even though he does not identify with his earlier suffering the fact that he has suffered on and on is specially terrible; if he did recover his memory and identify with the earlier suffering, this could make his present suffering more intense but that is a different point. Admittedly, when an individual suffers on and on, one of the reasons that this is bad, is that the person who suffers gets worn out and his subsequent suffering may be even more unbearable as a result; his memory of past suffering and his fear of future suffering may make his present suffering more unbearable. Such considerations could apply even on the reductionist view; for on the reductionist view, as long as one identifies with one's past and future selves, the consciousness of such past suffering and the fear of future suffering may well increase the intensity of one's present suffering.

But quite apart from the above mentioned bad effects, on the non-reductionist view the fact that the same individual has suffered on and on throughout his life is terrible in itself from the point of view of distributive justice. This is shown by considering the pathological case I just mentioned. On the the reductionist view suffering ceases to be a substantial evil from the point of view of distributive justice because it does not last long. Even when the present self identifies with the past and future selves, since the present self does not last for long, it does not have to bear the suffering for long.

If a family has suffered a lot for the last hundred years, the fact that a different individual suffers now from the one who suffered a few decades ago is better from a distributive point of view than if the same individual had suffered throughout this period. As we saw earlier the family is a complex unit and its suffering is borne by the different individuals who compose it. This remains true even though they all identify closely with each other. Now similarly, if the individual human being is a complex unit that is divisible into smaller units then the suffering would be ultimately borne by these smaller units. This shows that suffering is not so evil on the reductionist view or on the complex version of the non-reductionist view or on Dennett's functionalist view (where the rational system that constitutes the human being can be broken up into smaller and smaller units), as it is on the view that regards the self as a persistent and indivisible entity.

Marcus Aurelius[6] gives advice for making our suffering more bearable. He suggests that we should concentrate on the present suffering and not dwell on our suffering at other times. And some sages tell us to detach ourselves even from our present misfortunes. By ceasing to identify ourselves with our misfortunes we help to reduce the suffering. Such techniques may well reduce the total suffering, but for any given amount of suffering it is worse if the same indivisible entity undergoes it than if it is spread over a number of entities. So now we have seen that the view that the individual person is indivisible has profound practical consequences.

On the reductionist view it is a trivial truth that the same person can suffer on and on. That this is a trivial truth on the reductionist view can be seen from the following consideration. Suppose John Smith has suffered a lot for a few years and suppose that he identifies as the same person throughout this period. On the reductionist view if there had been branching (i. e. fission or fusion) during this period, it would no longer be true that the same person has suffered throughout this period. Yet it would be absurd to claim that therefore things would have been better off from the point of view of distributive justice.

It might be suggested that on the reductionist view it is how long the person survives rather than whether he continues to exist as the identical person that is morally important. But then, if reductionism is the truth about persons, why should the length of a human being's survival be any more relevant for distributive justice than say the extent to which a family or a tribe survives or the extent to which a corporation survives?

Earlier we examined the objection that on the reductionist view the moral unit is so short-lived that we need not worry too much about its suffering. We have seen that the attempt to merge the various units into larger ones by identification or appropriation will not succeed in increasing the duration of the rivulets of suffering. Such attempts may increase the amount of total suffering but the duration of the units will not alter. Since none of the units will last for too long we need not worry too much about suffering in the world! A similar argument could be used to show that we need not bother much about spreading happiness and joy in the world. What good is Nirvana if there is no long lasting entity that enjoys it! Even if there is no owner of the experience, at least the stream of experience should last for a substantial time. Is it really so good to have even billions of joyful experiences each of which form a unit that lasts for a very short time? Brief moments of joy that recur from time to time can be wonderful in the life of a person, but that is on the assumption that even though the experiences are momentary they are experienced by an individual that lasts for a substantial time.

So now we can see that though the reductionist view undermines a major objection to utilitarianism based on the separateness of persons, it also reduces the main charm of the utilitarian approach. A great deal of the attraction of utilitarianism is due to the belief that prolonged suffering is a terrible evil, and that prolonged happiness and joy are rather wonderful.

Section 2: Groups and Persons
Glover[7] argues that a human being could be just as deeply integrated and unified without a non-reductionist self. He considers the nation analogy. Some patriots may have believed that their nation had a soul. But one can be patriotic without such a metaphysical belief. One may simply believe that one's nation is deeply integrated. How far this belief is true is an empirical question. Just as a nation without a soul could be deeply integrated, so also an individual human being without an ego or soul could be deeply integrated. So the metaphysical views regarding persons may be a red herring.

This argument is not quite the same as the one I considered earlier according to which human beings can, even on the reductionist view, have a unity as long as they believe that they are non-reductionist selves and consequently identify with their future and past selves. On Glover's view we can have sufficient unity without our believing in the non-reductionist view. What are we to make of this argument? It is true that there is more psychological unity to a person's life than Parfit admits. Even when a person has a great conversion, the seeds of the new life are often found in the earlier life. For instance, Malcolm

Muggeridge in his younger days was in love with women. In his later years he was in love with God. He claimed in his later years that his earlier life too was in a muddled sort of way a search after God; it was his ignorance and weakness that made him indulge his passion.

Even if the reductionist view is true, the life of a human being can have considerable psychological unity. One must not exaggerate the extent to which people change psychologically. Even when they do change, their lives can be seen as a gradual unfolding of a potential that was there in the earlier days. And Glover has stressed that even if reductionism is true, human beings can to some extent create the character that they shall have in the light of their values and judgements regarding the sort of persons they want to be. But what has any of this to do with the problem of why the life of the human being should be regarded as a moral unit; why should psychological unity suffice for purposes of distributive justice, compensation, retributive justice etc? Suppose the early John Smith has suffered injuries at our hands and we are wondering whether we can compensate the later John Smith. Why should the extent of psychological connectedness be relevant to whether the two are the same moral unit for purposes of compensation?

On the reductionist view it would seem as if the particular psychology is being compensated, so that as long as the same psychology is there later on we can compensate it for the injuries inflicted on it earlier on. But does it really make sense to treat the particular psychology as having rights? Surely it is the owner, if any, of the psychology that is an end in itself; so if there is no owner then there is no persistent entity that is an end in itself. How can sets of character dispositions, memories etc., be regarded as ends in themselves? On the non-reductionist view it is the person who has these traits that has rights, such as right to respect and the right to compensation. Of course we can give the fact that human beings have a certain psychology as evidence of their being rather special creatures worthy of greater respect than animals that have less impressive forms of life and of consciousness.

One might believe in a non-individualistic ethic that advocates the promotion of certain forms of life not because they are good for the flourishing of individuals, but because it is intrinsically wonderful to realise such forms of life. One might treat human beings as means to the promotion of these forms of life. Such an ethic could go quite well with the reductionist view, but it would not be a rights based view.

There will be no intrinsic rights to fair shares, compensation, etc. Decisions about distribution, compensation etc, will either be by-passed or be made by an appeal to the goal of promoting the desirable ways of life.

Of course human beings may be required for the promotion of these ways of life, but any one human being is in principle replaceable. In its most stark form replaceability involves killing human beings such as unwanted foetuses and infants and replacing them with more productive people. In more moderate forms it can involve diverting resources from the unfortunate to the more useful members of society; the latter can replace the former as the recipients of scarce resources. For instance, if John Smith has been deprived of reasonable educational opportunities in the past and had a high proportion of his potential destroyed, we would now give resources to those who can now contribute to social welfare and not waste them on trying to compensate John Smith. Even on a rights based view, decisions about the use of scarce resources may partly be made with a view to promoting the common good, but on a rights based view fairness to individuals is at least one of the ultimate determinants of such decisions.

Admittedly, even on the reductionist view people would feel frustrated if they were not allowed to express their personalities and live their lives in the way they choose. But such frustration is something that a utilitarian approach can take into account.

Although psychological unity does not show why the life of a human being should be considered as one moral unit, the extent of psychological connectedness can be relevant in connection with some of our decisions about justice. In the case of punishment, for instance, reactions to punishment of serious criminals vary. Of those who approve of punishment, some would approve of the punishment of Eichman even if he was a reformed character as long as he was the same self as the Eichman who commited the crimes. Others would insist that he should be the same person in what I called the combined sense i. e. he should be the same self and have roughly similar character. Others such as Parfit in his moderate version would say that it is defensible to argue that the presence of substantial psychological connectedness by itself will suffice. This last position is I think untenable, for a replica of Eichman is not guilty of Eichman's crime. Some people would approve of the burning of an effigy of Eichman but one must resist the temptation to treat the replica as an effigy. For burning of the replica, unlike the burning of an effigy, would involve the suffering of the innocent.

The analogy with groups is again helpful, for similar arguments can be used with groups. Jonathan Edwards,[8] for instance thought that because we share a common psychology with Adam, his fallen nature, therefore we are responsible for and guilty of his crimes. In fact we cannot be guilty in any strong sense even if we share his fallen nature. For us to be morally guilty we must ourselves commit the crime or at least take steps towards committing it; moral guilt requires that the person being censured is the very same individual as the one who committed the wrong deed.[9] Perhaps it was because Edwards dimly realised this that he felt the need to argue that God, by an act of divine ascriptivism, made us all the same numerical individual as Adam.

Though moral guilt cannot be transferred across individuals, responsibility in the sense of liability to make amends can be transferred to some extent. If we belong to a group, we can be proud or ashamed of what the other members have done. If we have benefited materially, spiritually or culturally from belonging to a group, we may reasonably be expected to provide some compensation to those who have been victimised by our group. Though not morally guilty, to the extent that one identifies with one's group, one may feel polluted by its criminal activities even when one has not directly benefited from such activities or taken any part in them. To make amends to the victims of the crimes or to their families may be one method of purifying oneself. But how far do these considerations entitle us to punish one member for the crimes of another?

If punishment is taken to express moral condemnation, if it presupposes that the agent was morally guilty then punishment of one member for the crimes of another is unjust, however close the connection between them, unless the person being punished has contributed to the commiting of the crime.

Actually, I think a good case can be made for divorcing punishment from moral guilt.[10] If one severs the connection between punishment and moral guilt, one may more easily punish or penalise one member of a group for the crime of another. But one is still bound by considerations of rights and fairness. Is it fair to punish one person for the crimes of another? If the former has benefited from belonging to a group then he may be penalised in the sense of being asked to make amends, but the penalty should not be disproportionate to the benefit that he has derived. Germans now can only be asked to make amends to the victims of the Nazis to the extent that they have inherited resources from the Nazis. They may feel compelled to do more than that but that is a decision that is up to them. Suppose your father did awful things to my family and that I and my children are still suffering as a result. If you are prosperous now you could reasonably be expected to compensate me or my children even if your prosperity is not directly a result of your father's vicious way of life. If you identify with your family closely, compensating the victims may be one way of purifying your family's record. But if you do not so identify you would not feel polluted by the crimes of the other members of your family and you would not be expected to help the victims.

Notice that here identification seems more basic than psychological unity. Admittedly, sharing a common psychological nature is one important source of our identifying with others but it is neither a necessary nor a sufficient condition of our identifying with them. We sometimes identify with friends and relations who have a nature that is complementary to ours. And sometimes we dissociate ourselves from those with whom we share a common nature. I might recognise a common criminal nature between myself and a murderer. But I could distance myself from him by reminding myself that while he gave in to his murderous desires I control them. Even when I identify with a murderer because I share his psychology, it is not at all obvious that I could be punished for his murder. At most it would make it appropriate for me to make amends to the victim's family.

To summarise this discussion so far: to the extent that I have benefited from the way of life of a group, I may be required to compensate the victims. To the extent that I identify with the way of life of a group, I should (voluntarily?) help the victims as a method of purifying myself and the group to which I belong.

These considerations apply *mutatis mutandis* to the case of the individual human being if the human being is like a group or commonwealth. Though on the reductionist theory the later self is not morally guilty of the crimes of the earlier one, he can under certain circumstances be asked to make amends. But certain special problems arise if human beings are treated as groups consisting of smaller units. We have the problem of identifying these smaller units. When does one unit end and the next one begin? Then there is the problem of how we can penalise these smaller units. If we send John Smith to jail or if we extract money from him, he will now have a different set of experiences from what he would have if he were not penalised. So what happens is that certain flow of experiences are prevented from coming into existence, while other ones are brought into existence. But the unpleasent experiences that result from punishment cannot be said to be punished, rather they would not exist unless there was punishment. Who then is being punished on the reductionist theory? Is it John Smith? But John Smith is a logical construct. A logical construct such as John Smith does not suffer except in the sense that the items that it is made up of include the experiences of suffering.

Similar problems arise in the case of distributive justice and compensation. One cannot properly compensate a flow of experience; what one can do is prevent one set of experiences from coming into existence and let the person enjoy another set of experiences. Who then do we compensate? Is it the person? But the person on the reductionist view is a logical construct.

One might argue that a particular rivulet of experience has an essence and an identity that would survive change brought about by compensation. Thus if a flow of experience has begun with some suffering, then it would remain the same rivulet if we compensated it by providing some pleasant experiences as it would if we did not; for the rivulet could be individuated by an appeal to its origin *a la* Kripke. This view would imply that we should provide compensation immediately. It would also have the bizzare consequence that if a flow of experience has begun with substantial suffering then we must prolong this particular flow of experience so that we can compensate it. So that if a patient has suffered a lot continuously for the last few hours then we should not let him enjoy dreamless sleep before we have compensated the rivulet. For his experiences after the sleep, however happy, would be part of a different flow of experience and it will then be too late to compensate it properly. To meet such a difficulty reductionists can appeal to the notion of quasi-compensation.

The analogy with groups is again useful. We can sometimes partially compensate an individual by providing benefits to another. Parfit calls this quasi-compensation. Suppose a person has been injured and deserves compensation. Suppose it is not possible to compensate him directly because he is dying. We might try to quasi-compensate him by giving some of the benefits to those he would want us to help, such as his family or friends. Again, notice that his identification with the beneficiaries or consent to the transfer of resources to them is more basic than is his sharing a common psychology with them. If a person identifies with his children we should give them the benefits whether or not they share a common psychology with him. Similarly on the reductionist view, if we injure John Smith and he identifies with his future selves then we could provide quasi-compensation by giving them benefits, whether or not they have close psychological connections with him.

One does of course impose penalties on collectivities such as football teams and on corporations. And if we adopt the reductionist view perhaps we could treat a human being as a collective and impose penalties in a similar vein. The same applies to benefits. But in deciding what penalties and benefits are appropriate in the case of collectives, we use conventions which are ultimately justified by an appeal to the interests of individuals or of society. One does not treat a corporation as an end in itself. In deciding whether it should continue or whether we should destroy it and replace it with an alternative company, we appeal ultimately to the interests of individuals or of society. We treat such corporations as logical constructs and though we may treat them as persons in law, this is normally regarded as a legal fiction. Though corporations have legal rights do they really have natural rights or rights that are independent of human conventions?

If we really treated them as moral persons we would be much more worried than we are about replacing them with more efficient organisations. This reflects the fact that we take a reductionist view of corporations. There are people who regard corporations as moral persons and this view would become more plausible if one took a non-reductionist view of corporations. But the corporation analogy does not enable the reductionist, with regard to human beings, to show that the life of a human being would on his view be the ultimate moral unit for evaluating social policies. To make the analogy work one would have to argue not just that a corporation is an ultimate moral unit but that it would be so even if one took a reductionist view of corporations and regarded them as logical constructs.

It might be suggested that nations can have ultimate rights such as the right to self determination even if they are logical constructs and do not have a metaphysical unity. So why cannot human beings have some ultimate rights even if they are logical constructs and lack metaphysical unity? I would reply that if one took a reductionist view with regard to nations and regarded them as logical constructs, then the right of a nation to self determination would be understood as a right that its individual citizens, in certain relations to each other, have to self determination. Analogously one might argue that even if a person is a logical construct his fundamental rights can be understood as made up of the rights of the various members that it is made up of.

But in fact there is an important complication. Most of those who are reductionists with regard to nations combine this view with the non-reductionist view of persons, and so nations can have rights in the sense that its members can have rights. But if one takes a reductionist view of persons then can the person even have rights in the sense that is understood as its members having rights? For we have seen the difficulty of extending a rights based morality to its members. Thus we saw that if we try to promote the rights of certain experiences not to suffer then we prevent these experiences from coming into existence. Even on the non-reductionist view it can sometimes happen that the best way of promoting the interests of a possible person (such as a severely handicapped future being who would suffer a lot) is to prevent it from coming into existence, but normally there are ways of promoting people's interests and rights that do not involve preventing them from coming into existence or replacing them with someone else! Actual individuals would exercise their rights. On the reductionist view the actual experiences would normally be exercising not full rights but quasi-rights, for it will be their successors who would be the beneficiaries. Imagine a group where the main way an individual could exercise its rights was by promoting the interests of its successors. And the main way it could do this was by preventing some of them from coming into existence and allowing others to come into existence.

It might be suggested that as long as its members regard the group as the ultimate moral unit, the group should be taken as the moral unit. Thus there are societies where the family is regarded by its members as well as by others as the moral unit. In such cases we should treat the family as the ultimate moral unit for purposes of retributive justice and distributive justice. Would it be rational to so regard it even if we take a reductionist view of the family? Unless we answer in the affirmative the family analogy will not support the view that the life of a human being can be an ultimate moral unit even on the reductionist view.

One could suggest that the ultimate moral units are the individual human beings but since they regard the family as the ultimate moral unit, they transfer their moral sovereignty to the family. So the family becomes the moral unit by consent of its members, as it were. And this transfer of moral sovereignty would be effective even if the family could be analysed in reductionist terms. Similarly it might be suggested that the life of a human being can be considered as one moral unit because the various items of experience that are the original moral units transfer their sovereignty to it.

But now there is the problem regarding recalcitrant members. In the case of groups such as the family we may have a system where the wives do the hard work both at home and in the fields and the husbands get the rewards as the representatives of the family. This might appear just if the members of the family all consent to this transfer of moral sovereignty from themselves to the family and to regarding the husband as the representative of the family. In fact there will be many cases where the consent is not free and full. Indeed in cultures where the group such as the family or the tribe is regarded as the paramount unit the individual members are usually brought up and conditioned in a way that is heavily biased against their making free choices in such important areas. In India some advocates of Sati, the practice of women dying on their husband's funeral pyre, argue that this practice is all right because it is voluntarily undergone. But the truth is that there is enormous pressure brought to bear upon the women. There are many clear cases of force, threats etc, that are used against the women. The way they have been conditioned from childhood onwards makes it difficult for them to exercise a free choice in such a matter.

In the case of the life of the human being too there will be recalcitrant cases where the present self does not identify with some of the earlier selves and some of the later ones. And even in the case where the various selves do delegate their moral sovereignty to the person as a whole, they do it in the belief that they are all parts of the same substance. I identify with my future self because I believe that what happens to the future self happens to me. My primary egoistical hopes and fears presuppose a belief in the non-reductionist view. If the reductionist view is true then it would follow that I now transfer moral sovereignty to the larger unit on the basis of a false belief in the non-reductionist view. The decision to do so, if it is based on a false belief, is not a rational and free decision.

It is true that even if I get converted to the reductionist view, I could still identify with future selves that are psychologically linked with me. But why should I not also identify with other more talented people who can carry out some of my present projects better than my future selves could? So it is not necessarily the case that on the reductionist view it would be rational for the ephemeral selves to transfer their moral sovereignty to the whole life of the person. Similar doubts would arise if a reductionist engaged in Buddhist meditation. He may feel quite alienated from his past selves.

What then do we do with recalcitrant members. Do we treat them as ultimate moral units but treat the non-recalcitrant members as having transferred their sovereignty to a larger unit? But this would make the system of justice quite unworkable.

We have seen that if we get converted to reductionism the case for utilitarianism would become stronger in the sense that some of the objections against it will become weaker. But one need not adopt full blooded utilitarianism; the fact that on the reductionist view suffering would not be so evil, would tend to weaken the appeal of utilitarianism. One may try to combine a utilitarian outlook with a collectivist ethic where conceptions like pride, shame, collective responsibility, pollution, purification, etc. replace our modern ideas of personal guilt and the moral sovereignty of the individual person. What I think is very difficult is to retain our modern moral conceptions about the importance of the individual and apply them to the ephemeral 'individuals' such as the flow of experiences.

We already have at the present time a mixture of the individualist ethic and group or (collectivist) ethic.[11] We can be guilty of our own crimes and ashamed of our parent's crime. In chapter 4 section 3 we saw that individualistic and group cultures often co-exist side by side.

If reductionism is taken to be the truth about persons, then the individualist centred morality will be undermined and the group morality and utilitarian ethics will hold supreme, unchecked by individualistic ethics. Group morality may be quite appealing while it co-exists with individualistic practices, but it could be quite terrifying if it exists unchecked by individualistic constraints. Amongst some groups the women are treated as slaves and get exploited in the interests of the group.

If the person is a group or collective then the collective or group ethics will apply not just in our relations to each other but also in the relation that the various selves in the life of a human being have to each other. Some people would celebrate such a system where the barriers between persons have been broken, where it is irrational to have egoistical desire, where death and suffering are not so evil. But some grave consequences follow from this. If the distinction between persons is not important we can punish one human being for the

crimes of another[12] or in a war we can bomb civilians who are part of
the society against whom we are fighting a defensive war. For just as
on the individualist view we have the right to kill even a non-voluntary
aggressor in self-defense, on a holistic view we would have the right
to defend ourselves against the aggressive collective as a whole, which
includes civilians. If death is not such an evil then neither is murder.
If undergoing suffering is not such an evil then neither is inflicting
suffering or even torture upon a person for years, as bad as it appears
to the old fashioned!

It might be replied that even if the reductionist view is correct,
only the liberated sages will regard suffering and death with equanimity. The vast majority of people will be in the grip of the non-
reductionist illusion and fear death and suffering just as much as ever.
So causing them to suffer and killing them will involve just as much
suffering as it would on the non-reductionist view.[13] But this misses
the force of the objection. For as we saw earlier even if the total
suffering is the same, any given suffering is not so evil from the point
of view of distributive justice if it is undergone by many short lived
rivulets of experience than if it is borne by the same indivisible entity.

Buddhists think that their views once properly understood can act
as a therapy and get rid of our sorrows. For our sorrows arise from our
cravings which are a result of a false view of the self. The sages, unlike
the ignorant, are relatively free of sorrow. In chapter 8, we raised the
problem as to why the suffering masses should bother to seek Nirvana,
why not just commit suicide; and we raised the problem as to whether
it makes sense on the Buddhist view to seek one's own salvation. Now
we can raise another related problem for the Buddhist (as well as for
others who believe in the no-self view). Even in this life why should
one bother with the suffering of human beings; since on the
reductionist theory the duration of suffering is so short lived, why
should the Buddhists bother with the suffering of the ignorant?

In order to take seriously the suffering of humanity the Buddhists
need to argue that though our suffering is based on an illusion (i. e.
the illusion that we are persistent selves) the evil of the suffering is not
an illusion. It is because suffering really is an evil that we need
Buddhist therapy. But in this chapter we have suggested that on the
reductionist view suffering (including the suffering of the ignorant) is
so short lived that it would cease to be an evil. No doubt the ignorant
think that their suffering is long lasting and this false belief can
increase the intensity of their suffering. But for suffering to be a

substantial evil, it is also essential that it should really have a substantial duration. So why are the Buddhist sages better off than the ignorant? The traditional Buddhist answer is that they suffer much less. If my views about the nature of suffering on the reductionist view are correct, then reductionists should try to answer this question in some other way, perhaps in terms of the intrinsic value of knowledge, especially self-knowledge; the wise are better off than the ignorant because wisdom is intrinsically better than ignorance.

We have examined some of the views of the self and some of their practical and moral implications. In chapter 9 we saw that the view that we are each a separate self or person is crucial for formulating the objection that utilitarianism involves an unfairness or injustice to individual persons, that it treats them as mere means towards the maximisation of utility. We saw that on the reductionist view of persons this objection ceases to be a good objection. But we also saw in this chapter that the reductionst view of persons undermines the main charm of utilitarianism, for it makes it difficult for us to understand why suffering is such a terrible evil. What makes suffering a real evil is the combination of considerable intensity and duration. On the reductionist view one could have intense experiences but there is no one who undergoes them for long periods, indeed there is no one who undergoes them even for short periods.

The real ally of utilitarianism is not the reductionist view of persons but the cosmic self view or the collective self view. The cosmic self view, like the reductionist view of the person, undermines the objection to utilitarianism based on the separateness of persons.[14] But, unlike the reductionist view, the cosmic self view does not undermine the appeal of utilitarianism, which lies in its objective of removing suffering and promoting joy. Suffering remains a substantial evil as long as there is a self that keeps suffering intensely over a substantial period of time. Indeed in the case of the cosmic self, such suffering could be even a worse evil, if the same individual has suffered on and on from the begining of time. So the utilitarian goal of removing or reducing suffering would become very appealing, both because the existence of such suffering is a terrible evil and because (on the cosmic self view) its removal does not involve an unfairness to individual persons.

This discussion applies *mutatis mutandis* to the collective self. If we regard a group such as a State or a nation as an individual non-reducible subject of experiences, then perhaps it makes more sense to try to maximise the utility of the group. Also the suffering of such a group on this view would become an even greater evil than it would on the ordinary view. Thus if a nation has suffered a lot over centuries, the evil of such suffering is even greater on the assumption that the suffering of the group is all borne by the same enduring indivisible entity.

Of those who believe in the collective self as an irreducible subject of experiences and as an ultimate moral unit, some *also* regard the individual human being as an ultimate moral unit, while others like Plato do not. It is the latter view that goes most naturally with the goal of maximising the utility of the group. Such utilitarianism is however different from conventional utilitarianism where the welfare of the whole is merely the sum total of the welfare of its individual members.[15]

My own view is that groups do not suffer except in the sense that their members suffer. I do not deny that one can harm groups in the sense that one can fine them and as a result their bank balances may go down; one may also abolish a group such as a corporation, without killing the human beings who compose it.[16] One may also attribute hopes, beliefs and intentions to some groups in the functionalist sense. But one cannot make a group such as a corporation suffer in the phenomenological sense or be joyful in a phenomenological sense except in the sense that one can make its members have such experiences.

In chapter 4 section 3 I suggested that some of our intuitions about the importance of groups can be reconciled with the view that we are each separate indivisible selves. In chapter 2 I suggested that the sceptical case is stronger against groups having a mind in the strong sense than against human beings having a mind in the strong sense. I also suggested in chapter 2 that one could grant some of the claims of the holist with regard to groups without granting that the group is an irreducible subject of experiences. There may be social facts and sociological laws about the behaviour of groups that cannot be explained by an appeal to the behaviour of individual human behaviour in the way claimed by methodological individualism. To grant that some of the social facts and sociological laws are irreducible is not to grant that the group to which these facts and laws apply is an irreducible subject of experiences.

The view that it is individual persons, not groups, that are the irreducible subjects of experiences is consistent with the view that individual behaviour and even the content of individual consciousness can be profoundly affected by the group to which one belongs. Members of a close knit group may share a common heritage, common influences and even common consciousness in the sense that the content of the consciousnesses of the various individual members is qualitatively very similar and reflects the shared ways of life of the group.

One striking difference between a group such as a nation state and an individual person is that a nation state can often divide into two or more nation states whereas a person cannot, as far as we know, divide into persons. I have defended the conjecture that the self is indivisible. If it turns out that the self is in fact divisible, then I have suggested that the best solution would be to abandon the non–reductionist view. In the case of the nation state it is actually the case that it can often divide into more than one nation state. So one should be suspicious of the claim that the nation state is an irreducible subject of experiences. If we adopt the reductionist view about the experiences of a nation (e. g. the suffering of the nation is reducible into the suffering of its members), then splitting of such a nation presents no problem. But if we take a non–reductionist view of nations in the sense that we regard the nation as an irreducible subject of experiences, then we shall have the problem about what happens to this irreducible subject of experiences when the nation splits.

In chapter 5 we saw how difficult it would be for the non–reductionist view to explain splitting of persons, if it were to occur. Analogous difficulties apply in the case of the nation if one tries to defend the non–reductionist view of the nation as the subject of experiences. In the case of persons I suggested a way out of these difficulties by an appeal to the conjecture that persons are indivisible and that splitting is not possible. In the case of the nation the corresponding conjecture seems false and so it cannot be used to defend the non–reductionist view of nations. Even when a nation cannot split into nations (e. g. because it is too small to do so) its suffering does seem divisible in the sense that some of it is borne by one person, some by another and so on.

NOTES

1. Hume believed in the atomistic version for he believed that each perception is a distinct and separate existence and that we are 'nothing but a bundle or collection of different perceptions, which

succeed each other with an inconceivable rapidity, and are in a perpetual flux and movement'. *A Treatise on Human Nature*, book 1, part 4, section 6.

2. 'Consciousness, then, does not appear to itself chopped up into bits... It is nothing jointed; it flows... a "river" or a "stream" are the metaphors by which it is most naturally described' *Principles of Psychology*, Vol. 1, chapter 9, p. 239.

3. Adam Smith, *A Theory of the Moral Sentiments*, 1759, part 1 sec. 3 chapter 1.

4. Suppose a rivulet of suffering lasts an hour. Is it the case that the same rivulet suffers on and on for an hour? Suppose there had been branching of the rivulet after half an hour. Would the suffering have been less of an evil from the point of view of distributive justice?

5. Such cases actually occur in real life.

6. Marcus Aurelius, *Meditations*, Penguin Books, Harmondsworth, 1964, p. 129.

7. J. Glover, ' I ', *The Philosophy and Psychology of Personal Identity.*, p. 106.

8. *Original Sin*, part 4, chapter 3.

9. See F. H. Bradley, *Ethical Studies*, second edition, Oxford University Press, Oxford, 1962, chapter 1.

10. See my 'Excuses and Voluntary Conduct', *Ethics* 1986

11. In this book, when I refer to collective or group ethics I contrast it with individualistic ethics; the former treats the collective or the group as the moral unit, while the latter treats the individual as the moral unit. I do not here discuss collectivism in the sense which requires that there should be large scale collective or state action; that sort of collectivism does not necessarily assume that society or the group is the moral unit, for one may try to justify such collectivism on the grounds that it promotes the interests of individuals.

12. I have argued for this in more detail in my *Equality, Liberty, and Perfectionism*, ch. 7 sec. 2.

13. On this view is torturing a Buddhist sage less bad than torturing the ordinary deluded mortal who takes his suffering more seriously ? Incidentally, a similar problem arises for the utilitarian.

14. See chapter 9 footnote 1 and footnote 3.

15. See Peter France, *Collective and Corporate Responsibility*, Columbia University Press, New York, 1984, chapter 7.

16. Cf. A former Lord Chancellor is supposed to have said 'Did you ever expect a corporation to have a conscience, when it has no soul to be damned, and no body to be kicked.' Quoted by Peter France, *Collective and Corporate Responsibility*, p. 187.

Appendix A. *Nagel on the Subjective and Objective*

In his impressive book *Mortal Questions*,[1] Thomas Nagel distinguishes the objective, external or physical approach to the study of reality from the subjective, internal or mental approach. The former approach tells us, according to Nagel, about the way things are in themselves; the latter approach tells us about the way things appear from the point of view of the subject or group of subjects who apprehend them. Nagel claims that the objective approach gives only a partial picture of reality. Now this claim can be interpreted in two ways. There is the weak version according to which the objective approach gives an incomplete picture of reality; in order to get a more complete picture of reality we need to supplement the objective approach by the subjective one. And there is the strong version according to which the objective approach actually clashes with the subjective approach, and there is no rational way of resolving the clash.

This strong version leads to irrationalism and is much stronger and more controversial than the weak version which merely asserts that the objective account is incomplete, in need of supplementation by the subjective approach. It is clear that Nagel adheres to the strong version. He makes it clear that when he says that the objective picture is partial he means more than that it is incomplete: 'The proposal that I am considering is not that the objective picture is incomplete, but rather that it is in essence only partial' (p. 212). He believes that two natural and necessary ways of thinking, the objective and the subjective way, lead to collision' (p. 210), and that we have to put up with 'the co-existence of conflicting points of view' (p. 213). And he makes it clear that such co-existence of conflicting points of view 'is not just a practically necessary illusion but an irreducible fact of life' (p. 213); he believes in 'pluralistic discord over systematic harmony' and admits to being a romantic.

A curious feature of Nagel's position is that he combines irrationalism with realism. Bradley thought that if a view can be shown to be both true and false then that view does not pertain to the domain of reality but to that of appearances. Unlike appearances, reality cannot (according to Bradley) admit of inconsistencies and contradictions.

Again, Bernard Williams thinks that morality is not always rational and consistent, but he does not combine this position with realism in morals; indeed, he rightly suspects that if his views about moral conflicts are correct, they provide an important argument against ethical realism.[2] What is especially disturbing about Nagel's irrationalism is that he combines it with realism. How can reality admit of inconsistencies and contradictions? I shall argue that we should not accept Nagel's irrationalism. As against Nagel, I shall argue that the most that we are entitled to claim is that the objective picture is incomplete, in need of supplementation; I shall contend that Nagel's arguments do not show that the objective account is partial (in Nagel's sense), and that he has not made a case for the view that what is true in the objective view can clash with what is true in the subjective view.

Nagel illustrates his general thesis by considering various philosophical problems in turn. His view about the mind-body problem is that the physicalist or reductionist picture leaves out something very important, the inner life of the agent (see Ch. 12 and Ch. 14, pp. 201-2). The objective approach to the study of the bat's experiences leaves out what is essential to such experiences, namely what they are like for the bat (p. 173). The objective approach to the study of human experiences leaves out what is essential to such experiences, namely the human point of view. And he concludes:

'Certainly it *appears* unlikely that we will get closer to the real nature of human experience by leaving behind the particularity of our human point of view and striving for a description in terms accessible to beings that could not imagine what it was like to be us. If the subjective character of experience is fully comprehensible only from one point of view, then any shift to greater objectivity – that is, less attachment to a specific viewpoint – does not take us nearer to the real nature of the phenomenon; it takes us further away from it.' (p. 174)

Now, even if Nagel is right about this (and I am inclined to think he is), it only shows that the objective approach is incomplete; in order to understand the true nature of some aspects of reality, we have to resort to a subjective approach. But this does not show that the two approaches, the objective and the subjective, are in inherent conflict. Why may they not be complementary?

Some objectivists claim that mental states, such as pain, are identical with brain-states. Now if such claims are valid, then this would conflict with the subjectivist's claim that without their approach, certain aspects of reality, such as the mental experiences of human beings, will forever remain elusive to observers. If the view that our mental experiences are identical with brain-states is correct, then the subjectivists are clearly wrong in their claim; for since brain-states can be studied objectively, it would follow that mental experiences (assuming they are idenical with brain-states) too could be studied objectively. But if we reject the mind-brain identity theory, as Nagel and Kripke do, then the subjectivist's claim will not conflict with the objectivist approach, but rather be complementary to it – the objectivist approach would study brain-states, the subjectivist approach will be needed to study the inner mental states. In any case, even if the mind-brain identity theory were true, what this would show is that the subjectivist approach is in principle redundant; it would not show that the two approaches would be in collision.

Some objectivists (such as those who believe in the mind-brain identity theory) make grand claims for their approach. And such claims may well conflict with the claim that the subjectivist approach is essential to our understanding of some aspects of reality. But it does not follow that what is true in the objectivist's approach clashes with what is true in the subjectivist's approach. And so we do not get involved in irrationalism.

In his discussion of personal identity, Nagel again implies that there is an inherent conflict between the objective and subjective approaches. He seems to imply that from the objective point of view something like the reductionist view of the person holds; personal identity, on the objective view (according to Nagel), simply consists of various types of continuities and similarities, physical, mental, emotional, and causal (pp. 199-200). And he thinks that this objective picture conflicts with the subjective or internal view:

'Given that any proposed set of conditions is met, there still seems to be a further question as to whether the same subject or self is preserved under these conditions. This further question can be raised by imagining that you have the first of two experiences and asking about the other (which bears the candidate relation to it), 'Yes, but will it be mine?... From the point of view of the person himself, the question of his identity or non-identity with someone undergoing some experience in the future appears to have a content that cannot be exhausted by any account in terms of memory, similarity of character, or physical continuity... the self that appears to the subject seems to disappear under external analysis.' (pp. 200-1)

Now, is Nagel right in thinking that the objective and subjective approaches conflict with each other over personal identity? It seems to me wrong to assert that the objective view actually shows (or proves) the truth of the reductionist view.

The objective view does not disprove the non-reductionist view, it merely asserts that there is no objective evidence for it. So even if the subjective approach asserts the truth of the non-reductionist view it does not contradict the objective view; it merely goes beyond it. Compare: the objective view provides no evidence for the existence of God. But this does not make it incompatible with an internal view which asserts the existence of God.

Nagel might object that neither the reductionist nor the non-reductionist view harmonises with the internal point of view:

'It may seem that this further question involves the assumption
of a metaphysical ego which preserves personal identity. But
this would be a mistake, for the ego, if it is a continuing
individual with its own identity over time, would be just one
more thing about which the same problem would be raised
(will that ego still be me?). If on the other hand its only
identity over time is that of still being me, then it cannot be
the individual whose persistence preserves personal identity.
For its identity would then simply consist in the fact that
experiences had by it were all mine; and that cannot explain
what makes them all mine.' (p. 200).

What are we to make of Nagel's argument? Nagel is right in thinking that the view that the person consists of a metaphysical ego (or a persistent simple substance) does not enable us to answer sceptical doubts about the criteria of personal identity. But I do not think that he has shown that the non-reductionist view conflicts with the internal point of view. It seems to me that there are two ways of arriving at the view that the persistence of a person involves the persistence of a self or substance.

First, we may try to argue from the non-internal point of view that a persisting substance (or ego) is needed, e.g. because alternative views, such as the no-ownership view, according to which states of conciousness are not to be ascribed to anything, are incoherent. If one argues in this way, then it seems plausible to raise a further problem; but will that substance be me, the 'me' being understood from the internal point of view, an understanding that comes when the subject concentrates on his present experience and projects 'the temporal extension of its subject' (p. 200)?

But the second way (and the way that I favour) of arriving at the non-reductionist view is to do it via the internal point of view, by appealing to our hopes and fears and trying to show that they presuppose a persistent self or substance.[3] Now, if we take this route, there is no further problem about whether this substance will be me. For in order to create this problem one has to identify the substance through one route (e.g. the objective) and the 'me' through another (e.g. the subjective). If we get our grip on the idea of the self or substance by concentrating on our present hopes and fears, then it is not possible to distinguish it from the 'me' which is also identified by concentrating on our present experiences. In both cases we concentrate on our present experiences and project the 'temporal extension of the subject'.

At this point it might be objected that I have here simply taken up the subjective (or internal) view of the substance, and not reconciled it with the objective view of the person:

'It is the internal idea of the self that gives rise to the problem
of personal identity. Any (objective) attempt to conceive
persons completely as a kind of thing in the world persisting
through time will come up against this obstacle. The self that
appears to the subject seems to disappear under external
analysis.' (p. 201)

If Nagel is asserting the weaker thesis that the objective approach by itself does not provide us with any reason for believing in the self that we identify from the internal point of view, then what he says is true; but this would not provide any evidence for his stronger thesis, viz. that the objective account is in collision with the subjective account; it would at best show that the objective account is inherently incomplete, in need of supplementation. If one assumes that the objective account is complete, then this will leave no room for supplementation by the subjective account, and the two accounts could collide. But why should we assume that the objective accounts is complete?

Nagel is right in thinking that the metaphysical ego, if it is identical with me, cannot explain what makes my experiences mine or give an answer to the problem of criteria of personal identity. But it does not follow from this that the objective and subjective accounts of personal identity must clash with one another.

In Chapter Eleven (on brain bisection and the unity of consciousness) he thinks that there is objective evidence (arising from experiments with patients whose brains have been bisected) which undermines our concept of a unitary person and personal identity. He also
makes it clear (in Chapter Fourteen) that our ideas of personal identity
are derived from the subjective approach. If his sceptical and
pesssimistic views in Chapter Eleven are correct, they would show that
our subjective views regarding persons are false. But it still does not
follow that what is true in the objective approach clashes with what is
true according to the subjective approach, and so there is no descent
into irrationalism. At the end of Chapter Eleven he points out that it
is possible that 'the ordinary, simple, idea of a single person will come
to seem quaint some day, when the complexities of the human control
system become clearer and we become less certain that there is
anything very important that we are one of. But it is also possible that
we shall be unable to abandon the idea no matter what we discover'.
(p. 164)

The last sentence of the quotation suggests that even if our
subjective ideas of the simple self are shown to be untenable, we may
find it necessary to carry on with such ideas as a practically necessary
illusion. But of course this does not show that what is true in the
objective approach clashes with what is true in the subjective
approach; it does not provide evidence for Nagel's strong claim at the
end of his book that the 'co-existence of conflicting points of view, is
not just a practically necessary illusion, but an irreducible fact of life'.

Another example that Nagel considers to illustrate his general
thesis is the problem of free will. He thinks that if we study human
behaviour from an objective standpoint there is no room for free will:
'As the external determinants of what someone has done are gradually
exposed, in their effect on consequences, character, and choice itself,
it becomes clear that actions are events and people things' (p. 37). It
is not just determinism that undermines free will; the absence of
determinism is no more congenial to free willl. For uncaused acts are
just random events and are no more attributable to the agent than
those caused by antecedent circumstance. In order to make sense of
the idea of agency we have to understand it from the subjective point
of view.

'It is just that when I pick the shiny apple instead of the rotten
one, it is my doing – and there is no room for this in an
external account of the event, deterministic or not. The real

problem stems from a clash between the view of action from the inside and any view of it from the outside. Any external view of the act as something that happens, with or without causal antecedents, seems to omit the doing of it' (pp. 198-9).

It is interesting to compare Nagel's objective-subjective distinction with the Kantian distinction between the theoretical and practical. One difference is that whereas Nagel thinks that the objective approach gives us insight into the way an object is in itself, Kant does not think that reason in its theoretical use can give us such insight; for Kant all our knowledge is knowledge of appearances. Indeed for Kant it is reason in its practical use that enables us to believe in our freedom at the noumenal level. We do not come across instances of free will at the phenomenal level, but postulate it at the noumenal level, for it is presupposed by the Moral Law, which fills us with such awe. So for Kant it is the practical use of Reason, rather than its theoretical use, that gives us some sort of insight into the way things are in themselves. Another difference is that for Kant there is no inherent clash between the theoretical use of Reason and its practical use, whereas we have seen that Nagel thinks that the objective and subjective approaches are inherently liable to clash. Nagel's view is irrationalist in a way that the Kantian view is not. For Kant, faith ought to be rational in the sense that it must not conflict with reason.

There is one important problem that neither Kant nor Nagel have solved, viz. how to distinguish actions that are free from actions that are not. Nagel (Chapter Three) is sympathetic to the pessimistic and sceptical view according to which there is no rational way of making the distinction from the objective point of view: 'The area of genuine agency, and therefore of legitimate moral judgment, seems to shrink... to an extensionless point' (p. 35). Nagel (Chapter Fourteen) does seem to think that from the subjective point of view we are free, but even here he gives no way of distinguishing free actions from unfree ones.

Nor does Kant solve this problem. The view that morality presupposes free will does not tell us when individuals act freely and when they do not. While Nagel distinguishes the objective level from the subjective level, Kant distinguishes the phenomenal level from the noumenal level. While these distinctions are by no means the same, both Nagel and Kant think that men are free at one level but not at another. This sort of solution is too general and does not in the least help to answer the specific problem of distinguishing cases of free actions from cases of unfree ones.

Is Nagel right in thinking that there is an irreducible and insoluble clash between the objective and the subjective approach over free will? There are two views worth distinguishing. First the view that the objective approach does not by itself give us any understanding of, or reason for believing in, the existence of actions, agency, free will, etc. Secondly, there is the view that the objective approach actually disproves the existence of actions, agency, free will etc. Now, it might be contended that the most that Nagel is entitled to assert is the first view; he has not really made a proper case for the second. The second view does not follow from the first any more than the view that the objective view disproves the existence of the non-reductionist view of personal identity follows from the view that the objective view provides no evidence for the non-reductionist. Once one grants that the objective view is incomplete, in need of supplementation by other methods of understanding reality, then we can see that something can be the case even though the objective approach cannot show it to be the case.

If our belief in, and understanding of, free will, agency, non-reductionist view of personal identity, etc., is founded on the subjective approach, this is quite compatible with the view that the objective approach provides no reason for believing in such things. Again, the view that the objective approach cannot enable us even to understand terms like 'free will', 'agency', etc. is quite compatible with the view that such terms can be understood through some other approach. Perhaps Nagel believes (see his discussion of moral luck in Chapter Three) not only that the objective account cannot enable us to understand such terms, but also that it shows such terms to be incoherent and/or illusory. If this view is correct, then it would indeed conflict with the corresponding subjective claims, such as that we have free-will; we would then have to admit that our subjective claims are false even if we find it natural to continue to adhere to them as practically necessary illusions. So again, there would be no need to embrace Nagel's irrationalism.

In cases of post-hypnotic suggestion the subject who has been hypnotised feels and believes himself to be acting freely, yet the objective facts are that he has been hypnotised to do the relevant actions and so his subjective feelings of freedom are shown to be based on an illusion. Now, some people would claim that our objective approach commits us to a belief in determinism and so it is incompatible with the existence of free will in general. I am not at all convinced that the objective approach does commit us to the truth of determinism, but even if it does and determinism is incompatible with free will (as I believe it is), then it would follow that our subjective claims to free will are illusory. We may still, as practical agents, not be able to abandon belief in free will, but this only shows that we may have to retain it as a practically necessary illusion. It would not show that that what is true in the objective account clashes with what is true in the subjective account, any more than the case of post-hypnotic suggestion shows this.

Nagel does mention the posssibility that 'we may dismiss the deliverance of a subjective viewpoint as an illusion' (p. 210). He gives no good reason why we should not do so even when these deliverances clash with what is true from the objective viewpoint. As far as I can see, the only argument that he has is that the subjective standpoint is not reducible to the objective standpoint. But this argument is vitiated by the failure to appreciate that the view that the subjective viewpoint is not reducible to the objective, is consistent with the view that the deliverances of the subjective viewpoint are an illusion when they clash with objective facts.

We should admit that when the claims made from subjective viewpoints clash with the objective facts, then the former claims have been shown to be false. This is what happens in the case of post-hypnotic suggestion that we discussed.

The mere fact that the subjective point of view exists apart from the objective point of view does not imply that the conflicting claims made by the subjective and the objective points of view must both be true. Compare: the Nazi point of view is irreducible to the Liberal point of view; it does not follow that the conflicting claims made by the Nazis and the Liberals about the inferiority of the Jews are both true. The Nazi claims are false, the Liberal claims are true, even though the Nazi claims are irreducible to the Liberal claims. No doubt the Nazi and the Liberal viewpoints are not both as necessary and natural as the objective and the subjective points of view are, but this does not affect the point I am making.

Nagel is probably right in thinking that the subjective point of view is essential for an understanding of such problems as personal identity, free will, agency (see p. 200). But this too is compatible with my view that when the deliverances of the subjective viewpoint clash with objective facts, the former should give way.

What then should our views be regarding the deliverances of the subjective viewpoint? Even though we admit that there is such a standpoint we should grant that its deliverances can only be true when they do not clash with the objective facts. When such deliverances do not clash with the objective facts we may believe them to be true. Such beliefs often involve a kind of faith or, if you are more scientifically minded, a kind of conjecture. For though they cannot normally be proved by objective facts, they are falsifiable, at least in the sense that if certain objective facts were to occur then the relevant subjective beliefs would be undermined. In this respect the relation between the subjective and the objective has certain analogies to the relation between scientific theories and empirical testing and refutation; for scientific generalisations too, like our subjective deliverances, cannot be proved by objective facts, though they can (as Popper and others have stressed) be refuted, or at least undermined, by counter-examples.

The fact that our subjective judgments cannot be proved but can be sometimes disproved, has the effect that the relevant criteria tend to be defeasible. We often assume that human beings acted freely, until this presumption is defeated in particular cases by objective facts. Similarly we assume that the non-reductionist view of personal identity is correct; it is presupposed by so much of our moral and practical life. But this presumption in its favour would be defeated if, for instance, human beings, started splitting in an amoeba-like way; if such splitting took place our faith in the non-reductionist view would be undermined or at least weakened. If so, the non-reductionist view is not so unfalsifiable and unscientific as it has sometimes been alleged to be.

Some of our moral and practical life presupposes free will as Kant, Strawson, and others have stressed. But none of this constitutes a proof of the existence of free will. It is possible that our practices are based on a grand illusion. The fact that such practices are necessary for us to live a civilized life may only indicate how necessary the illusion of free will is to our civilized life.

Earlier, I said that a curious feature of Nagel's position is that he attempts to combine irrationalism with realism. Another curiosity is that he combines irrationalism in the strong sense with a profound respect for scepticism. One of the important virtues of Nagel's books is that he is not impressed by easy solutions to difficult philosophical problems, such as the problem regarding the criteria of personal identity or the problem as to whether we are ever morally responsible.

In several areas of philosophy, he makes us aware of the strength of the sceptic's challenge.[4] Now scepticism makes us suspicious of knowledge claims. But irrationalism in the strong sense arises from not being suspicious enough, it arises when we suffer from an overdose of knowledge claims. If you are impressed with scepticism then you can apply it to reject some of the conflicting knowledge claims of the objectivist and subjectivist approaches, and the conflict between what is true in the two approaches will disappear. Admittedly, scepticism leads naturally to irrationalism of a sort. For instance, if you are suspicious of attempts to demarcate science from superstition, then this would have the effect of making 'superstitious' views more respectable. But there is no reason why scepticism must lead to irrationalism of the strong kind that Nagel believes in.

There are other areas too where Nagel does not work out the full implications of scepticism. Take, for instance, scepticism with regard to other minds. Such scepticism applies, if anything, with even greater force in the case of animals than it does with human beings. But Nagel assumes that animals such as bats have a point of view, an inner life, that there is something it is like to be a bat. He then poses the problem about how we can capture the flavour of what it is like to be a bat. This last problem will not arise unless we grant that animals have an inner life. How do we know that they do? Now it might be replied that animals have minds because without postulating such minds we cannot explain much of animal behaviour. But as we saw in chapter 2, the trouble with such arguments is that though they show that we need to postulate a mind in some sense, they do not show that we need to postuate a mind in the strong sense or an inner life. As Nagel himself says, the subjective character of experience cannot be captured by any reductive analyses of the mental, for all of them are logically compatible with its absence. How then does he assume that animals have an inner life? He does say (p. 170) that because we cannot know what it is like to be a bat, we must not infer that bats do not have an inner life. But he does not give any reason for thinking that we are entitled to infer that they have an inner life. It would seem that scepticism would lead to agnosticism with regard to the inner life of bats.

Like many sceptics Nagel in the end seems to fall back on our commonsense intuitions. In the case of bats he simply assumes that bats have an inner life. His discussions of moral issues as well as metaphysical issues in the book are usually based on the assumption that our intuitions are sound. He points out that he trusts intuition over arguments; when arguments and theoretical considerations clash with our intuition, something is wrong with the arguments and the theory rather than with our intuitions (p. x). Now, trust in our intuitions may be quite sensible in cases where intuitions do not clash with arguments, and this may justify Nagel's belief that bats have an inner life. But he carries this trust too far. In fact, it is this excessive trust that leads to his irrationalism. For as we saw earlier if we are willing to abandon some of our subjective intuitions, we could avoid the clash between the subjective and the objective approaches.

In his chapter on 'Brain Bisection and Unity of Consciousness' he seems to make an exception to his doctrine that our intuitions are sound. In that chapter he is very suspicious of the commonsense views about the nature of the person. But he gives no reason why in this case we should make an exception to his general policy of trusting our intuitions over arguments. At the end of the chapter he suggests that our ordinary intuition about the person may be retained as a necessary illusion.

But in the last chapter of the book he seems to change his mind, without giving any reason; he seems there to illustrate his irrationalist thesis by treating our subjective views about the person, not as practically necessary illusions but as truths which clash with certain truths revealed by the objective approach.

To conclude, there is no need to embrace Nagel's irrationalism. When there is a clash between the objective approach and the subjective approach, it must always be possible to take one of the following ways out. First, the objective account does not really establish what it claims to; secondly, when the claims made by the objective account are true, the subjective account (however natural it may be to believe in it) does not establish what it claims to. No doubt, when one knowledge claim conflicts with another, the sceptic may take the line that we do not know which of them is false. But this view of the sceptic is consistent with the view that at least one of the conflicting knowledge claims is false.

Appendix B. *Madell's Self*

Geoffrey Madell[5] has attempted to combine the Reid–Butler view that personal identity is simple, primitive and unanalysable with the denial of their view that the self is a substance. Madell follows McTaggart in regarding the self as a property like redness. According to Madell the experiences are the basic particulars; all my experiences have the simple unanalysable property of being mine. But, unlike McTaggart, who regarded the self as a property of the substance, Madell thinks that nothing is gained by postulating a substance.

Madell's view cannot make sense of some of our current ideas of responsibility for our actions, or of our guilt for our misdeeds. Unless the agent has brought about or caused or guided his actions[6] it is not clear why he should be morally guilty. Madell seems to adopt the Humean view of mental causation. Some mental events, such as volitions, are followed by events in the physical world. No doubt a Humean could make room for some kind of action, and some conception of guilt and blame. Hume himself tried to show how the reconciliation could work. Briefly, he argued that we blame people and punish them when their harmful actions reflect their characters, for it is against their characters that our resentment is directed. Even if they have no control over their character, our resentment against them does not become any less. But to the extent that our practical life presupposes an active agent, the Humean account will not square with our practical life. For instance, libertarian freedom of the kind that Chisholm and C. A. Campbell have argued for, requires some kind of active agent who can at least sometimes act against our character. If acts of volition simply occur, why should the agent be held morally blameworthy ?

Madell might argue that he does allow for the existence of a self and so he can account for the activity of the self; we are responsible to the extent that our self is involved in our action. But if the self is just a property like redness it is difficult to see how the self can influence actions. Redness is manifested in red objects, but it can hardly be said to cause or influence their redness, and if we did regard the property of selfhood as some kind of concrete universal that did actively cause or influence our actions, then would such an active view of the self not make it rather like the substance view of the self?

Madell is suspicious of bringing in talk of substance or ego for the reasons given by Nagel. I have in Appendix A tried briefly to show that Nagel's arguments against the substance view are not conclusive. I argue that we do not have to objectify the substance; we can admit that the substance view does not solve the problem of what the criteria of personal identity are, but that is not its purpose, it is there because it is presupposed by much of our subjective and practical point of view.

Another respect in which Madell's view is different from the current view is that he allows more than one stream of consciousness per person. Thus his solution to the splitting problem is that if A splits into A1 and A2 then A1 and A2 can both be the same person. I have argued that our present views presuppose unity of consciousness and so do not admit of more than one stream of consciousness at any one time per person. On my view if full blooded splitting did start taking place we would be compelled to admit (at least at the theoretical level) that our present ideas of personal identity have been undermined. We may then seriously consider one of the alternative views of the person, such as the reductionist view or the view that the person is a concrete universal. But to say this is not to say that these alternative views are the current ones.

Appendix C. *Persons as Perdurers?*

In his valuable book *Personal Identity*, Harold Noonan, following Quine and D. Lewis, distinguishes persons as perdurers and persons as endurers. On the former view persons are four dimensional objects that persist by having temporal parts. On this view persons extend both in space and in time. Persons are made up of successive person stages. On this view when a person is present at two different times he is only partly present at each of these two times. This view can be contrasted with the conventional view according to which a person does not have temporal parts but endures over time in the sense that he is wholly present at each of the times that he exists.

The view that ordinary persons are made up of person stages has different versions. There is the Parfitian reductionist version according to which each person stage is made up of various experiences and dispositions. And there is the Lewis-Noonan version according to which person stages are not so reducible. On this latter view a person-stage does many though not all the things that a person does. It thinks, it has beliefs and desires, it talks and walks, has a size, shape and location. It even has temporal duration, but because it does not last long it cannot do the things that require a long period. On this view person-stages not only resemble persons, but are short lived persons; so persons rather than experiences remain the basic category.

It would seem that the view that persons perdure is inconsistent with much of our moral and practical thinking. For instance, our system of moral and criminal responsibility presupposes that the person to be blamed or punished must be the very same individual that performed the past action. And does this not require that the individual should endure through change, so that he is wholly present both at the time of punishment (or blame) and at the time of the past action?[7] Noonan rejects such arguments on the grounds that the view that persons perdure does not deny that persons persist over time, it simply tells us what it is for a person to persist over time.

What are we to make of this reply? On the view that persons perdure, the later person stage, which is a kind of short lived person, is being punished for the deeds of the earlier person stage. Is this not unfair and unjust to the later person-stage? Nor can it plausibly be replied that talk of unfairness or injustice does not apply to person-stages but only to persons. For remember that on this view a person-stage is a kind of person.

These remarks also apply to some of John Locke's well known views about punishment and personal identity. Noonan points out that on Locke's view there are thinking substances which are related to persons in ways that resemble the relation of person-stages to persons on the Lewis view; an immaterial substance on Locke's view does think, feel etc, somewhat in the way that person stages do: 'R. M. Chisholm brings the matter into clear focus. If, as on the Lockean theory, I am placed in a thinking substance but not identical with that thinking substance, he asks, "If I want my dinner, does it follow that the two of us want my dinner? Or does the thinking substance wants its dinner but not mine?". . . .

The answer the Lockean must give, to be consistent, is that the thinking substance wants me to have my dinner, but the only way it can think this thought is by thinking "I want my dinner"... David Lewis's much admired theory has the same consequence, modulu the substitution of person-stages for thinking substances.'[8]

Locke also thought that for purposes of accountability, what is relevant is personal identity (which he analysed in terms of sameness of consciousness) rather than identity of substance, somewhat as on the Lewis-Noonan view it is personal identity rather than identity of person-stages that is relevant. But there are differences between the two views. On the Lockean view, while it is possible that the life of a person involves a succession of thinking substances, it is also possible that there is just one such substance that persists throughout a long life of the person. His official view was that though there are such substances, identity of substance is not required for accountability. However, at one point, Locke departs from his official view. He is impressed with the argument that his view allows for the possibility that one immaterial substance might be punished for the crimes of another. For if one substance can transfer its consciousness to another, then the latter may be punished for the sins of the former. His solution is that this danger is there in theory, but in practice the good God will not allow one substance to transfer its consciousness to another:

'... why one intellectual substance may not have represented to it, as done by itself what it never did, and was perhaps done by some other agent... will be difficult to conclude from the nature of things. And that it never is so will by us, till we have a clearer view of the nature of thinking substances, be best resolved into the goodness of God, who as far as the happiness or misery of any of his sensible creatures is concerned in it will not, by a fatal error of theirs, transfer from one to another that consciousness which draws reward or punishment with it.'[9]

Noonan thinks that Locke should have been quite happy with his official version according to which it is personal identity rather than identity of substance that is relevant for moral responsibility: 'whether punishment falls on a given person on Judgement Day not only does but should depend solely on what sins have been committied by the thinking substance it then involves. But if so there is no fatal error involved in condemning a thinking substance to Hell for a sin it never committed – as long as it is the same person as the thinking substance that did commit the sin then the punishment is quite appropriate.'[10] Presumably, Noonan would offer a similar defence of the Lewis-Noonan view against the objection I raised earlier; he would say that it is perfectly just (on the complex view of persons) to punish a person phase for the crimes of another person phase, as long as the two phases are phases of the same person.

But I do not find such reasoning any better than the following reasoning: It is perfectly just to punish the current members of the Smith family for the crimes of their parents because they are all parts of the same family; it is the same family that committed the crime as is being punished now.

The reason why such punishment is unjust is that the family is a complex unit made up of members, each of whom is a separate moral unit. Similarly *if* persons are complex units, an aggregate of person phases, each of which is a kind of short lived person, then it would seem that these short lived persons are separate moral units. Even if the aggragate as a whole is a moral unit, its members too could be separate units. As long as they are separate units, we should beware of making one such unit suffer for the crimes of another.

It is true that in the case of the family, the current members do not have memories from the inside of the crimes committed by their parents, whereas the later person phase normally has such memories of the crimes committed by the earlier person phase. But this does not affect the point that whenever there is a complex unit such as the family or the nation which has members that are moral units, we should be careful about what happens to these members when we punish the complex unit.

On the four dimensional view of things, as Noonan tells us, the familiar persisting things of everyday acquaintance are only a sub-set of the totality of things that there are. There are all sorts of other objects such as the object of which George Washington is the first spatio-temporal stage and Ronald Reagan the second. These unusual objects are ontologically on par with the everyday objects. It is just that we single out the familiar objects because of pragmatic considerations.

It is wrong to think that such a view harmonises with our system of moral and criminal responsibility. In our system it is considered essential for responsibility that there should be identity through time. The person being punished should be the very same person as the one who committed the crime. Noonan says that this requirement is consistent with the view that persons perdure. But it seems to me that the four dimensional view goes against the spirit of this requirement. For the point of this requirement is to insist that the pursuit of pragmatic goals such as reduction of misery should be qualified by considerations of fairness to the individual. But on the four dimensional view the principle of fairness would itself be cashed out pragmatically, so how can it offer a proper check to the pursuit of pragmatic considerations? We could punish Reagan for the crime committed by a former President by treating the several Presidents as forming one four dimensional object. We could punish the son for the crimes committed by his father by treating them both as belonging to the history of the same four dimensional object.

NOTES

1. All the page and chapter references in this appendix are, unless otherwise stated, to *Mortal Questions*.
2. B. Williams, *Problems of the Self*, pp. 204-5.
3. The view that our hopes and fears presuppose the simple view is ably defended by R. G. Swinburne, 'Personal Identity', *Proceedings of the Aristotelian Society*, Vol. 74 (1973-4), pp. 231-47.
4. See, for instance, chs. 2, 3 and 11 of *Mortal Questions*, which is dedicated to his father who is described as a passionate sceptic.
5. *The Identity of the Self*, Edinburgh University Press, Edinburgh, 1981.
6. H. Frankfurt, 'The Problem of Action', *Journal of Philosophy*, 1971.
7. See D. H. Mellor, *Real Time*, Cambridge University Press, Cambridge, 1981, p. 106.
8. H. Noonan, *Personal Identity*, Routledge, London, 1989, p. 76.
9. J. Locke, *An Essay Concerning Human Understanding*, ed. J. Yolton, Dent, London, 1961, Essay 2, chapter 27, section 13.
10. H. Noonan, *Personal Identity*, p. 55.

Index